Word of Mouth

CALIFORNIA STUDIES IN FOOD AND CULTURE

Darra Goldstein, Editor

The labels on the fruit stand read:

THE GRAPES OF WRATH · THE ORANGES OF INDECISION · THE FIGS OF FEAR · THE KUMQUATS OF LONGING · THE MELONS OF LOST DREAMS

METAPHORIC CONSUMPTION. Laden with cultural meanings, food is always more than matter. If we are what we eat, we also eat what we are—or imagine ourselves to be—and we use food to show us how to be. As this fruit stand reminds us, food is rife with metaphor. With its biblical resonance (Revelation 14:18–20) the "grapes of wrath" entered American culture during the Civil War through Julia Ward Howe's immensely popular (in the North) "Battle Hymn of the Republic" (1861). John Steinbeck's novel of 1939 and John Ford's movie the following year extended the reach. Decades later, these grapes produce a world that turns every fruit into metaphor. W. B. Park, The New Yorker Collection / www.cartoonbank.com.

Word of Mouth

What We Talk About When We Talk About Food

PRISCILLA PARKHURST FERGUSON

UNIVERSITY OF CALIFORNIA PRESS

Berkeley Los Angeles London

University of California Press, one of the most
distinguished university presses in the United
States, enriches lives around the world by
advancing scholarship in the humanities, social
sciences, and natural sciences. Its activities are
supported by the UC Press Foundation and by
philanthropic contributions from individuals and
institutions. For more information, visit www.
ucpress.edu.

University of California Press
Oakland, California

University of California Press, Ltd.
London, England

Library of Congress Cataloging-in-Publication Data

Ferguson, Priscilla Parkhurst.
    Word of mouth : what we talk about when we talk
about food / Priscilla Parkhurst Ferguson.
        p.   cm. — (California studies in food and
culture ; 50)
    Includes bibliographical references and index.
    ISBN 978-0-520-27392-4 (cloth, alk. paper) —
ISBN 978-0-520-95896-8 (electronic)
    1. Food—Social aspects.   2. Food—Cross-
cultural studies.   3. Food habits—Cross-cultural
studies.   I. Title.
GT2850.F46   2014
394.1′2—dc23   2014005773

Manufactured in the United States of America

23   22   21   20   19   18   17   16   15   14
10   9   8   7   6   5   4   3   2   1

In keeping with a commitment to support
environmentally responsible and sustainable
printing practices, UC Press has printed this book
on Natures Natural, a fiber that contains 30%
post-consumer waste and meets the minimum
requirements of ANSI/NISO Z39.48-1992 (R 1997)
(Permanence of Paper).

To the memory of Neale Sargent Parkhurst, who first taught me to prize Eager Eaters, and to Robert A. Ferguson, who pushed me to think about them

CONTENTS

He likes bread and butter,
He likes toast and jam,
That's what his baby feeds him,
He's her lovin' man.

Well . . . I like bread and butter,
I like toast and jam,
That's what my baby feeds me,
I'm her lovin' man.

He likes bread and butter,
He likes toast and jam,
That's what his baby feeds him,
He's her lovin' man.

She don't cook mashed potatoes,
She don't cook T-bone steaks,
Don't feed me peanut butter,
She knows that I can't take.

He likes bread and butter,
He likes toast and jam,
That's what his baby feeds him,
He's her lovin' man.

Well, I got home early one Monday,
Much to my surprise,
She was eating chicken and dumplings
With some other guy.

No more bread and butter,
No more toast and jam,
He found his baby eating
With some other man.

No, no, no. . . .
No more bread and butter,
No more toast and jam,
I found my baby eating
With some other man.

    The Newbeats, "Bread and Butter" (1964)*

STORIES ABOUT FOOD

Food talk takes many forms and does many things. When we talk about food, we share our pleasure in what we eat. But we conjure the dangers of consumption no less than we convey its delights. Sometimes we talk about food simply to talk about food. Yet as often as not we talk *through* food to speak of love and desire, devotion and disgust, aspirations and anxieties, ideas and ideologies, joys and judgments. Given the many connections between food and what humans do in the societies that we make, what we say about food offers a wonderful medium for exploring the social world. Food surely can be construed as a "total social phenomenon," as Marcel Mauss defined it—that is, as a set of experiences and practices so pervasive that we could not imagine our worlds without them. From the kitchen to the dining table and beyond, the talk generated by food draws our attention because of its connection to our social selves.

The song lyrics quoted above offer a case in point. As aficionados of 1960s popular music will no doubt recognize (and the rest of us can discover on the Internet), "Bread and Butter" was a 1964 megahit by the vocal trio the Newbeats. A first viewing of the video shows it to be very much a period piece. From the vantage point of the more aggressive, insistent popular music of the twenty-first century, this performance seems very old-fashioned indeed—the flip hairdos of the teenage girls in the audience provide instant transport back a half century.

Yet if the Newbeats sing from another era, the story that they tell resonates today—if, that is, we take the time to give the song our full attention. "Bread and Butter" turns out to be food talk at its most engaging. Unlikely though it may seem, this song is archetypal food talk. It displays and dramatizes the power of food to shape our lives. And it does so by telling a story.

"Bread and Butter" is a love story—alas, one with an unhappy ending, at least for the narrator. It tells of a love affair gone wrong because the lovers think about and use food so differently. Food, it becomes clear as the stanzas progress, is shorthand for life. In particular, food means doing love. In life as at table, ill-matched tastes bode ill. The man tells his story, putting the listener off track by adopting a screechy falsetto that wavers between a whine and a scream. The narrator's opening (the text in roman above) and backup chorus (in italics, sung by two men) evoke a gustatory paradise where bread and butter, toast and jam satisfy every appetite. These elementary foodstuffs satisfy at once culinary cravings and amorous desire: "That's what my baby feeds me, I'm her lovin' man."

Predictably, this gastronomic Eden proves a temporary sojourn. The narrator turns out to suffer from a severe case of arrested development. The simple life of bread, butter, toast and jam are the stuff of a child's world—poor preparation for the "real" world of adults. The foods he prefers are childhood standbys that adults tend to relegate to breakfast, and not even a real breakfast at that. The archetypal American breakfast of eggs, bacon, and possibly pancakes makes a real meal; starch, dairy, and sweets do not.

The culinarily attuned among us will not be surprised at the consequences of such dietary deprivation. Returning home unexpectedly, the narrator finds that he has been replaced—at the table and in his girl's affections. Until now she has existed to feed her man. She does not cook, she feeds. Does *she* like bread and butter? All we know is that she makes neither mashed potatoes nor steak and stays clear of peanut butter "she knows that [he] can't take." The result of this imbalanced diet and inadequate meal? "Much to [his] surprise," the narrator comes home to find her consuming a meal of her own, "with some other guy." A new culinary couple sits at table. Fed up, his "baby" has grown up. Abandoning the surrogate motherhood of nursery feeding, she has taken to eating proper (adult) food with a proper (adult) dinner companion.

Betrayal at table says everything anyone needs to know about a love affair gone wrong. The new culinary couple is having a "real" meal, a dinner for adults. Unlike bread and butter, chicken and dumplings have to be cooked. Supplying protein as well as carbohydrates, this dish, like steak and mashed potatoes, answers standard nutritional requirements for a good—that is, balanced—meal that contrasts with the dietarily and gastronomically impoverished snack of dairy, starch, and sugar.

Furthermore, along with the peanut butter that the narrator refuses to touch, this iconic dish integrates this dinner into a particular social setting. Chicken and dumplings is a common dish in the American South, and steak and potatoes is representative American fare. In refusing its foods, the narrator rejects his country, just as his refusal of a "real" meal refuses a "real" relationship. Bread, butter, toast, and jam are side dishes, not the real thing. Making a time-honored conjunction, this song all about food turns out to be all about sex after all.

SOCIOLOGICAL UNDERSTANDINGS

However improbable a cultural indicator, "Bread and Butter" takes us to the heart of food talk. This pop song tells what it means to talk about food and why we do so. This talk lays bare the food world. It articulates the values and norms of that world and comments on its practices. Most succinctly, food talk—the ways we talk about and represent food—structures our experience of food, from kitchen to table, from menu to meal. As the drama of "Bread and Butter" illustrates so vividly, food is part of the social relationship that it expresses, sustains, and occasionally alters. Food talk recounts the ways that food affects our lives. More than that, it shows how food can help us live those lives. We talk about food to both craft identities and construct social worlds.

The reflection that *Word of Mouth* places on food talk and its creation of social worlds is a sociological enterprise. As the undergraduate promotional brochure for my department has it, sociology studies associational life. Instead of focusing on people as individuals, sociologists look to the relationships that bring people together. In other words, we look at what people do when they are with other people, and we pay attention to how people talk and write about what they do—in this case, about the many ways they think about and do food.

The question is how to get at the food talk that is all around us. The limitations of eavesdropping and direct observation impel cultural sociologists to raid the arsenal of the historian and the literary scholar. Like them, we scrutinize texts. Traditionally, the texts most often consulted were literary works and historical sources of unimpeachable consequence that looked at the social world "from above." In the past half century, as critics and scholars have become more concerned with looking at society "from below," there has been a corresponding shift in the material that we use to reconstruct social worlds. We look at writings and representations of a great many sorts, not as cultural monuments but as signs that reveal ways of doing and thinking in a particular culture in a given time and place.

These documents come in many guises. Like others before me, I draw on a miscellaneous assortment, unequal in importance and significance, each of which gives a glimpse into the world I am examining—in this case, our contemporary food world. The ephemeral plays its part, as does the classic; a pop song turns up in *Word of Mouth*, as do the novels of Marcel Proust and Virginia Woolf. Fleeting by definition, journalistic reporting offers powerful insight on cultural ephemera. Images and representations of every sort have a concentrated, visual impact that makes them illuminating. The force, and the appeal, of film lies in its conjunction of images and stories. Texts describe and analyze the food worlds that literature animates, images represent, and film stages.

Cultural forms have their specificity. Each has its own public, follows its own rules, uses idiosyncratic methods, and makes a singular appeal. Even so, and as dissimilar as these cultural markers assuredly are, the analytic lens that I have adopted sees them as equal. It is not useful for my purposes to distinguish among the different indicators, either theoretically or empirically. To understand food talk and the food world that this talk creates, I take each both on its own and as part of the cultural reading proposed in *Word of Mouth*.

This methodological eclecticism takes its cue, and its inspiration, from Walter Benjamin's endlessly fascinating excavation of nineteenth-century Paris. In *The Arcades Project*, Benjamin reconstructs the city through cultural texts of all sorts. The incongruent nature of these texts along with his apparent disregard for conventional intellectual hierarchies make Benjamin the very model of the scholar as scavenger. Almost anything written offers him a clue, however insignificant it may seem to any other reader, about the people, place, and period of the city that he famously celebrated as the Capital of the nineteenth century. Snippets of mostly forgotten plays find their place next to the iconic poetry of Baudelaire; journalistic essays receive serious attention alongside the work of esteemed historians. *The Arcades Project* all but drowns the reader in its stories, tales, and anecdotes of nineteenth-century Paris. Readers navigate the swirling currents as best they can.

The opening essay of *The Arcades Project*, "Paris, Capital of the Nineteenth Century," proposes straight off the reasoning behind what Benjamin knows will seem like a scattershot approach to the past. The very first sentence announces his working premise: that the "essence" of history is to be found in the conjunction between Herodotus and the morning newspaper, between classic historiographical texts and the ephemera of everyday life. The writer known as "the Father of History" takes his place alongside whatever sensational tidbit turns up in the latest news.

That same search takes me to scholarly studies of food and to a vintage pop song about a meal gone wrong, to extensive interviews with chefs and emblematic cartoons about dining. It makes the most of cookbooks and films about cooking and eating. In brief, rather like the cook who makes use of what turns up in the larder, in this cultural chronicle I pick up the documents that I find at hand.

This pursuit takes me on a Benjaminian treasure hunt for the telling example, the vivid illustration, and the revelatory quote. My concern is not with individuals or events. What counts are modes of being and kinds of behavior. I work through social relations to construct models of relationships much as Benjamin looked to character types (the flâneur, the collector), typical places (arcades and shops), and contemporary conventions (fashion, exhibitions, and advertising). Benjamin does not spend much time on discrete portraits or singular occurrences for their own sake. Even his discussion of the Paris Commune—the spectacular uprising of 1871 and its bloody repression by governmental troops—frames events as exemplary, not singular. Benjamin takes the figures that he picks out—Marx, Fourier, Saint-Simon, Baudelaire, Daumier, Hugo—as exempla of the modernity that made Paris the Capital of the nineteenth century.

Taking the exemplary over the singular puts me in good sociological company. Georg Simmel, to cite one of the founding fathers of the discipline, prizes form over content and structure over substance. He explains social phenomena by constructing patterns and configurations. Simmel looks to the forms of what he calls *sociation*—that is, forms of social interaction. Two of his most celebrated essays, "The Metropolis and Mental Life" and "The Stranger," show these social forms in action. The modern city dweller is a social type, and so is the stranger. Each is the creature of a distinctive social space; each exposes a social relation that simultaneously unites and divides, setting the insider apart from the outsider, the self from the other.

All of us recognize something of ourselves in Simmel's types. That's one reason why his essays work so well in the classroom. Just looking around shows students how the space that they inhabit fosters the attitudes and behaviors that Simmel identifies. None of us is anywhere near fully one type. As Max Weber would later insist, ideal types never coincide with reality. Their concentrated features are dispersed in ordinary life, making them more real than reality and exceptionally useful tools for the sociologist. Though I talk about people and events, my aim is formal. I propose forms of connection, types of relationships, modes of action. I take the cook, the chef, and the diner as types, categories, styles, modes of association. Instead of proof, I offer my own text as document, illustration, and example, the better to connect with the reader's own experience.

QUESTIONS

Every book begins with a question. Whether the whodunit of the mystery story, the epistemological conundrum of the philosophical treatise, or any number of variants in between, questions set the stage for the interpretive drama under construction. *Word of Mouth* asks questions about food—how we think about it, what we do with it, and what effect it has. Why do dining and cooking preoccupy so many in contemporary society? Despite the highly unequal distribution of food both across and within societies, why is need surprisingly muted in discussions of what makes our contemporary food world so different from what it was not all that long ago?

Crucial to understanding this strikingly assertive food world is food talk. In every culture, people talk about, write about, and portray food for all sorts of reasons. Today we contend with an extraordinary array of foodstuffs brought within easy reach by a globalizing economy. We confront unmatched culinary diversity. We take note of arresting changes in food practices, which some of us work to alter further. New modes of production and consumption, new requirements of supply and demand, and new forms of dining push us to think about food both more often and more intensely than ever before. The explosion of food talk in the past twenty-five years—in articles, blogs, and television shows, cookbooks and memoirs, films and, yes, scholarly studies—is a sure sign of our times. Benjamin, for one, would have leaped at the opportunity.

Talk anchors this food world by making it possible for us to share the unshareable—that is, our sensual, powerfully private experiences of eating. Chapter 1 shows the conversations that occur in the kitchen and at table, along with the writings and images that take this talk beyond those spaces. Firmly rooted in place, these ways of using food connect us to a culinary country. Food talk is instrumental in making us aware of that identity.

At the same time, in the markedly mobile food world of the twenty-first century, no culinary country operates on its own, if it ever did. It cannot do so because every country is part of a larger food world that favors exchange. The greater the exchange, the more blurred the identities. In the culinary conversation that *Word of Mouth* tracks most closely, France and America have exchanged culinary products and practices for three centuries and counting. Yet they maintain their distinct culinary identities even when archetypal French croissants turn up in American supermarkets and fast food outlets, from McDonald's to Kentucky Fried Chicken to Starbucks, dot the French landscape. Chapter 1 suggests some of the means by which croissants remain French and McDonald's stays American, and why, in this global market, it is vital that they do so. "McDo" sells burgers, to be sure; it also sells America. Croissants convey, however faintly, a certain idea of France. That culinary nationalism is very much of our times comes to the fore in two films: *Haute Cuisine*, from France, and *Le Grand Chef*, from South Korea.

What do we actually say about food? How have people talked about it? What about food fears? Every time we put something in our mouths, we put our lives on the line, although few see the situation in such dire terms. As chapter 2 points out, the hope of gustatory delight wins out over the fear of poison, as it must if we are to survive. It then becomes a question of what we can do to minimize the dangers and maximize the delights. The tension between the two makes our relationship to food exceptionally tentative. Food talk guides us through this dilemma. Rhetoric sits at every table, helping diners think through the standoff between danger and desire. The film *Chocolat*, the perennial favorite children's story *Winnie-the-Pooh*, and Dagwood, from the long-running comic strip *Blondie*, all propose models of consumption that prize gluttony over gastronomy, enthusiasm over discrimination.

Chapter 3 moves from the talk to the talkers. From the Greek writer Athenaeus in second-century Rome, unquestionably the greatest food writer of all time, to the utopian philosopher Charles Fourier in the nineteenth century, from the great chef Marie-Antoine Carême to the critics Alexandre Balthazar Laurent Grimod de La Reynière and Jean Anthelme Brillat-Savarin, the different genres of food talk take a stand. Each articulates positions in a cultural field—that is, a configuration of intellectual and social positions that structure cultural practices. As danger and delight shape our personal experiences of food, so these exemplary food talkers stake out the positions and perspectives on food in the larger society. In working with and against one another, these genres of food talk sustain a cultural field—a configuration of interlocking positions that operates on its own, largely according to its own rules. The food world of the twenty-first century is very like a loosely connected cultural field.

Then there are those who do food for the rest of us: the cooks and chefs who stamp the food world with their personalities and their conceptions of what it means to cook and eat. Chapters 4 and 5 recount America's culinary coming of age, via the cooks who brought French cuisine to the home front and the chefs who altered what it meant to dine out. Investing food with intellectual and aesthetic value, prizing eating no less than cooking as a legitimate cultural pursuit, the French model proved crucial—in translation. To take hold, French cuisine had to be rendered in American terms. By the mid to late twentieth century, American cooks and chefs had joined the culinary conversation and started the work of translation in earnest.

Chapters 6 and 7 shift the spotlight to consumption and the consumer. The past half century has radically redefined consumption. It is no easy matter to decide today between dining in and dining out. From take-out and order-in to food trucks to pop-up restaurants, ever more inventive means of connecting food and consumer obscure the dissimilarities between once distinct, even incompatible, activities. As more people consume more food in an ever-greater variety of locations, a pervasive informalization blurs the boundaries between cooking and eating, as between dining out and eating in. Design magazines propose that the ideal kitchen has its own dining space. The dining room, I was advised when I was moving to New York City, is the least-used room in the apartment. Rather than indulge in an apocalyptic lament that "no one" cooks anymore or eats a "proper" (i.e., sit-down) meal, we might do well to ask, as I do in chapter 7, who cooks what, why, when, and for whom. Who dines with whom, on what occasions, and to what purpose?

The unsettled, exceptionally mobile food world of the twenty-first century has spawned its own characteristic culinary construct: haute food. Chapter 7 details the striking shift from haute cuisine to haute food. Haute cuisine understands the parts—dishes, ingredients, techniques—in relationship to the whole and the principles by which that whole is defined. French cuisine, for the most striking example, is such a strong culinary system because it has a strong sense of the whole and the tradition on which it depends.

Haute food, by contrast, takes the particular taste, dish, ingredient, or technique on its own. Driven by an insistent culinary individualism, haute food as I see it prizes personal taste over tradition, a single dish over any culinary system. The weight placed on culinary creativity and innovation at all costs pressures chefs to come up with something unrecognizable. Insofar as the ultra-new dish is a context unto itself, haute food undermines culinary principles and conventions. It also redefines the meal by according diners the right to their own food, regardless of anyone else's preferences. Haute food disconcerts and excites in equal measure.

To counter the song about eating that opened this book, I close with a film about cooking. *Ratatouille* (2007) is a food fantasy of the first order, precisely what is expected of a Disney production. That fantasy has lessons for anyone concerned with the meaning of food. It is a food story that, in effect, summarizes all of the themes in the previous chapters. The hero is as unlikely as his career trajectory. Remy the rat conquers Paris with cooking that works wonders, creating happiness. Learning to cook and learning to dine, *Ratatouille* tells us, is learning to live.

PART I

From Talk to Text

CHAPTER ONE

Thinking About Food

Thirty or forty years ago, doomsayers predicted that in a more or less distant future, we would all be eating the same food in the same kinds of places. The culprit was globalization—or, in food terms, fast food. All the more invasive because it markets a highly standardized and controlled system of preparation, fast food works its magic—or its devastation—across the board. From hamburgers to croissants to fried chicken to pizza, no food is off limits. For many people, fast food means lots of food available inexpensively. During a football trip to Europe, one of my students, who loved French and Italian food, couldn't afford to eat much of it on his budget. So, it was off to McDonald's to stave off his hunger.

Contrary to predictions, fast food has not done away with difference. Food, especially in the elaborated form of cuisine, speaks of place and particularly of country. In these days, when people and products cross borders with ease, culinary nationalism insists on identity, on the idiosyncratic ways a country "does" food. Although he resorted to the familiar, my football player student recognized, and appreciated, the difference in the foreign foods that he encountered.

Today, the questions raised by globalization tend to be more nuanced. Some of the most interesting discussions turn on the ways that moving across cultures changes the foods themselves, as well as what they mean. With McSushi in Japan, vegetarian fare in India, and a host of other "non-American" innovations elsewhere, even the hyperrationalized McDonald's adapts to local customs and food preferences—so successfully that younger Asians may not think of this quintessentially American food as American at all. Someone invariably brings up the perfectly plausible (if apocryphal) anecdote of the teenage Japanese visitor who marvels that Chicago—the home of Hamburger University, after all—boasts a McDonald's just like back home!

Connections, then, are not a one-way street. They are part of an exchange, a conversation between cultures. Consider sushi. Americans have scarcely been known for their fondness for raw fish. Yet, over the past fifteen years or so, sushi turns up just about everywhere, from corner delis to food outlets of every sort, few of which make any claim to be Japanese. My immediate Manhattan neighborhood offers sushi in at least three general markets and an Italian deli, in addition to a "pan-Asian" restaurant, not forgetting the university dining halls and snack bars. Far from the metropolis, local supermarkets satisfy the craving for sushi in places where the very term was unknown only a few years ago. Of course, Americans have their say in this conversation. Early on, the avocado-stuffed California roll became a sushi classic in the United States (substitute mango for avocado in Peru). Sushi purists might object to the cream cheese in the Philadelphia roll, but few of us are purists, not even the Japanese. There is, after all, a restaurant in Tokyo that specializes in "New York sushi."

While many elements prepared the way for sushi's popularity in the United States, including the growing sophistication of American tastes, the ease with which sushi became "naturalized" still astonishes. Though, upon reflection, it should not. After all, what is sushi but "fast fish"? It fits surprisingly well with American consumption habits that emphasize snacks, food eaten with one's hands and on the go, and informality of consumption. Sushi started out in nineteenth-century Japan as street food, and that is exactly how many Americans treat it, making them, perhaps, more "authentic" consumers than the connoisseurs in high-end sushi restaurants.

For an even more striking instance of assimilation I propose Spam. Yes, Spam: the handy, inexpensive can of processed pork shoulder, gelatin, and lots of salt that hit the market in the 1930s. Older Americans likely associate Spam with soldiers' rations, meals during the Great Depression, or the "mystery meat" of institutional dining halls. In the age of the computer, virtual "spam" epitomizes the unknown and the unwanted. Yet this indelibly American processed food product turns up in a number of Asian cuisines. It has become a dish of choice for Asian Americans longing for a taste of home. Brought to Asia by American GIs during World War II, Spam was a cheap source of protein. Unexpectedly, it also became a favorite, most likely because it lent itself well to Asian seasonings, such as soy sauce.

Today, demand for Spam is so great—with South Korea, Guam, the Philippines, and Hawaii the leading consumers—that it has spawned Chinese knockoffs. One owner of a Chinese restaurant in New York recalls that when she set out for the United States at the age of seventeen, some twenty-five years earlier, her mother carefully packed a can of Spam to give her a taste of home to take with her. Today, in her Manhattan restaurant, this woman from Hong Kong serves Spam—sautéed with greens and soy sauce—to other Spam nostalgics. Like every food that travels, Spam acquires different uses, and different meanings, in different settings.

It is precisely because food travels so easily that distinctions matter. The UNESCO cultural heritage program assumes as much. In November 2010, the international agency recognized "the French gastronomic meal" (not French cuisine) as an "intangible cultural good" worthy of notice and protection. Along with Spanish flamenco dance, traditional Mexican cuisine, and the Mediterranean diet, the archetypal French meal—with its regulated conviviality and rules of order—joined the roster of worldwide cultural heritage manifestations. The bid for international recognition can be seen as the latest in a long string of assertions of superiority. On the other hand, the very fact that the French applied for international endorsement also signals that they no longer take that authority for granted.

For centuries, France has considered food and cuisine central to what it means to be French. What's more—and it is no mean achievement—France has managed to convince others that French cuisine and culture are central to what it means to be *civilized*. Since the seventeenth century, French chefs have spread French practices abroad. Culinary nationalism surfaces in a manifest sense of superiority: in recipes that tout French connections and French savoir faire; in governmental policies protecting French products and consumers; and, finally, in the cooking competitions that promote French cuisine. More generally, a sense of manifest destiny enables the French to imagine themselves as a community—that is, as a country.

France is not alone in creating an imagined national community around food, though the French are and have been notoriously vocal about the "Frenchness" of French cuisine and the superiority of French food. America has as much at stake, though the stakes are different. In many important ways, food and cooking in America are indelibly American. One of the most striking developments over the past half century is the growing awareness among Americans of these connections and their importance. In these few decades, America and its foods have come into their own—the United States is not simply a purveyor of fast food—through conversation and occasionally conflict with culinary France. For America, as for many other countries, France is not just another country; the prestige of France's culture, cuisine included, has long made it a model—to be emulated or rejected, as the case may be. From the spectacular banquets of the seventeenth century to the show of cooking contests in the twenty-first century, French cuisine is a model to be reckoned with.

CULINARY FRANCE

> Animals fills themselves; people eat; intelligent people alone know
> how to eat.
>
> Jean Anthelme Brillat-Savarin, *The Physiology of Taste* (1826)

Culinary distinctiveness is not a new phenomenon, and certainly not for the French. For the past three and a half centuries, the French have aggressively defined France in terms of culinary excellence. Equating distinction with superiority, early modern France exercised a virtual monopoly on the European imagination. The first cookbook published in France for more than a century, *Le cuisinier françois* (The French chef, 1651), proclaimed its Frenchness loud and clear. Later chefs followed suit, never losing an opportunity to trumpet the achievement that made French culture the very model of civilized society. Only in Europe, wrote one chef at the end of the seventeenth century, is there good taste; only in Europe are foods properly cooked; and only there, "and especially in France, can one take pride in our excelling over all other nations in these matters, as we do in manners and in a thousand other ways." By the early nineteenth century, the great chef Marie-Antoine Carême was even more unqualified: "France is the only country for good food; foreigners are convinced of these truths."

French cuisine is all the greater, the story runs, for reaching far and wide. It takes ingredients and dishes from all over and transforms them into an unquestionably French product. So even though *sauce espagnole*, the basic brown sauce of French cuisine, came to France to celebrate Louis XIV's bestowal of the Spanish throne on his son, "we have perfected it so much since then," writes Carême 150 years later, that it no longer has anything much to do with whatever concoction the Spanish sent to France in the mid-seventeenth century. French chefs have similarly transformed *sauce allemande*, the basic white sauce that originated in Germany, making it "as unctuous and as smooth as it is perfect." "These foreign sauces," Carême concludes grandly, are so altered that they "have long since been entirely French." In short, French savoir faire Frenchifies the exotic—and a good thing too, since "no foreign sauce can be compared to those of our great modern cuisine." The emphasis falls on *our*. Whether at home or abroad, everyone agreed that French cuisine was at once universal and very French. It is only to be expected that Paris came to celebrate itself as the culinary capital of the world.

Later on, notably in the dark days after the enormous losses of World War I, tributes to French traditions came fast and furious. Cuisine figured right up there with literature and the arts. "Grand, noble cuisine is a tradition of this country," wrote Marcel Rouff in the introduction to his novel *La vie et la passion de Dodin-Bouffant-Gourmet* (The life and passion of Dodin-Bouffant-Gourmet, [1924] 1994), "a time-honored and noteworthy element of its charm, a reflection of its soul." In Rouff's outsize conception, the hero, Dodin-Bouffant, is "a gourmet as Claude Lorrain is a painter, as Berlioz is a musician," both quintessentially French artists.

The dishes themselves carry this inimitable excellence: "A quiche lorraine . . . or a Marseillaise bouillabaisse . . . or a potato gratin from Savoy has all the refined richness of France, all its spirit and wit, its gaiety . . ., the seriousness hidden beneath its charm, . . . its wit and its gravity, . . . the full soul of its fertile, cultivated rich earth." And, as both a cause and a consequence of this heightened culinary consciousness, in a takeoff and homage to Brillat-Savarin, Rouff decrees: "Everywhere else, people eat; in France alone, people know how to eat."

Nor were men alone in waving the flag, though they dominated gastronomic discussions (as they still do). Marthe Allard Daudet, to name one prominent woman, was a prolific journalist whose "incomparable recipes" and "delicious books" earned the praise of Marcel Proust. Writing under the pen name Pampille, in *Les bons plats de France* (The good dishes of France, 1913), Mme. Daudet, patriot that she was, looked to history and literature for cultural legitimacy for her recipes. Good game can be found only in France because the animals themselves possess an uncommon sense of duty to the meal. The hare, partridges, quail, and pheasants all eagerly participate in the meal of which they will be part. They "seem to know," she tells us in the section on game, that they appear in traditional French fables and chronicles. "You might even say," the author speculates, "that they are trying hard to justify their reputation for excellence."

Over the top? Tongue in cheek? Of course. Yet Pampille is dead serious about the indissoluble link between history and cuisine—that is, *French* history and *French* cuisine. You may well say, so what? Why should we care about the permutations of French cuisine? Let French chefs boast all they want. Why should it make any difference to us? To which I would respond, because it *does* make a difference. Convinced of their authority, the French have convinced many others as well. That talk about excellence and quality is more than vain boasting because it can count on the support received from both everyday practices and governmental policies. In the first place, French chefs have been carrying French cuisine around the rest of Europe since the seventeenth century. Vincent La Chapelle, then chef to the Earl of Rochester, wrote *The Modern Chef* in English in 1733; only two years later did it appear in French. Carême himself, the "king of chefs and chef of kings," traveled to England at the behest of George IV, but he pined for Paris and stayed just long enough to brag that the king had no attacks of gout when *he* was running the kitchen!

The exodus continued through the nineteenth century. Elite cuisine in England was French, thanks to chefs such as Alexis Soyer, the longtime chef to the Reform Club, who was a fixture in mid-nineteenth-century London. Later in the century, again in London, Auguste Escoffier worked in tandem with the hotel owner César Ritz. His kitchen at the Savoy and then the Ritz Hotel in London offered superlative training grounds for the thousands of French chefs that Escoffier proudly dispatched across the globe—emissaries

"No one attacks quite like the French."

Figure 1. CUISINE AND COUNTRY FOOD IN FRANCE. Deployment of food identifies the French in every situation. This view from America insists on the identification of cuisine and country—and in particular on the elegance of the meal—as integral to French priorities, even in war. Christopher Weyant, The New Yorker Collection / www.cartoonbank.com.

of French culture to the hinterlands and purveyors of French products. His highly influential *Guide culinaire* (1903) came out in English as *A Guide to Modern Cookery* six years later. To this day, Escoffier remains a basic reference point for culinary trainees in the United States as elsewhere.

Where, we may ask, was everybody else? The Italians? The Germans? The English? Why didn't Italian chefs do for Italian cooking what the French did for French cuisine? Germany has wonderful food, as does England—what happened? Or, perhaps more importantly, what did *not* happen?

The short answer is that France had the decided advantages of a centralized government and concentrated cultural life that long took the court as its model for sophisticated behavior and practices. English government, from the sixteenth century on, to the contrary, centered in the country seats of the aristocracy. Queen Elizabeth took the court with her on regular "progresses" to the countryside; a century later, Louis XIV required the attendance of the aristocracy in Versailles. French culture carried so much clout that it was identified with the civilizing process itself. The Europe that counted looked to France. "Everyone" spoke French. They also, even more assiduously, *ate* French.

Such cultural ascendancy simply did not obtain elsewhere. Italy and Germany did not exist as nation-states until the late nineteenth century. Their cuisines were perforce regional, as, to a remarkable degree, they still are. Given that the Italian monarchy dates only from 1861, it should surprise no one that the first cookbook considered Italian did not appear until 1891. Pellegrino Artusi's *La scienza in cucina e l'arte di mangiare bene* (Science in the kitchen and the art of eating well) was the work of a retired silk merchant, not a chef. The recipes that Artusi included from all regions of Italy justifies the position of *La scienza* as the founding text of Italian cuisine. Yet it is surely worth noting that the title says nothing about Italy at all—in pointed contrast to *Le cuisinier françois* almost two and a half centuries earlier, with its unequivocal commitment to France and Frenchness.

A brief look outside Europe confirms the primacy of regional cuisines in countries that lack political, social, religious, or cultural unity. India, for one example, covers a vast territory and did not come into existence as a state until 1947. In many respects, the country is a legacy of the British colonial regime. Think of the regional cuisines of the subcontinent—from Bengali and Gujarati to Pakistani, Punjabi, Nepalese, and Tamil. There was, as in France, a complex aristocratic cuisine, although the dishes elaborated in the imperial kitchens of the Mughal empire necessarily came up against the different practices and principles of largely Hindu India.

The centralizing influence came not from any court, but from the British colonial administration. The dish that most people outside India firmly associate with Indian cuisine—curry—is not a dish at all. Nor is it the generic ingredient that the ubiquitous little bottles of ground spices on supermarket shelves would have us believe. In India, each region, each family, and each cook draws on a mixture of spices, not a prepackaged "curry." From afar— from New York, Paris, and especially London and Liverpool—"curry" was, and remains, the ultimate sign of an "Indian" cuisine constructed from the outside. Patterns of continuing immigration ensured the Englishness of curry. So English was curry that the historian Tony Judt, growing up in London in the 1950s and 1960s and overcoming his definitely non-English Eastern European Jewish roots, could claim that eating Indian food made him feel more English!

A prime ingredient in the dominance of French cuisine was its conspicuously secular orientation. The discourse of gastronomy makes food its own end. Sensual pleasure needs no justification. For most Indians and Chinese, Hindus, Buddhists, or Confucianists, on the other hand, food cannot be separated from philosophical or medicinal directives. Similar orders dominated Western thinking about food through the seventeenth century. The notion inherited from Greco-Roman medicine of the four humors—black bile (melancholic), yellow bile (choleric), phlegm (phlegmatic), and blood (sanguine)—held that these temperaments required foods that would counter the excess of one or another humor. If the separation of cooking and philosophical or medical concerns is always imperfect, for cuisines such as Indian or Chinese, it hardly exists. Systems that subordinate the sensual pleasures of taste to philosophical or ideological principles endow food with a purpose beyond itself. Food becomes a means, not the end in which a secular gastronomy delights.

Every state looks to its national interests. What has set France apart are the many ways in which the government has associated those interests with food, with the excellence of preparation and elegance of presentation. In the modernizing economy of the nineteenth century, the French government naturally looked to export French products. Escoffier's chef-ambassadors carried those products all over the world, and carried, too, a model of culinary excellence. Similarly, Louis Pasteur's work on wine (*Études sur le vin*, 1866) endeared him to Emperor Napoleon III. French wines were spoiling, and exports were falling. Pasteur's discovery that gentle heating eliminated the noxious bacteria without compromising the wine turned the beleaguered French wine industry around. The celebrated (and influential) 1855 order of Bordeaux wines is one manifestation of the drive to classify quality.

In the twentieth century, pride became a matter of policy. The French government instituted a number of measures to ensure quality of produce and of personnel. Beginning in the 1920s, the AOC (*appellations d'origine contrôlées*), or regulated names of origin for wines and foods, identified ingredients and their sources, geographical origins, and mode of preparation. Roquefort was the first cheese to receive an AOC, and since 1925, no cheese can call itself Roquefort unless it meets all the official specifications (milk from one of three breeds of sheep, injected with the fungus *Penicillium roqueforti*, and ripened in the caves of Mont Combalou in Roquefort-sur-Soulzon). Product is technique, and it is place.

France pushes hard to defend these products. Battles in the European Community (EC) can be fierce. A few years ago France lost the great chocolate war when the EC decided that "pure" chocolate did not require 100 percent cocoa butter. The news was bad for Belgium, France, Italy, Spain, Luxembourg, Germany, Greece, and Italy, and good for Great Britain, Ireland, Denmark, Portugal, Austria, Finland, and Sweden, which could continue using vegetable substitutes as they always had. Their "pure" chocolate was still chocolate—for the EC if not for connoisseurs.

Competitive Cooking

People, too, are vetted. Again in the 1920s, the competitions for Meilleur Ouvrier de France (highly skilled French worker), or MOF, were set up to promote crafts, from carpentry to landscaping . . . to food. Chefs figured prominently among the closely monitored artisans. Competitive cooking came to the fore, realizing a dream of Carême's from over a century before. Cooking contests, he thought, would be good for French cuisine. No doubt he had in mind the guilds or corporations of artisans (*corps de métier*) that regulated artisanal production from medieval times on. To rise from apprentice to journeyman to master craftsman demanded rigorous training and demonstration of competence as judged by the masters of the trade. Despite abolition of the guilds in 1791 and the consequent restructuring of workers' lives, this ideal and practice of artisanal excellence retained substantial cultural currency. The MOF continues the tradition today.

Because French chefs have been cooking competitively for a long time, when competition went international, the French had a big advantage. For the general public the best known of these international contests is probably the Bocuse d'Or, a biennial mega cook-off held in Lyon, France, that was founded in 1987 by celebrated French chef-entrepreneur Paul Bocuse. Hosted by the Salon international de la restauration, de l'hôtellerie et de l'alimentation (SIRHA), with sponsors ranging from Perrier and San Pellegrino to All-Clad cookware and the City of Lyon, the Bocuse d'Or brings together chefs from Singapore to Sweden, South Africa to South Korea, survivors of preliminary trials in Asia, Latin America, and Europe. (Canada and the United States enter in the individual category.)

The competition proceeds according to strict guidelines, with the base ingredients specified only at the moment of competition. The slick videos and hype, the sports-type arena where the competitions are held, and especially the teams that represent their countries are so many reminders of the Olympics. Each national team enters the stadium with its coach, pumping fists. The audience in the stadium waves flags, brandishes placards of support, and cheers frenetically. Beyond the Olympics, the Oscars and similar film ceremonies loom large in the media-hyped presentations, right down to the gold, silver, and bronze statuettes of Paul Bocuse brandished by the winners. Beyond the three main prizes, additional prizes go to Best Commis (assistant), Best Fish, Best Meat, Best Poster, and Best Publicity.

As with the more artistic Olympic events, such as figure skating or ice dancing, questions arise as to the standards by which to judge these culinary productions—performances, really. Despite the formidable organizational work and the ever-widening reach of the Bocuse d'Or into Asia, Australia, and the Americas, the competition retains a noticeable French inflection. Only two candidates from outside Europe have placed (Singapore and Japan, who took home bronze medals in 1989 and 2013, respectively). Beyond the actual prizes won by French competitors, French cuisine itself figures importantly in the training and work of many of the competitors and, most importantly, the winners. The 2009 Swedish silver medalist spent a numbers of years training at two Michelin three-star restaurants. The coach for the 2013 Japanese bronze medalist (and for the two preceding competitions) holds the title of MOF and currently runs a Michelin one-star restaurant.

There is little reason to expect otherwise. French techniques and base preparations continue to play a big role in the training of chefs around the world. Training competitive cooks takes vast amounts of time. Many of the French contenders and coaches have already won the MOF. The competing chefs and judges proudly sport the blue, white, and red MOF ribbons and medals when they bound on stage. As New York-based French chef Daniel Boulud has noted, it takes a good year of honing competitive skills to make a viable candidate. In contrast to most of the Europeans, who had been preparing for years, the American team competing in 2009 had only a few months to prepare after winning the trials the previous October. Sixth place wasn't so bad, in view of the Americans' subsequent tenth place in 2011 and seventh in 2013, and this despite the increasingly intense period of training and preparation.

The United States wants to do better, and Paul Bocuse, his eye on the American market, wants it to do better. Training competitive cooks takes time and money, and lots of it. The prize monies (€20,000 or $27,000 for the gold, €15,000 or $20,000 for the silver, and €10,000 or $13,500 for the bronze) do not come close to recouping the investment needed to ready a team for competition. Making the United States' ambition a reality is the goal of the Bocuse d'Or USA Foundation, founded in 2009. In the summer of 2010—in time to drum up support for the competition in 2011—the foundation launched *Bocuse d'Or USA,* a glossy magazine that aims to "inspir[e] culinary excellence." The foundation also sponsors a series of fund-raising dinners across the country to give the final candidate a series of trial runs.

We may well ask why—and how—French cuisine maintains its edge when both judges and judged come from all over the world. The French origins and organization of the contest, along with the long-standing prestige of French cuisine, are not unimportant. They are also not decisive. The larger context of competition weighs heavily in favor of the French, for whom culinary competition is a way of life that extends beyond any given competition—beyond the MOF or the Bocuse d'Or. In 2013, before, during, and after the Bocuse d'Or, eighteen French competitions were held over several days, ranging from World Pastry Cup, with its Carême-worthy sculptures, to the Golden Shell contest, with its tests of speed and dexterity at opening oysters. Many are ambitiously international (World Latte Art Championship, World Barista Cup, International Catering Cup); a couple are European (European Sugar Championships, European Trophies for Butchering display); and still others are French either explicitly (French Bread Cup, National Cheese Contest) or implicitly (Best Wine Chef). For a French contestant, the path to the Bocuse d'Or may well start with the grand prize for the Lycées of the Rhône-

Alpes region (around Lyon). Competitors who start at this high a level this early in their careers can only have an edge in competitions down the line.

Another factor is the character of French cuisine itself. More emphatically than for many—probably most—other cuisines, the governing principles and practices of French cuisine structure a system. Unlike foods tied to place, this system travels easily. It is, to use the language of economics, highly portable. A French restaurateur in New York a number of years ago invoked the importance of solfège—the rules of harmony—in any understanding of French cuisine. Once you learn the basic rules and understand the whole system, then—and only then—you can start cooking wherever and with whatever. Codes define French cuisine—not place, not products, and not people. The roster of winners of the Bocuse d'Or confirms that you do not need to cook in France or use French products or, for that matter, be French to cook French. Even so, as more than one French restaurateur in New York City observed, it certainly helps to know the French scene from the inside. A stint in France remains essential for ambitious chefs today.

Just think of all the French culinary terms that have become standard English. The 1943 edition of Irma Rombauer's classic and thoroughly American *Joy of Cooking* finds no explanations necessary for French techniques (à la mode, sauté, blanch), soups (consommé, bouillon, vichyssoise), sauces (béarnaise, béchamel, hollandaise, mayonnaise, poulette, velouté, vinaigrette), or desserts (compote, crêpes, mousse, soufflé), not to mention omelettes and pâtés. And this list does not count the organization of the professional kitchen. Cuisine, like ballet (another contribution of seventeenth-century France), speaks French in every language.

Haute Cuisine

For a vivid illustration of just how much culinary identity matters in France, I propose the 2012 French film, *Haute Cuisine* (*Les saveurs du palais*, "The flavors of the palace"). This food story translates French exceptionalism into everyday life. It dramatizes culinary France, a community imagined through its foods, cuisine, cooks, and consumers. It shows food talk connecting cuisine and country.

The palace to which the French title of the film refers is not just any palace. It is the Élysée Palace, located just off the Avenue des Champs-Élysées in the center of Paris, which serves as the official residence of the president of France. The central personage, however, is not the palace's official occupant but the cook—a special cook—and her sometimes close but more often distant relationship to her even more special patron. The French president has asked this relatively unknown woman from the Périgord region in southwest France (known for its truffles), Hortense Laborie, to be his private cook—to cook for him, his family, and his close acquaintances. All the official, public meals are the province of the head chef and his staff.

Hortense Laborie is the only woman in these kitchens, and her regular run-ins with the male staff and especially the ill-tempered, defensive head chef say a lot about the tensions of the professional kitchen, where women, even today, are not always welcome. Jealous guardians of their prerogatives, the men do not take kindly to the interloper in a skirt and high heels who insists on being called by her first name." She refuses the hierarchy that sets chefs apart. Hortense is adamantly *not* a chef.

Sexual innuendos are rife. The men can come up with only one reason why this woman should be muscling in on their domain—sex. They nickname her "du Barry" after the influential, extravagant, and pushy last official mistress of Louis XV in the decadent waning years of the ancien régime. One put-down leads to another. A final instance of sabotage pushes Hortense to the edge: "du Barry," she yells at one point, "says 'up yours.' "

The title in French, *Les saveurs du palais*, has a second sense, and it is ultimately the more important because it takes us to the heart of French culinary exceptionalism. *Palais* is French for "palate" as well as "palace." This film does not just bring to light the many *cuisines* (French slang for undercover machinations as well as "kitchen" and "cooking") in the palaces of the high and mighty, though these revelations are all part of the fun for the spectator. Hortense in effect creates a palace for the palate, and it is very much to the point that it is a *French* palate as well as a *French* palace.

The names of the dishes themselves are magic—*filet de boeuf en croûte de sel* (beef filet with salt crust), *brouillade de ceps au cerfeuil* (scrambled eggs with cèpe mushrooms and chervil), *tarte pâtissière aux fruits rouges* (red fruit pastry tart) . . . The list rolls off the tongue as Hortense announces the dishes that she prepares and whose preparation the film follows in sensuous detail. We never see the diners at table. Hortense has to ask whether the president liked the dish or not. The kitchen, not the dining room, cooking, not consumption, centers this culinary world. As in so many of the best food films, which focus on the process of preparation—the splendid *Babette's Feast* (1987) is a wonderful example—the camera of *Haute Cuisine* lingers lovingly on the food as it is transformed into a proper culinary creation. The drama opens with the painstaking layering of salmon and cabbage and moves on to the poaching of the reconstituted whole cabbage, followed in due course by the cutting of individual portions and the final plating.

The iconic truffle plays an even bigger part. At what seems to be a secret rendezvous on a street in Paris, Hortense picks up a box of enormous black truffles, delivered by hand from her farm in the south. That evening, drawn by the news and perhaps the pungent aroma, the president unexpectedly appears in the kitchen. Hortense serves him a slice of country bread with more and bigger slices of truffles than most of us see in half a lifetime. Given the traditional association of truffles with France and French cuisine, the president in effect incorporates the country that he presides.

The stories told by this kitchen tell of a country, its culture, and its traditions. Culinary nationalism comes to the fore in the loving presentation of this cuisine that restores body and soul. "I need to rediscover the taste of things," the president explains to Hortense early on. His taste for life itself is in question. Moreover, he knows where to find that taste: "Give me," he pleads, "the best of France." To recreate a menu for a special family gathering, Hortense spends hours on the phone and more at the stove, coming up with the most authentic recipe, which is also the best.

That best lies in the land—Hortense uses only products straight from farmers whom she trusts—and the women who guard its traditions. Her ideal, as she tells everyone who will listen (and even those who do not), is her grandmother's cooking. Why so many dishes named "Julia"? "If anyone asks who Julia is, tell them that she was my grandmother," Hortense proclaims. She can give her assistant no higher praise than that he flawlessly executed "Granny's custard sauce": nothing exotic, nothing fancy—just eggs, milk, sugar, flour, and a vanilla bean—but rendered to perfection.

That a film so infused with culinary nostalgia should spend so much time talking about food and showing its preparation should surprise no one. Hortense takes visible pleasure in reciting the dishes as she proposes them to the officials who must approve the menu. She talks her way through her recipes as she prepares them. The president, too, loves to talk about food and takes particular delight in quoting—from memory—cookbooks that he read as a child. Appropriately enough, his favorite cookbook was Édouard Nignon's *Éloges de la cuisine française* (In praise of French cuisine, 1933). Nignon's evocations of the countryside by France's great writers allow the president to indulge his twin passions for good food and great literature—both, of course, French.

The president sends a copy of Nignon's book to Hortense, who, predictably, finds the text as delicious to read aloud as he did. It makes perfect sense that he wonders if he might not do better to spend his time on cuisine instead of politics. In this vision of perfect communion between cook and consumer, French cuisine reaches to a perduring ideal of a better world. The film resurrects a childhood world of nurturing women, grandmothers' cooking, "real" food, and the tastes rooted in place that the French call *terroir*. It also reminds us that, in France, the meal comes first.

Haute Cuisine pledges its allegiance to the culinary rear guard. There is no place here for today's disconcertingly mobile food world of restaurants that range over many cultures, of exciting taste experiments that call on innovative techniques and unexpected products. Anything vaguely reminiscent of "modernism" or the avant-garde remains totally off screen.

The enemy on screen is an old one—haute cuisine, here equated with gratuitous spectacle. The president goes on at great length about the sugar roses that his chefs kept foisting on him: "I cannot abide sugar roses." Still, so tenacious is the hold of haute cuisine that eliminating the superfluous sugar roses from the presidential menu takes an executive order. Too much time spent on appearance, not enough on taste. There is no personality. The dessert exceptionally prepared by the chef for a family meal disappoints. Hortense and her young assistant agree: it's a generic dessert, whereas every dish that Hortense makes is unquestionably hers. It is hers because it tells the story of country that she wants it to tell. By contrast, the chef's dessert "has no author," no context, no ties to the land that the president and Hortense seek. All the food talk in the film puts us on the side of her "real" French cuisine—that is, home cooking—with a difference. If few French actually cook these dishes at home, most recognize them as part of a distinct—and distinctly French—tradition.

It is instructive of differing conceptions of culinary excellence that this film, with its adamant stand against haute cuisine, turns up outside France under the title of . . . *Haute Cuisine*. For Americans, the skirmishes between Hortense and the sugar-rose chefs come down to the confrontation between chefing (male and macho) and cooking (female and nurturing). For the French, the film pits haute cuisine against *cuisine bourgeoise*—not exactly home cooking but, in France, most certainly connected to home and hearth. For others, this cuisine and its traditions are foreign, even more unlike what most of us cook at home than they are for most French.

This cuisine—the idealized version conveyed by the film—has its place in a very personal relationship. Although the president appears in few scenes, he—or rather, his taste—is a constant presence. To please this guest, Hortense needs to know his likes and dislikes. She wants to know his favorite dishes. The two form the ideal culinary couple: the cook and the patron who make great food their common cause. The cook is also a sophisticated version of the mother who feeds him, and him alone. But the dream ends, as it must. After two years, Hortense quits, leaving the Élysée Palace to return to its old ways.

The dishes whose preparation is followed here in such detail are neither simple nor cheap. Quite as much as any creation of haute cuisine, these recipes take a great deal of time and require very particular ingredients, from the best butter to the biggest truffles. Like the greatest of chefs, Hortense patronizes farmers who spare little expense to resurrect heirloom produce. Her own expenses eventually land her in hot water with the budget-conscious bureaucrat in charge of the kitchen account. How can she cut back and still please the president? Do justice to the recipes? Create a meal worthy of France? The answer is that she cannot.

Even so, the two culinary worlds are closer than the film would have us believe. Indeed, the power of French cuisine lies in these connections. This cook is not nearly the outsider that the professional chefs assume. She makes a point of setting the kitchen staff straight. Far from coming from nowhere, Hortense has worked with chefs from around the world to introduce them to French cuisine. She comes to the Élysée Palace on the recommendation of Joël Robuchon, a fabled three-star chef in Paris, the epitome of the professional chef, and a bona fide star of haute cuisine.

Haute Cuisine puts culinary France on stage. It dramatizes the profound connection between cuisine and country. The film talks about food—French food—and what it means for France. It is, in short, ideology in action, in the etymological sense of a story—*logos*—about an idea—the idea of French cuisine. But we would do well to remember that *logos* also means "interpretation." Just as sociology—*socio* + *logos*—tells the stories of society and offers interpretations of that same society, *Haute Cuisine* tells a tale about the food world today that reveals its dynamics, lays bare its tensions, and momentarily resolves some of its conflicts.

CULINARY AMERICA

And America? What kind of a culinary country are we? There is no American culinary code, no systematic construct that distinguishes American cuisine. That said, Americans recognize and prize a distinctive style of cooking and eating. Despite the many dishes routinely cited as quintessentially American (fried chicken, hot dogs, hamburger, steak, apple pie, corn . . .), attitude and style, not food, define culinary America.

First off, America is the land of plenty. "America the Beautiful," sung by generations of schoolchildren, pays tribute to the "amber waves of grain" and the "fruited plain." This American doxology conceives the abundance of the land as a token of divine blessing. The belief in the never-ending bounty of the earth is essential to any understanding of the distinctive ways Americans think about food. It helps explain, to name one striking characteristic of American ways of eating, the preoccupation with volume of food and size of servings. Foreign travelers early on noticed the American fixation with size. Every country has beef in one form or another, but compare the archetypal American steak with, say, the *steak frites* of French cuisine, where size is not an issue.

Americans, on the other hand, typically make much of the quantity of food served. Diners are urged to do justice to the food provided. Restaurants promote their full sixteen-ounce steak and advertise "all you can eat." One roadside restaurant in upstate New York proudly proclaimed its buffet as a "Belly Buster," and McDonald's promotes its quarter-pounder hamburger, double quarter-pounder, and Big Mac. Remember my student who hightailed it to McDonald's in Rome just to fill up. No wonder that Julia Child and her coauthors had to adjust the recipes in *Mastering the Art of French Cooking* (1961) to accommodate the American appetite. As they specify in the foreword, the amounts in the recipes are double what would be usual for a French meal.

Size is key to an American style of production and consumption. Thus, Thanksgiving is a meal rich in rituals that center on food. Unlike any other country I can think of, Americans share a national meal. As practiced in the twenty-first century, Thanksgiving harks back to the now-legendary meal that the Pilgrims shared with Native Americans in 1621 to give thanks for the abundant harvest and amity that allowed the settlers to survive a very harsh winter. Linking America's present to its past, Thanksgiving reminds us of our heritage. It acknowledges diversity as it honors abundance. It is, in every way, a foundational meal.

The turkey that the president has pardoned every November since 1989 reminds us that the turkey centers the meal—alive, in the oven, on the table, and adorning any number of decorations and greeting cards. For weeks ahead of time, newspapers, magazines, television programs, and blogs testify to the national obsession. Thanksgiving preoccupies the nation. Cooks weigh the merits of fresh over frozen turkey and consult all kinds of recipes for endless variations on the obligatory stuffing. Bread? Cornbread? Oysters? Chestnuts? Sweet potatoes with marshmallow topping or without? Turnip or rutabaga? What about pies—mince, apple, or must you have pumpkin? Families mediate Thanksgiving traditions—your mother's mashed potatoes or my grandmother's sweet potatoes?

As impressive as the meal may be, the actual food at Thanksgiving dinner is notably plain: roast turkey and stuffing with gravy (no fancy sauce), potatoes, cranberry, and pie. Perhaps even more important, this dinner is not simply abundant; it is a cornucopia. Americans want plain food, and they want lots of it. In the standoff between mashed and sweet potatoes, the logical "American" solution—the only way to do justice to the banquet—is to do both. Thanksgiving does not follow the restaurant model that gives the individual consumer the right to choose. The conviviality of the communal table, laden with celebratory bounty typically prepared by many hands, creates an obligation to consume. We are enjoined to sample the white meat of the turkey and the dark meat as well, the sweet potatoes and also the mashed, the cranberry sauce along with the jelly. Mince pie without pumpkin just wouldn't be a proper Thanksgiving. Eating to excess on this special occasion has nothing to do with fear of famine and everything to do with proclaiming one's allegiance to the country that set the table. The citizen-consumer's every mouthful makes the connection between cuisine and country.

Competitive Eating

The American competitive-eating contests that have become increasingly prominent in the past decade turn patriotic consumption into a full-fledged spectacle. The best known and oldest of these competitions, sponsored since 1916 by the hot dog company Nathan's Famous, started as a patriotic promotion of a local food on Independence Day. That first year, four recent immigrants determined to demonstrate their allegiance to their new country by consuming this all-American food, which was already a Coney Island specialty. If eating American makes you American, it follows that the more you eat, the more American you become. You are as American as you eat, and America depends on its eaters. Which is why the 2008 contest made competitive-eating history: that year, the coveted Mustard Belt awarded to the winner finally "came home" to the United States. After a string of six victories by Takeru "The Tsunami" Kobayashi, Joey "The Jaws" Chestnut showed American mettle. He has continued his victories ever since, thereby assuring that consumption remains proof of patriotism.

Japan and America chow down for the Mustard Belt. Since 1916, every Fourth of July the hot dog–eating contest on Coney Island sets up consumption as patriotic duty. In 2009 it was vital that the championship remain in America to solidify the connection between food and nation.

In crucial respects, such excessive eating is anachronistic, harking back as it does to a time when food supply was uncertain, dependent on the vagaries of the weather, the vicissitudes of harvests, and the depredations of war.

Eating beyond hunger makes sense when you do not know when you will be eating next, what you will eat, or whether there will be enough. Competitive eating has little to do with the food itself. Taste is not a factor. Quantity alone counts.

Ritual overeating exists in many cultures. Like the "cook-offs" that award prizes to the best pie or chili or whatever, "eat-offs" have long been part of local farm festivals in the United States and elsewhere, often tied to consumption of a local specialty. It is easy to dismiss these displays as so much gluttony, and the amateur contests do nothing to discourage the association. But the highly organized and regulated overeating of competitive eating is not gluttony. The loss of control that led the Catholic Church to classify gluttony as one of the seven so-called deadly sins simply does not obtain. It is not how much one eats that defines gluttony but how much attention is paid to food—how much one is ruled by appetite.

Competitive eaters are not gluttons, no matter how much food they consume, because their goal is to control the body, not yield to its urges. Consumption is divorced from appetite, from desire. For competitive eaters, food is neither fuel nor pleasure. It is the enemy to be vanquished by forcing the body to extreme consumption.

Following the lead of the Japanese, Americans have worked diligently to transform amateur eat-offs into the competitive eating of the twenty-first century, organized and promoted as a sport. Consumption becomes a spectator sport with a vast audience. This contest is now in the big time, both in terms of the number of hot dogs (with buns) consumed during the allotted ten minutes—sixty-nine is the record set in 2013—and in terms of the number of spectators—an estimated forty thousand at Coney Island and over a million and a half behind their television screens. The abundance of which Americans are so proud justifies these feats of consumption. As in every sport, whatever the rules, the numbers speak for themselves—the fastest, the furthest, the heaviest wins the game, the race, the match, the contest. Most is best.

Figure 2. BABY BLUES. Some old-fashioned consumers remain skeptical about competitive eating, but its fans know a sport when they see one, with all the extras and ratified by television. BABY BLUES ©2011 Baby Blues Partnership Dist. By King Features Syndicate.

Competitive eating belongs in culinary America, just as competitive cooking fits culinary France. It is only a slight exaggeration to classify both as glorified food fights. Certainly both are far removed from the cooking and consumption of everyday life, behavior that has little in common with what most of us do in the kitchen or dining room. Divorced from everyday life, they are both extreme forms of cooking and of production. Where one empowers the chef, the other promotes the consumer.

The model of competitive cooking that prevails in French culture sets competitors less against one another than all of them against a standard of excellence, their accomplishments judged by acknowledged authorities. Unlike in sports events, in these sorts of competitions, it is entirely possible that there will be no winners—that is, no one deemed worthy of designation as, say, a Meilleur Ouvrier de France (MOF). Of course, this model imperfectly accounts for actual practice. In the absence of winners, the Bocuse d'Or would most certainly lose the commercial sponsors that finance the contest. If no candidate qualified as MOF, the whole enterprise would be jeopardized. This elite, like every other, depends on new recruits.

For a sense of the personal investment in competitive eating, I turn to the recent novel *POW!*, by the Chinese author Mo Yan, winner of the 2012 Nobel Prize for Literature. *POW!* is a book about meat and about a Chinese boy who cannot get enough of it, who is irresistibly drawn to it. Yet his gluttony is of a different order. It is extraordinary, even epic. Mo Yan's protagonist, Luo Xiaotong, takes his place in the line of overeaters headed in Western literature by Rabelais's Gargantua.

A series of competitive-eating contests structures chapter thirty-six of the novel, building up from an unremarkable chili pepper contest and a heroic fritter battle won by the narrator's father years before the narrator's own marathon encounter with meat. The power dynamics are clear, as are the stakes. Winning this contest will set the twelve-year-old Luo Xiaotong up as a person to be reckoned with: "What I really wanted was to establish my authority at the plant [the meat-processing plant where he works] and make a name for myself in the world." The contest, then, is not a simple case of consumption. It is a display of prowess of every sort. "[I wanted] the opportunity of displaying my special skill . . . —not just my skill but my artistry." It was "not only a test of strength or stomach capacity, it was also a test of will." That skill, that artistry, and especially that will make a case for gluttony outdone, and hence redefined.

This novel parts company with the usual practice of competitive eating in the special relationship between the contestant and the food that he is to consume. It is very much to the point that this contest involves meat. From birth, Luo Xiaotong has had an intimate, visceral identification with meat. He can never get enough. He loves meat with a passion—and what's more, the meat knows it. In an encounter heavy with sexual innuendoes, the meat actually calls out to him to be consumed: "I used . . . my hands—I knew the meat preferred the feel of my skin. When I gently picked up the first piece, it gave out a joyful moan and trembled in my hand. . . . As I brought the piece to my mouth, glistening tears gushed from a pair of bright eyes staring passionately at me. I know it loved me because I loved it." This outsize competitive eater transforms the food into an eager sexual partner. Not only does the meat to be consumed by his competitors wail in distress, but their messy, disorderly eating contrasts with his deliberate and refined mode of consumption. Luo Xiaotong transcends the animal even as he identifies with the meat. Sloppy eaters with no method, the ordinary gluttons who are his competition deserve to lose, and of course they do.

Competitive eating is not for the weak or the undiscerning. *POW!* makes the case for true competitive eating as gluttony without the glutton. Fiction makes the impossible possible. As practiced on Coney Island, competitive eating works hard to be a sport like any other—"the fastest-growing sport worldwide," according to the television announcement in 2013. Still, for all that competitive eating fancies itself a sport, and for all that the competitors work to control their bodies, gluttony hovers over the crowd. As the 2013 Mustard Belt champion acknowledged, the spectacle "is not pretty."

CULINARY NATIONALISM

Concern for culinary identity is hardly limited to the French, nor is pride in indigenous foods confined to Americans. The Japanese are every bit as concerned about authenticity and defining "our food." The status of imported rice is worrisome; it may not be Japanese enough. Echoing the French conception of learning cuisine through the rules of its harmonies, the successful chef-restaurateur Nobu Matsuhisa comes down squarely in favor of savoir faire: "So long as you keep your feet planted in the techniques of Japanese cookery, new Japanese dishes can be created anywhere in the world."

Le Grand Chef

Nationalism works through produce and dishes, through images and text—in a word, through the talk that ties us to place and, beyond, to nation. To see culinary nationalism in action, I propose a film, *Le Grand Chef (Shik Gaek)*, from South Korea (2007). Based on a popular television series, itself based on an equally popular graphic novel, *Le Grand Chef* tells the story of the contest for a legendary knife that had belonged to the last imperial chef. So intense was his devotion to the emperor that, rather than practice his art for the Japanese occupiers, the chef chopped off his hand. The Japanese conquerors confiscated the knife.

The film has melodrama and comedy, good guys and bad guys, a love story, filial devotion, great shots of food preparation, and lyric landscapes—all in the service of connecting cuisine and country. With a media frenzy that echoes the Bocuse d'Or, a series of trials (best fish, poultry, game, and beef dishes; even the best charcoal, which imparts incomparable flavor to meat; and best butchering of a cow) pits the top chefs of Korea against one another. Not until the final trial do the high stakes of this competition become apparent—the task is nothing less than recreating the soup that made the last emperor weep, just before his death as the Japanese advanced to destroy the royal dynasty.

In a complicated twist, the two finalists, the Hero (Sung-chun) and the Rival (Bong-ju), are grandsons of apprentices of the last chef and have been adversaries since their own early days as apprentices. The Rival's grandfather, who had cooked for the Japanese, became chef-owner of an immensely successful high-end restaurant, while the Hero's grandfather, staunchly Korean, retired to the countryside and gave up cooking. The Rival prepares an exquisite soup—from a recipe left by his grandfather that had been approved by the Japanese. But with soy sauce as an ingredient, the soup tastes Japanese.

The winning soup is ordinary—a peasant soup prepared lovingly following the recipe bequeathed to the Hero by his grandfather. This is the soup that made the emperor cry. The Korean judges offended by the presentation of such an ordinary dish in competition cannot appreciate what is so evident to the Japanese businessman who is returning the legendary knife to Korea (son of the official who had tasted the exemplary soup)—namely, that this humble soup contains the very essence of Korea. As he explains in detail, each ingredient is tied to the land, to this people, and to their history. Only an exceptional chef can put it all together.

Le Grand Chef dramatizes the dynamics of culinary nationalism. Notwithstanding the unremitting focus on all things Korean, the international context defines national identity. Only the Japanese outsider recognizes the Koreanness of the dish, and the film articulates this identity to the outside world—where it must compete with other cuisines and with other films. This competition—the gentle Hero's ambition to be the best, the rapacious Rival's skullduggery, the media that promote the contest, the journalist angling for a scoop—drives the film.

Korean cuisine is the sum of ingredients that are themselves part of a landscape that envelops the viewer. The camera lingers on the lush countryside, on the abundance of country markets, and on the generosity of the people. The nation, like the film, subsumes produce, inhabitants, and landscapes. (A key shot zooms in on Korea's national flower, the rose of Sharon.) *Le Grand Chef* casts viewers as "consumers" of a nation imagined through its food and what its great chefs and humble cooks alike do with that food. Almost every frame of the film impresses upon us the notion that cuisine, indeed, *is* country.

+ + + +

Who disagrees? Certainly not the members of the United States Congress who in 2003 demanded (and got) "freedom fries" to replace "French fries" on the menu at the cafeteria of the House of Representatives in retaliation for France's failure to support the U.S. invasion of Iraq. Nor those who boycotted foie gras. And French cheese and wine. And Perrier (until they discovered that PepsiCo owned the company). Nor again, after a Danish newspaper published cartoons deemed to caricature Muhammad, the Iranians who renamed Danish pastries quite wonderfully as the "Roses of the Prophet Muhammad."

No disagreement either from those of us who delight in American deep-dish pies and French *tartes* and prize the difference, who long for "authentic" foods, however vague we may be on what we mean by "authenticity." In the perceptive words of a great French chef, we eat more myths than calories. We eat, in sum, with our imagination.

CHAPTER TWO

The Perils and Pleasures of Consumption

Even as food practices pledge our culinary allegiance, so to speak, they reveal a fundamental ambivalence at the heart of every relationship to food. Every eater is wary of food. We are ambivalent about food because consumption is so uncertain. We know that we must eat, and experience tells us that eating can bring great pleasure, but we are all aware that food can also put us in grave danger. It is scarcely an exaggeration to say that every forkful, every spoonful that we take puts our lives on the line.

Will it do me in or will it do me good? That most of us do not ordinarily think about our meals in such drastic terms has much to do with food talk. Every human must settle how to live the paradox of food. Talk tells us how. It helps us figure out how to navigate the pleasure and the pain that consumption entails, how to reconcile the necessity of eating and the luxury of consumption, and how to ascertain the foods that deliver both fuel for the body and fancy for the soul. The articulation of these choices assumes that they matter. Perhaps, this food talk suggests, we ourselves are in control of our food, and hence ourselves.

Never has our talk about food been more critical than at present. The profusion and variety of foods so widely available make choice increasingly problematic. Everything that we hear about new foods, or unusual foods—not to mention contaminated foods—exacerbates anxiety. The greater the number and kinds of foods among which we must choose, and the more that we know about those foods, the more complex the venture of eating becomes. The more we read or listen or watch, the harder it is to construct a viable diet that maximizes pleasure and minimizes pain. Paying attention to the newly prominent dangers of consumption, modern media aggravate even as they allay the fears inherent in all consumption.

FOOD FEARS

Culinary consciousness is at an all-time high. Time and again, and across the social spectrum, consumers show awareness of what food can do, both for good and for ill. There is marked apprehension about the dangers of food— for us personally, for our families and our communities, and for the planet. All this attention paid to the perils of consumption leads a great many people to spend a great deal of time worrying about food, its place in their lives and the world about them, and then talking about it.

In the globalizing world of the twenty-first century, anxieties are rampant. A new crisis surfaces almost every day as foods travel far and wide and pass through many hands and machines. It is hardly possible to open a newspaper without coming across a food scare or scandal of some sort. Menus of ordinary restaurants warn customers about the risks of food-borne illnesses in seafood, meat, and just about everything else. Compared to a century or more ago, when most of what we consumed came to us from near rather than far, the food system of the twenty-first century exposes every one of us to many foods from a great many places farther and farther away.

This extraordinary array of foods opens us to ever-greater dangers. Industrialization altered both the conditions of production and the methods of preparation. The late twentieth century brought societies across the globe into the era of mass food. Consumers are at risk, whether they know it or not, though these days the fragility of our food supply is so present in everyday life that it is difficult to ignore the risks. Exposé after exposé tells us of foods gone wrong—and then there are all the dangers that do not make the headlines.

Food fears are not all the same. Or rather, fears about food vary seriously—from one individual, one culture, and one era to another. They vary by social class, ethnicity, race, gender, and age; by country, city, and even neighborhood. What frightens one society need not coincide with what worries another. Yet this superficial variability misleads. Radical transformation of the conditions of production, distribution, and consumption of foodstuffs triggered a distinctly modern set of food fears. The preindustrial world feared things that mean little to us today, just as the inhabitants of that world had no idea of, and mostly no need for, the fears that dominate today.

Humans have always paid particular attention to those who cook and serve the food that they consume. The food threat that jumps to mind is outright poison. We stand in awe, and fear, of those who know their way around natural substances, herbs, and powders. The villainous Emperor Nero went so far as to appoint a personal poisoner, Locusta, on the strength of her reputation as a dispenser of lethal herbal concoctions. Remedies may be beneficial, but the same substance may just as easily be noxious. Their task of preparing food has long associated women with this "weapon of the weak." Secret and surreptitious, poison is—or is seen in countless stories as—more "feminine" than a sword or a gun. Poisonings are staples of history, legend, and fairy tales. Dramas of deceit and seduction are invariably compelling. Crime fiction brings poisoning into modern times, while the occasional high-profile trial reminds us that this old-fashioned means of doing someone in can still be highly effective.

In a world swarming with malefactors, it stands to reason that we take steps to keep our plates clean and our food safe. The taster offered a solution in premodern times, efficacious though highly inefficient and profligate with human life. In ancient Rome the job fell to a slave, the *praegustator*, literally the "pretaster." However many precautions are taken, no system is foolproof. With Locusta's potions, Nero outwitted the royal tasters and did in his rival Britannicus. Potential glitches in the system notwithstanding, royalty continued to rely on these surrogate selves for many centuries, and even today, the practice has not altogether disappeared.

Undeniably dramatic, visions of enemies armed with lethal draughts intent on deadly deeds do not trouble most of us. For the most part, we indulge our morbid fascination for these poisonous enterprises from the safe distance of a comfortable armchair, book open or television on.

That we do not worry much about intentional poisoning does little to alleviate our anxieties about the food we consume. We do not have the option of sitting it out. There is no safe distance. People—ordinary people, not just royalty—have always been afraid of food, not so much because food can carry poison from an external source but because food itself can be, or turn into, poison. A natural product, food is always in the process of transformation. Left to itself, food ripens, ages, rots. Cooking turns produce into something else yet again. Potential dangers await at every point along the food chain. Consumption is scary, not because of probable poisoners but because of potentially toxic food.

To deal with these food fears and the conditions that prompt them, societies adopt various strategies. In small, traditional communities where produce was grown relatively close to the site of consumption, it was essential to see the foodstuffs, to judge quality with one's own eyes. Seeing was believing, which explains why, in medieval Europe and for some time thereafter, slaughtering of animals took place within city walls. Customers—butchers, anyway—could see, touch, and assess the animal whose state on the hoof was taken to guarantee the quality of the meat on the table. With the population explosion attendant upon urbanization and acting on a different conception of hygiene, latter-day municipal authorities moved slaughterhouses out of central cities, a relocation that both reflected and generated marked changes in food behavior.

The development of mass food further separates producers and consumers. Today's customers rely little on their eyes and still less on their noses. Packaging conspires to keep us distant. Plastic, whether in the form of wrap or containers, prohibits sensory connection, though few of us have either the knowledge or the training to judge much beyond gross defects. Moreover, contemporary scientific standards make sensory connection pretty much irrelevant. Although some damage is readily visible—an obviously diseased animal—we now know that the most toxic elements cannot be seen nor smelled nor touched. We have no alternative but to entrust our food safety to others. Mass-produced food forces choice by proxy. We place our well-being in the hands of the preparer (the cook), the supplier (the local butcher), in habit ("this has always been good"), and in presumed inspection by authorities of one kind and another, fallible though we know them to be.

Systems of surveillance break down. One strain of the deadly *E. coli* bacterium turned up in ground meat in the United States in 1994, and another, previously unknown strain appeared in vegetables in Europe in 2011. When the Food and Drug Administration falls down on the job, the consequences can be dire. Even when it is working, there is room for doubt about its efficacy. We are at the mercy of the very security systems that we set up. We cannot possibly know everything that we need to know to be 100 percent sure that what we put into our mouths is 100 percent safe. The numbers are staggering—seventy billion eggs produced annually in the United States, sometimes more than 150,000 hens squashed together in a single barn. A half billion eggs were recalled for salmonella in 2010. Adequate supervision is impossible, even discounting producers' inevitable resistance to inspection—eggs in this instance, but any other food will do, from beef to cheese, chicken to pork.

Then there is the totally unforeseen, idiosyncratic disaster—like the pea that went down the windpipe into the lungs of an unsuspecting diner instead of taking the usual route from esophagus to stomach. The errant vegetable created a health problem as severe as it was bizarre. The pea sprouted and grew into a plant that collapsed the unlucky swallower's lung and required a major operation. The story is compelling—it would not have turned up on the wire service otherwise—but such a fluke that no lesson suggests itself. It would be silly to avoid peas on the strength of this one example. Even the usual admonition to "watch what you eat" is not helpful.

A slip anywhere along the food chain—and anyone who spends time in a kitchen knows that appalling slips occur all the time—can prove fatal. Packing flour and dried fruits in my local food co-op, mindful of all the posted governmental regulations for cleanliness, reminded me how much our nutritional well-being depends on countless pairs of hands all over the world.

More troubling still, as we have heard often enough, you are what you eat. Food becomes part of who we are in the most profound sense. Our bodies take what they can use and literally eliminate the rest. In the set-to between consumer and consumed, the consumer feels, and needs to feel, in charge. We need to believe that we control the food that we eat, and not the other way around.

Just how crucial this power differential is to our sense of self became clear to me several years ago when I saw a poster in the subway on the west side of Manhattan that featured an advertisement for the Bronx Zoo (located at the end of the subway line). The poster showed a close-up of a big brown bear. Fair enough; every zoo worthy of the name has a bear or two. But the caption made me look again: "If you are what you eat, this is one funny looking salmon." It's amusing because, of course, the bear looks nothing like a salmon. The bear wins this food encounter. The caption grabs our attention and reassures us at the same time. We are what we eat, to be sure, but, in strictly physiological terms, there are, thankfully, limits. Like the bear, we come out ahead in an unequal contest. We control our food. The poster tells us so.

Perhaps not. We may not be so sure that we will come out ahead in our own food contests. We all worry about the transformative powers of food—about what it can do, will do, and might do to us. It would be disconcerting for the bear to turn "salmon-y." More than health, identity is on the line. We need to believe that the bear overcomes the salmon, given the times that food wins.

With allergies, which in their severest state are life-threatening, food takes over. A recurrent nightmare, stimulated as I recall by an against-all-odds adventure survival article in *Reader's Digest* years ago, has me lost in a jungle. Starvation looms. Eventually, I hear the sound of an airplane—supplies, salvation! Alas, it is not manna from heaven that drops from the skies but peanut butter—nutritious no doubt, but to me, with my peanut allergy, deadly. Between starvation or anaphylactic shock, which do I choose? Wasting away by starvation would be less painful; the violence of anaphylaxis would speed the dénouement.

Salmonella is toxic for all humans, and so eggs are recalled. Arsenic will do anybody in, but allergies pick and choose. The peanut that sets me into anaphylactic shock delights millions of fans of Mr. Peanut. Which is why allergy sufferers have to be their own vigilantes. We don't leave home without an EpiPen. We read labels compulsively; we scrutinize menus and interrogate waiters ("Yes, I know nuts and peanuts are not the same thing, but I'm allergic to both"); and we justify apparent inconsistencies ("Pine nuts aren't nuts").

No matter how alert we are to the perils that lie in ambush for us at every turn, we cannot do it alone. As the general population depends on general systems of food surveillance, allergy sufferers have to rely on individuals and institutions. We cannot check labels if the manufacturer fails to specify the ingredients, we cannot read menus that have no detail, and it does no good to badger waiters who have no clue about either allergies or kitchen preparations. In time we acquire a network of guardians on the lookout for our special poison. A friend checks her supplies ("The new jar of jam is just for you, untouched by peanut butter-laden knives"), a spouse puts a restaurant on notice ("We have an allergy at the table"), and a restaurant tracks preferences ("Madame cannot have the chocolate cake").

That allergies are on the rise gives them a significant public presence. Until I went to college I knew no one else who was allergic to any food. Certainly, there was not much talk about food allergies, which remained relatively uncommon well into the 1970s. Today, in the United States, they seem to be ubiquitous. Schools routinely forbid any child to bring a peanut butter sandwich for lunch and segregate allergic children in a separate lunchroom. Some schools have become entirely peanut free. Before airlines stopped handing out anything at all to eat, pressure from passengers led many of them to stop distributing peanuts as snacks. A full third of major-league baseball teams offer peanut-free seats at some of their games, and one minor-league team has an annual peanut-free day, with an allergist in attendance. It is impossible to say how many fans are attracted, though it is clear that freedom from peanuts has turned into a powerful marketing strategy.

Chocolat *and Chocolate*

The power of food to radically change lives for the better is a staple of fantasy food stories. So in preparation for my course on food and the social transformations that it can provoke, I took another look at the film *Chocolat* (2000), which I remembered as just such a story of transformation. Vianne, a mysterious itinerant chocolate maker (the incandescent Juliette Binoche), arrives with her exotic chocolates and her daughter in a very conservative, tradition-bound French village. Right at the beginning of Lent she opens up a chocolate shop. Vanquishing the inevitable resistance, the amazing confections that Vianne creates shake up individual lives and the life of the entire village, where no one has seen—much less tasted—chocolates like these: dark chocolates, flavored with chili power or in erotic shapes with suggestive names like the "nipples of Venus" (chocolate mounds with white frosting tips in the middle). The right chocolates restore conjugal affection, galvanize dilatory suitors, give a battered wife the courage to leave her abusive husband, liberate the priest, and turn the unhappy, straitlaced mayor into an ardent sensualist.

It seemed only fitting, then, to treat myself to chocolate of my own as I watched *Chocolat*. Suddenly, one individually wrapped milk chocolate ball—from a well-known and much-advertised manufacturer, and as far as I could tell identical to the one I had consumed the day before with impunity—tasted wrong. Familiarly wrong. The reaction, to my dismay, was equally familiar, and the routine as well. Lulled by my peanut-free good fortune over the previous few years, I had allowed my EpiPen to go woefully out of date. So after a dose of antihistamine, a hasty trip to the emergency room was in order. I wasn't released from the hospital until the next morning—sadder certainly, but how much wiser? Full of resolutions, I fervently hoped that, contrary to what one nurse hesitantly suggested, I had not become allergic to chocolate.

Starvation might be preferable after all.

All of which is simply to recall that every consumer courts danger all the time. *Chocolat* makes the stakes of our choices clear with the story of Armande. Once this old woman (played by the incomparable Judi Dench) discovers Vianne's thick, dense hot chocolate, which conjures up her childhood, she takes to frequenting the enticing chocolate shop. Armande knows full well the dangers of this regime since, as is revealed only late in the film, she is a diabetic for whom chocolate is a much more than ordinary indulgence. Armande chooses death by chocolate, which she prefers to being packed off to the nursing home where her daughter wants to dump her. Pleasure trumps prudence. Armande dies contentedly after a glorious celebratory meal.

As Armande's deliberate disregard of her diabetes illustrates to perfection, our physical well-being is only one of the factors that determine food choice, and often not the deciding one at that. Given that health is a highly variable concept, the best that can be said for any of us, as a doctor once said to me, is "You're fine—for now." However loath we are to admit it, no consumer, no eater can claim any more about the food we eat.

Food is always more than just food. Every act of consumption says something about the universe that we make for ourselves. A whole range of food choices engages fundamental beliefs that connect the individual to a group, a community, and a country. We also eat our conscience. Our food choices bear witness to our moral universe. Whether keeping kosher, following halal, or renouncing a favorite food for Lent, food practices express religious beliefs and tie us to a community that practices food the way we do. To be sure, these religious convictions and their dietary directives are hardly new. What *is* new and marks these food choices as modern is the dependence of food today on an elaborate system of production and distribution whose geographical reach complicates surveillance immensely.

PLEASURE TALK

Whatever the many food perils we know about, and however mindful of those we do not, we keep on eating. We do so not only because of commitment or need for a variety of nutrients. A simpler answer, beyond sheer hunger, is that we like to eat. Appetite conquers anxiety; anticipation of delight wins out over fear of danger. I eventually returned to chocolate, although it took some time for the suggestive images of *Chocolat* and the happiness of the chocolate-crazed villagers to push the memories of the IV tubes in the emergency room to the back of my memory box.

Images and memories of pleasurable tastes take over. Adhering to the principle of calculated forgetfulness, we retell ourselves stories of pleasure and relegate the pain of bad experience to the back burner. We forget as we remember—selectively. We want to eat, but that's not enough because we are not content with the same old thing. Pleasure, too, is problematic. We certainly could choose to stick with foods that we think safe. Comfort food is, above all, familiar food. But we do not.

We may rationalize our actions, but playing with our senses puts us constantly on the lookout for new tastes. In the right frame of mind, we revel in taste adventures. We look forward to the excitement of the culinary unknown. Every time that we try something even slightly out of the ordinary, we come upon new territory.

Comfort food is not the answer to our food fears. Even the foods typically cited in the comfort category—say, mashed potatoes, for many Americans—will pall after a time. They will comfort, perhaps, but they will also bore. A steady diet of mashed potatoes would dull our taste buds, no matter how much butter and cream are added, or how flavorful the potatoes are to begin with. My mother, who disliked desserts and rarely made them, once bought several cases of Raggedy Ann canned peaches in heavy syrup. Presumably, the price was right, and she had a default dessert. So, for more time than I care to remember, Raggedy Ann peaches appeared on the dining table with appalling regularity. A collective sigh of relief arose when the last can was dispensed with (it may even have been donated to a worthy cause). I have not touched a canned peach since.

The very idea of culinary boredom sends shivers down any cook's spine. The original meal cannot be reprised too many times, lest the family groan, more or less audibly, "Oh no, not again . . . " What to do with the ham after the feast is a test of ingenuity in anyone's book. Many of us faced with a still-laden table might well think ruefully of the definition of eternity attributed to the satirist Dorothy Parker: two people and a ham. My mother-in-law, for one, found this quotation particularly apt. Like most domestic cooks, she had faced mountains of leftovers in her years in the kitchen. Food talk helped her cope.

Because humans are social animals, enmeshed in a social world, consumption is tied to certain meals, specific foods, particular people. We trust food because we trust the people we associate with it—the cook, the supplier, the friends whose choices we follow, the waiter, the chef, the farmer, the governmental agency in charge of safety. Will you pick up food dropped on the floor? What is your time limit? Ten seconds? Twenty? My mother liked to say that you eat a peck of dirt before you die anyway, so there is no point in being fussy. Her pickup rule was probably around twenty-five seconds, though—to be fair—she, like most of us, worked off the knowledge of the floor in question, however faulty that standard had to be. Even though a scrupulously clean kitchen floor does not exist, my mother's own kitchen passed muster. It is not clear to how many other kitchens she would have extended her tolerance.

For all the dire tales about the perils of consumption, most of us continue to eat, and eat with gusto. Surely one element of this enthusiasm is that we listen to other stories—to stories that tell of the pleasures of food, not its threats, to those that emphasize the delights that await us, not our vulnerability. Along with, and no doubt in reaction to, the many warnings about the dangers of consumption, culinary pleasure preoccupies the food world today. Selling food has always meant marketing pleasure, and today more than ever before, marketing pleasure calls on the senses and exploits sensuality, sometimes quite shamelessly.

The inability of language to get across the experience of tasting foods helps explain the power of images, from traditional still lifes to today's websites and glossy food magazines, that vie to convey the sheer sensuality of food. We are caught between perils and pleasures. Accepting that we cannot know everything and that we cannot control our food, we opt for the pleasure of food. What did the pea eater who sprouted a pea plant in his lung eat for his first meal, when the operation was all over? Why, peas, of course! And laughed about it.

It is still more gratifying, and consumption all the more legitimate, when pleasure is patriotic. The United States enthusiastically identifies foods with country. The entire month of July is officially National Ice Cream Month. Specific days are set aside for National Ice Cream Day, National Ice Cream Soda Day, National Vanilla Ice Cream Day, National Ice Cream Flavor Day, National Peach Ice Cream Day, and, perhaps best of all, Hot Fudge Sundae Day.

Yet, even with America's emblematic treat, there can be too much of a single good thing. The specter of culinary boredom looms—for chefs as much as, perhaps even more than, for consumers. July kicks off with National Creative Ice Cream Flavor Day. A look around will confirm that ice cream makers frequently turn to startling effect in an effort to tempt consumers into new taste territory, with flavors ranging from prosciutto, peanut butter curry, and hibiscus-beet to balsamic-caramel and cucumber ice milk.

Beyond patriotism, boredom, and indulgence, how we approach eating depends on how we think about food. And how we think about food— whether we consider it friend or enemy—in turn depends on the food talk that we listen to. Works like *Chocolat* tell tales of beneficent transformation. Seeing, smelling, touching, and finally—when they can resist no longer—tasting Vianne's extraordinary confections lays food fears to rest. The transformations are all to the good—for the individuals and for the village. The chocolates are transformative, and we are the better for it. "One taste is all it takes," as the publicity for the film proclaims. It is a profoundly reassuring food story.

The Happy Glutton

> "When you wake up in the morning, Pooh," said Piglet at last, "what's
> the first thing you say to yourself?"
> "What's for breakfast?" said Pooh. "What do *you* say, Piglet?"
> "I say, I wonder what's going to happen exciting *today?*" said Piglet.
> Pooh nodded thoughtfully. "It's the same thing," he said.
>
> A. A. Milne, *Winnie-the-Pooh* (1926)

In contrast to *Chocolat*, which promotes the pleasure of food through the wondrous changes brought on by consumption, *Winnie-the-Pooh* makes its bid for pleasure with reassurances that indulging our appetite brings no dire consequences. Rather than change us, this classic children's story tells us, food makes us more ourselves. For Winnie the Pooh, food is unalloyed pleasure. To be sure, mishaps occur, but Pooh on the whole is a happy bear, and he is happy at least in part due to the abundance of the food that fulfills his deepest desires. We can have our cake and eat it too, and be none the different for it.

Pooh is the very model of what my mother called (approvingly) an Eager Eater. For such enthusiasts, eating is an adventure and food a source of infinite pleasure. He—and we—look forward to breakfast, lunch, dinner, and all the treats in between. Like Pooh, Eager Eaters anticipate the culinary excitement that awaits at the next meal. And, like travelers to far-off lands who return home with many tales, Eager Eaters can scarcely wait to tell their stories of exploration at table. Recalling the adventure, food talk replicates the pleasure.

At the same time, misadventures are part of every adventure. Pooh's begin when he falls out of a tree looking for honeybees. Then, so avidly does he seek out every last taste of honey that he gets his head stuck in a honeypot. And though he is a good soul who truly cares for his friend, this honey-loving bear cannot refrain from eating the honey that he had set aside to give Eeyore for a birthday present.

In short, Pooh is a glutton. He thinks overmuch about honey and has no notion of moderation. But Pooh is a glutton with a difference—a big difference. In no way does the toy bear resemble the archetypal glutton, with his insistent, enveloping physicality, outsize body, gross eating behavior, and craving for meat—often in the form of animals consumed whole. Represented as a sin, gluttony is meant to be, and is shown to be, repugnant.

Pooh is nothing like. He is a glutton oddly untainted by gluttony. In the first place, he is not obese. He is little, his girth well within the parameters of toy bear-dom. Nor does he show any interest in the meat that marks the glutton as an aggressive carnivore. Fixed in a childhood paradise of milk and honey, Pooh turns out to be a contradiction in terms: a lovable glutton. He is untouched by the negative traits, disgusting characteristics, and offensive behavior that Western cultures have associated with this vice, or sin, these several centuries.

This wonderland of extravagance metes out no real punishment. Pooh is immoderate, to be sure, but moderately so. When he overindulges during a morning visit to Rabbit, his tummy expands so much that he cannot get out of Rabbit's hole. There is nothing to be done except wait until he thins down enough to squeeze through. Which turns out to be a whole week. "*What about meals?*" Pooh plaintively inquires. Alas, there will be no meals for this greedy bear. Stories about food must do. So Pooh requests "a Sustaining Book" for his week of deprivation, and Christopher Robin obligingly reads Pooh a story about jam. Food talk saves the day, though, predictably, the ever-ravenous bear finds it a poor substitute for the real thing.

For the rest of us, however, food talk is no substitute. "Sustaining Books" like *Winnie-the-Pooh* are the real thing because they tell us that food is good, that eating brings great pleasure, and, best of all, that we can indulge with impunity. If there is a problem, food talk will take over. Food is an adventure for Pooh, and he is an example to us all—by no means solely to the children targeted by the book. Will the food do me in or do me good? *Winnie-the-Pooh* answers this urgent question with a resounding hurrah for pleasure. We come back to these stories again and again to renew our pleasure in reading, much as we renew our pleasure in eating.

Lest any reader be tempted to dismiss a children's story as too obviously a fantasy, a never-never land, happy gluttons are not confined to children's stories. Other texts in contemporary culture bring us the same message. The comic strip *Blondie* features a glutton who is both comic and likeable. The strip, which has been running continuously since the 1930s, never tires of showcasing Dagwood Bumstead's inordinate love of eating, his propensity to eat anything and everything at hand at every possible opportunity and to think about food when no food is to be had. Food controls Dagwood's eating life and his fantasy life as well, from his dreams to the books he reads, and, in more recent times, the television shows that he watches.

Dagwood has a prodigious food memory. Despite the fact that he cannot remember "little details" like the name of the restaurant where he and Blondie had their first date, he has total recall of what he ate ("I ordered the roast beef, medium, an end cut, and it was kind of chewy" [14 August 2006]). Even his bedside reading turns on food. The biography of the inventor of barbecuing on a gas grill [21 November 2006] honors a great culinary hero. A cookbook proves so "inspiring" that Dagwood rushes off to raid the family refrigerator for a midnight snack (*Blondie's Cook Book*, [1947] 1996).

Where *Winnie-the-Pooh* takes readers to a fantasy childhood in an equally make-believe English nursery, *Blondie* gives us a protagonist straight from middle America. Dagwood is an all-American (over)eater, through his favorite food, his eponymous sandwich, through the ordinary diner that he frequents, and through his voracious enthusiasm. Of course, like any comic character, he has setbacks—in a recent strip depression sets in when his favorite chef gets booted from the television program "Top Chef."

As with Pooh, neither adventure nor misadventure changes him one whit. He never learns because he never has to. A true comic character, he is always ready to start over. Then, too, just as there was always more honey for Pooh, food never lacks. Dagwood never encounters an unstocked refrigerator when he gets out of bed to make a midnight megasnack. And, again like Pooh, Dagwood has none of the negative traits of gluttony—he is not overweight and he is an exemplary family man, if inclined to laziness (his fondness for naps figures right up there with his love of eating). Food is important, but his family comes first. Dagwood is happy and serves as a model for us all because he has none of the stigma associated with gluttony.

Such is pleasure talk at its most effective. Again and again, readers return to stories such as *Winnie-the-Pooh* and the ever-evolving, yet never-changing story of *Blondie,* and we do so, at least in part, because we see in their adventures a model for our own lives. Their happy relationship with food justifies our own. If Winnie and Dagwood can be happy gluttons, so can we.

CHAPTER THREE

Texts Take Over

Food talk—the right kind, the kind that we want to listen to—equates food with pleasure. A culinary paradise is ours for the eating. It is also, it seems, ours for the talking. For it is here that we find a sense of the pleasures that attend our encounters with food. Speaking about food both before and after the event sharpens our pleasure.

Small wonder, then, that the true Eager Eater hungers not just for food but also for food talk. Strictly construed, of course, we are mostly talking about writing, not talk. To work its full effect on the individual and on society, to transform the individual act of eating into the social phenomenon of consumption, food talk needs texts. The written word opens worlds beyond our ken. It allows, as talk alone does not, access to others.

Notwithstanding the long history of writing about food, modern times have made such writing central to the very notion of modernity. As food came to be seen as an urgent concern, more writers and thinkers, statesmen and rulers, came to recognize just how central it was to their interests, however different these might be. The France that emerged out of the Revolution paid a good deal of attention to food, as the French along with everyone else scrambled to make sense of the new century. Few of those who thought about social change remained oblivious to the dynamic role that cooking and gastronomy played in a world that was changing before their eyes. Food writing exploded into a multiplicity of genres that took stock of, made the most of, or simply tried to understand what food meant for the changing times. An expanding publishing industry accelerated the pace of change, intensified the sense of social dislocation, and prompted the production of culinary writing of all sorts.

FROM TALK TO TEXT

Tell me what you eat, and I'll tell you what you are.

Jean Anthelme Brillat-Savarin, *The Physiology of Taste* (1826)

The originality of Brillat-Savarin's aphorism does not lie in the connection that it makes between eating and being. The German "Man ist, was er isst" or the English "You are what you eat" say almost as much. In contrast to the German or English affirmation of a physiological correlation between food and consumer—after all, eaters literally incorporate the food that they ingest—the French critic places the material and physiological fact of eating in a social context. He insists on the conversational connection. The eater eats, and, even more importantly for everyone else, the eater talks, and, in the best of circumstances, the talker writes. To know our place in the world made by eating, Brillat stipulates, means talking about it.

Why this need to talk about food? Why is food talk so important? First off, eating is a deeply private affair. Because we cannot share the actual food that we consume, we talk about it. We do not share food; we share the experience of food. In so doing we propose our private dining for public perception. We want to convey the great pleasure that we find in food, and we take it upon ourselves to warn others of our displeasures, our disgusts, and, at times, our deadly food encounters. Food talk completes the culinary circuit, turning the private into the public, embellishing the personal, and memorializing the idiosyncratic.

The most memorable meals are not the ones that we eat, and certainly not at the moment of consumption. The really important food is the food that we think about, dream about, and talk about—meals that trace our lives and connect us to a tradition. Passover and the Last Supper are founding meals in the Judeo-Christian tradition. With the exception of the First Meal in the Garden of Eden, none has occasioned more food talk. Even though most of us are not apt to think of such commentary as food talk, sacred texts have a good deal to say about food and the transformations that it effects. Food supplies the medium for the message—translated into a shared language that allows us to pass on the experience to others.

Food talk, and more precisely food writing, creates the cultural artifact—whether Carême's writings, or contemporary television programs that take us step by step through recipes, or the blogs and magazine columns that make celebrity wedding cakes front-page news. Reaching back a bit, there is the over-the-top cake that Gustave Flaubert baked for Emma Bovary's wedding, with its Carême-inspired colonnaded temple, turret, and lakes of jam and boats of slivered hazelnuts topped with a pastry Cupid caught in midair on a chocolate swing. Today, as in the nineteenth century, no formal wedding is complete without the bride, the groom, . . . and the cake that materializes the vows, realizes the celebration, and obliges guests to actively participate in the ritual.

Like food, talk disappears, and that shared ephemerality explains why food talk matters and also makes clear why talk is not enough. Texts allow, and indeed encourage, the comparisons that make judgment, criticism, and analysis possible. By extending the reach of localized culinary practices, these texts lay the foundation for a true culinary culture. To have an effect beyond the individual cook or diner, cooking has to get out of the kitchen; feasting must exit the dining room. That job of conveyance to the larger food world is what food writing does.

If writing about food has been around for as long as records exist, not until modern times, roughly the nineteenth century and particularly in France, did there emerge a consciousness of food writing as a distinct genre born in response to the conditions of contemporary society. For some, food became a social issue; for others, a fashion; and for still others, a lens through which to examine and imagine the new world coming into being around them.

To appreciate the distinctive nature of the modern food world, to grasp what makes it modern, we must remember that food talk has to do with cultural figures, not individuals. For the same reason, food writing is most usefully thought of in terms of the collective rather than the particular—that is, in terms of genres that structure individual works.

The Enthusiast: Athenaeus's Culinary Tourism

Enthusiasm about food is essential to all food talk—all good food talk, at any rate, the food talk that gets, and keeps, our attention. Absent enthusiasm, food talkers would be talking to themselves. The Enthusiast of all Enthusiasts, the writer who set patterns for food talk that continue millennia later, was a Greek living in late second-century Rome. By every standard, *The Deipnosophists* (The scholars at dinner) of Athenaeus (A.D. 170–230) serves up a bizarre banquet. This work, whose first French translator in the seventeenth century appropriately called it "delicious," fills page upon page with a jumble of culinary facts and fabulations, anecdotes and narratives, apparently selected at random. Athenaeus concocts a narrative meal out of seemingly endless discussions of Homeric dinners and diners, table manners, lists of dishes and foods that go on forever, seasoned with commentary taken from poetic, dramatic, philosophical, historical, and medical works relating to food and feeding, cooking and consumption, products and producers.

As classicists have long recognized, *The Deipnosophists* is a compendium of Hellenistic Greece. Its fifteen extant books refer to some fifteen hundred works, most of which, notably the comic dramas, exist today almost entirely through this weird work, which, like so many ancient texts, itself survived through a combination of perseverance and sheer luck. Were it not for Athenaeus's enthusiasms, many of the eight-hundred-odd authors whom he cites would be no more than names. Athenaeus is food talker extraordinaire with whom, even more than classicists, cuisinologists ought to keep company. What better inspiration than this author who encounters no person, place, thing, or event related to food without talking about it at great—at times, interminable—length, and then had the greatest inspiration of all: he wrote it down.

This text that does not end (literally, since so much of it is lost), recounts a meal that never ends. It is a symposium gone bulimic, a dinner without apparent rhyme or reason for either the dishes served or the tales told. The founding fiction is the sumptuous feast to which a Roman citizen has invited a number of his fellows, though the veritable orgy that ensues is less culinary than linguistic. Athenaeus's dinner guests manifest a greater appetite for words than for food. The banquet—three meals, as it turns out—prompts and sustains the narrative—the *logodeipnon,* the meal of words, to use the neologism invented by the first compiler of the work.

There is no end to Athenaeus's stories about food. There are disquisitions on drinking cups, utensils, agriculture, luxury-loving peoples, women and flowers, literature, music and dance—all tied to food or eating. Athenaeus jumps from one topic to another so jauntily that transitions hardly exist: "Well enough of cooks. I must speak of the conger-eel" (3:317). He looks at *The Iliad* and *The Odyssey* and wonders why these meat-eating heroes snub all the fish that surrounds them. He is absolutely fascinated by fish, which turn up just about everywhere. There is also a good deal about wine, its benefits and its drawbacks. He lets us know that wine from Lesbos "will seem to you to possess the glory of ambrosia rather than wine" (1:129). In case of ambrosial overindulgence, the ever-considerate author thoughtfully includes his remedy for hangover (boiled cabbage, to be taken after a nap).

Not surprisingly, cooks are the stars of *The Deipnosophists*. After all, "it isn't given to every man to season a sea-lizard nicely" (1:297). Then come the exotic dishes, such as the "fecund matrix" of the *vulva eiectitia* (sow that has miscarried). The cook's transformative genius comes to the fore in preparing a turnip to taste like anchovy. The reader who loves anchovy (or turnip) can only agree with Athenaeus that "the cook and the poet are just alike: the art of each lies in his brain" (1:33).

Fortunately for Athenaeus, cooks talk a good deal, at least in the comedies that supply the bulk of the material of *The Deipnosophists*. One cook goes so far as to put talking and cooking on equal footing: "A yearning hath crept upon me to come forth and tell to earth and sky how I dressed the dainty" (3:288). Why is it so important that he apprise the world of his great talent? The claim is not a small one. It is nothing less than life itself: "I have found the elixir of life: men already dead, once they but catch a whiff from the dish, I cause to live again" (3:288-290). One would be hard pressed to find the most megalomaniacal of contemporary celebrity chefs pressing a similar claim of resurrection.

Clearly, "the complete cook is made on a different plan" (3:307). As artist, savant, and military commander rolled into a single package, the cook "must acquire many arts held in high esteem . . . painting . . . astrology, geometry, and medicine. . . . It is a matter of military tactics as well—this use of reason and harmony" (3:307-311). Ultimately, in a claim that will echo throughout history, cookery makes civilization possible: "From a bestial and lawless life that art has freed us; from disgusting cannibalism she has led us to discipline . . . a populace came together, cities became civilized, all through this art, I repeat, of cookery" (7:41-43).

In the midst of abundance—a sumptuously laden table centers the narrative—Athenaeus dreams of still more, and since words have the great advantage of ingestion with impunity, no indigestion is to be feared. Food comes to the eater unbidden, begging to be consumed: "Let it snow barley-meal, sprinkle wheat-loaves, rain pease-porridge; let broth roll its lumps of meat through the streets, let a flat-cake give orders to be eaten" (3:213). In this golden age, food produces itself, comes to the table of its own accord. Since no work is required, no servants are needed. Agriculture is bypassed altogether.

> What need have we any longer . . . of seed or vine-propping? Why! Rivers of black broth, gushing forth copiously of their own accord over the cross-roads with rich spice-cakes and barley-cakes of finest meal, will flow from the springs of Plutus all ready to be ladled up. And Zeus will rain smoky wine and drench your tiles like a bathman; and from the roofs conduits of grapes, in company with cheese-cakes, stuffed with cheese, will draw off rills of hot pease-porridge and polenta made of lilies and anemones. The trees on the mountains will put forth leaves of roast kids' guts, tender cuttlefish and boiled thrushes. (3:211)

What one would not give for a taste of lily-anemone polenta!

And so on, and on, and on. The temptation is to keep quoting as Athenaeus comes up with yet another quirky incident, fantastic anecdote, or striking fact—say, about the copulation of dolphins (slow) as opposed to that of other fish (rapid) (4:101). There is always so much more to say about Athenaeus. What is important in the context of food talk, though, is not *The Deipnosophists* as a single text, amazing as it is. Rather, this work offers a template for all food talk. In its own way, *The Deipnosophists* reaches back to Homer and to Plato. Like these illustrious predecessors, Athenaeus reaches forward to talk to us today.

That *The Deipnosophists* continues to offer succulent sustenance after so many centuries attests to its extraordinary culinary diversity and unparalleled gastronomic scope. Most of all, *The Deipnosophists* owes its place in culinary history to the irrepressible exuberance of the author for everything and anything to do with food. Athenaeus is the first, and still unrivalled, tourist of the table—a cuisinologist of unflagging curiosity and indefatigable zeal.

Figure 3. THE MODERN ENTHUSIAST ENERGIZED BY FOOD WRITING. The all-American everyman Dagwood epitomizes the modern Enthusiast, who sees everything in terms of food. Reading a cookbook inspires him to raid the refrigerator. Gluttony is a way of life, the appropriate term not just because Dagwood eats great quantities of food whenever he can but mostly because his life revolves so importantly around food in every form. BLONDIE © 2004 by King Features Syndicate, Inc. World rights reserved.

All kinds of food talk can be found in this mammoth work, whether or not *The Deipnosophists* is acknowledged or, for that matter, known. Athenaeus's enthusiasm infuses food talk everywhere. Food talkers are all Enthusiasts.

Although food talk has been around for a very long time and well before Athenaeus set to work, modern times altered almost beyond recognition the conditions in which it is formulated and attended to. From urbane gastronomes in search of the latest taste sensation in the fanciest restaurant to ordinary eaters worried about their budget, the publics for food talk multiplied prodigiously. The nineteenth century ushered in the age of print, and print reconfigured popular culture as much as elite culinary culture. An expanding publishing industry took advantage of technological inventions like the roller press and cheap paper made of wood pulp, commercial innovations such as advertising, and literary enticements such as the serial novel. The public was voracious.

Food writing was everywhere—in cookbooks, journals, and newspapers, in books of every sort, all of which promoted an awareness of food and a conviction of its importance. The times were propitious for discussions of food and food practices. The Visionary, the Practitioner, the Critic, and the Analyst flourished. The oddball philosopher Charles Fourier (1772-1837), the great chef Marie-Antoine Carême (1784-1833), the first gastronomic journalist-critic, A. B. L. Grimod de La Reynière (1758-1837), and the social analyst J. A. Brillat-Savarin (1755-1826) were all writing in Paris in the first three decades of the nineteenth century. Together and separately, their work taken up by scores of others, these writers laid the foundations of the modern French food world. Each in his own way raised culinary consciousness to an exceptionally high level—precisely the level that French and foreigner alike commonly ascribed to French cuisine and in many quarters continue to do so.

The Visionary: Fourier's Gastrosophy

A slight acquaintance with Athenaeus makes clear just how much the Enthusiast is of this world. Food delights in the here and now. The Visionary, on the other hand, thinks of food very differently. Rather than the end that it is for the Enthusiast, food offers the Visionary a means to reach another—better—world. The nineteenth century hatched a great many schemes of social reorganization, from revolutions in the street to new societies that live on the printed page. One of the most remarkable is the vision of Charles Fourier, which is all the more noteworthy for the place that food and gastronomy played in making the world a better place. Fourier envisioned food in order to imagine a better, infinitely more fulfilling collective existence. To alter the way life is lived was Fourier's goal, and he used food as a fundamental building block.

Fourier's ideal society put pleasure—sensual pleasure—to good purpose. Like Athenaeus he enthusiastically embraced the material world of food. No detail was too mundane for his attention. Sex and food—or, in Fourier's lexicon, love and gourmandise—will sustain the new social order beyond our comprehension, benighted as we are by society as we know it. "The resources of Civilization," he wrote, "can give no idea of the resources of the Combined Order. . . . The events resulting from this Order will give you, not the objects of your desires, but a happiness infinitely superior to all your desires" (1:169–170).

Fourier premises his entire system on material abundance as the guarantor of spiritual abundance—that is, happiness (1:77): "God . . . must have forced us to focus on the most useful attractions. In this treatise these are love and gourmandise, which should be deified to make them more dear to men and to establish religious unity on the most powerful instruments of enthusiasm" (7:20–21). The increased production of Harmony—Fourier's term for his ideal society— will spread abundance throughout society.

People will change. Under this new regime, everyone's prodigious appetites will need five meals a day plus two snacks, men will be seven feet tall, easy digestion will make children strong, and life expectancy will be 144 years (1:180n1). The first meal of the day will be so terrific that everyone will leap out of bed at 5 A.M. (8:482)! Sweetness literally reigns in Harmony since sugar will replace bread (4:19–20). Children—those especially inclined to sugar—will be given a lot (8:121). Moderation is counterproductive, a "travesty of nature" (6:256): "The more this science [gastronomy] is useless and unknown in our indigent societies, the more we should sense that it will occupy the first rank in a social order where there will be no calamities to fear except the surplus of subsistence that will come from industrial perfection" (7:138).

Fourier had to decide how to convey his vision. All the details about life in Harmony, like the unremitting attention to everyday life in most material elements, respond to readers' needs to have an idea of what he was talking about. Hence, like Athenaeus, and with almost as much enthusiasm, Fourier spends considerable time on cooking and cooks. Whereas a cook in our "civilized" society enjoys little prestige, a cook in Harmony "becomes a savant of the first order" (5:115). Cooks can become saints, and—absolutely exceptionally for the period—for Fourier, these cooks included women as well as men. And why not, since cooking "of all the arts is the most revered in Harmony, the linchpin for all agricultural work and the principal space for education." So important is food preparation in Harmony that everyone is trained to be more or less of a cook. Cooking is "everyone's science" (7:131). Likewise, on the consumption side, this society will no longer dismiss gastronomy as a frivolous waste of time and resources. To the contrary, it will recognize in "gastrosophy" a "science of advanced social politics" (4:130).

And so Fourier built what one contemporary called "a gastronomic throne surrounded by culinary institutions," a new monarchy in which diners, producers, and cooks come together to partake of this "high gastronomic wisdom" and benefit from a "deep and sublime theory of social equilibrium" (4:30). For all that Fourier worked to construct a logically ordered society, he was a Visionary, a poet and a prophet, whose writings raised food to transcendental status. It is this sense of limitless possibility in the most ordinary of activities that captured the imagination of the nineteenth century and has a good deal to say to the twenty-first.

The Practitioner: Carême's Treatise

It is hard to conceive of any writer more wedded to the material, the quotidian, and the daily duties of cooking than Marie-Antoine Carême. Yet, Carême had a strong sense of what cooking was and could be. Where Fourier modeled a new society, Carême established a cuisine and a profession. This celebrity chef when there were no celebrity chefs routinely signed himself (with royal approval) simply "Carême de Paris." Known as "the chef of kings, and the king of chefs," Carême was chef to Napoleon's foreign minister Talleyrand, whose delicate diplomatic negotiations relied on Carême's equally delicate cuisine. He subsequently became chef to the Prince Regent of England and then, once again with Talleyrand, supervised the French kitchens at the Congress of Vienna that decided the fate of post-Napoleonic France. His final post saw him serving the wealthiest of the wealthy, Baron Rothschild. The sumptuous yet natural meals that Carême prepared were legendary. Of his patrons, he asked only that they not stint on his provisions: "The man born to wealth lives to eat, and supports the art of the cook," he decreed, adding for good measure that "a miserly rich man lives in mediocrity." Few patrons lived up to Carême's standards. When the proper provisions for cuisine as he understood it were not forthcoming, the great chef quit the service of Tsar Alexander I in a snit, leaving Saint Petersburg without preparing a single meal.

His vision of fine dining made Carême a creature of the ancien régime. He stressed the magnificence of French cuisine, the spectacularity that gave such scope to his acclaimed skills as a pastry maker. The great banquet table had all his care. The so-called French service—all the dishes for a given course on the table at once—was the only mode of presentation that did justice to the splendid pastry centerpieces (*pièces montées*) that were responsible for his quasilegendary status among his contemporaries.

Carême's heart may have been firmly set in the eighteenth century, but his practice and his principles made him very much a chef of the nineteenth. He saw his cuisine as modern: "modern cuisine will owe to me its elegance and notable progress." This modern cuisine was of its century. "Nineteenth-century French cuisine," he declared, "must be the example for centuries to come."

This conviction that he was creating a new world at table is crucial to appreciating Carême's reputation. His most important contribution to French cuisine came, as he well knew, not from his unequaled talent as a chef but from the cookbooks that translated his cooking from the kitchen into the food world at large. Carême did not just collect recipes. Others had done so and would continue to do so. Carême's work stood apart because it worked out a culinary system. Recipes made sense in relation to a rationalized system of preparation. "The analytical spirit of the 19th century" informed all his work.

So alert was Carême to the possibilities offered by the printed word in a rapidly changing social and culinary landscape that he self-published his cookbooks, making sure to include engravings of his own drawings of his confections. He took his cue from the illustrious predecessors whom he revered. These great chefs never wrote a word. Think of the loss to the art of fine cuisine! Carême would not follow suit. His cuisine was modern, it was French, and it was for everyone. Like Fourier, however different the perspective, Carême intended his food talk to have a general utility. The care that he took with the drawings meant that even women would be able follow the recipes. It was his fervent wish for "every citizen in our beautiful France to be able to eat delicious food." His writings about food brought this vision of the Practitioner at least into the realm of possibility.

The Critic: Grimod de La Reynière's Gastronomic Criticism
Alexandre Balthazar Laurent Grimod de La Reynière gave little thought to the ordinary run of either diners or dinners. He directed his attention to what counted gastronomically, which meant those able to afford this most exigent and newest of social practices. Like Carême, though operating in a different social sphere, Grimod intended his work to be "useful." That reason alone, he announced in the preface to the *Manuel des Amphitryons* (Manual for hosts, 1808), led him to undertake writing. Ever the pedagogue, Grimod aimed his instructions at those whom he considered in need of learning to live well, which, for him, meant dining well. The new society had not altered the duties of either hosts or guests, "but it wasn't the same people who fulfilled them." Absent the *savoir vivre* that comes from connection to a tradition, these new age, would-be gastronomes needed to learn how to practice gastronomy correctly. Grimod offered his "science" and his services.

The *Manuel des Amphitryons* offered lessons to these new elites on the traditions and practices of gastronomy, from carving meat to folding napkins. (These topics are less idiosyncratic than they might seem to modern readers, since both carving and napkin folding were standard subjects in a number of earlier cookbooks and treatises.) These and other fine points of dining did more than embellish eating. They were not "extras." They laid the foundation of good dining, a veritable art, and as such necessary to the proper practice of gastronomy. Grimod took the etymology of gastronomy seriously. He attended to the laws of the stomach, or, in his rendering, the rules of civilized consumption. Gastronomy, as Grimod preached its gospel, is all about order and control of individual appetite in the name of the art of living well. His was the voice of experience and the wisdom of tradition.

The contrast with Carême is striking. Both Carême and Grimod took aristocratic dining of the ancien régime as their model. But Carême, who was born to lower-class parents only a few years before the Revolution, took his notion of that world from the books in the Royal Library, which he frequented assiduously, and from older colleagues. Grimod, just over thirty years of age in 1789, had himself been part of that society. In some respects his writing was an exercise in nostalgia, a vehicle for resurrecting a world that was lost to him and to France. Like many others who lamented the ravages of the Revolution on polite society, Grimod mourned a bygone era. Unlike most others, he endeavored to recreate at least some of the traditions of that world.

The title page of the *Manuel* gives the scope of Grimod's ambitions: the book contains a treatise on carving (the technical French term is *dissection*) meat at table and a program of the newest menus for every season (a "celebrated restaurateur" advised him in setting it up). But the most important, and certainly the most revelatory, sections of Grimod's food talk are the fundamentals of *politesse gourmande,* which translates imperfectly as "courtesy at table." A host worthy of the name needed to master all of these practices to live up to Grimod's exalted conception of what the host should do—indeed, what the host should be. The typically wordy nineteenth-century title page proclaims this work "indispensable for all those desirous of eating well" and "to have others do so as well." The *Manuel*, as he summed it up, was "a sort of catechism" on "the art of living well."

That gastronomy, as Grimod notes in the preface to the *Manuel*, had become fashionable was in no small measure due to his own *Almanach des Gourmands*, the journal that he published from 1803 to 1812. The term *gastronomie* had come into usage only in 1801. In a few short years it was everywhere: in kitchens and society drawing rooms, libraries, and even in the theater. The first critic to take food seriously in terms of the market, Grimod made a great and lasting contribution to food talk by creating gastronomic journalism. He remains the model of the food critic as judge.

For all his allegiance to the formalities of gastronomy and adherence to the culinary traditions of aristocratic society, Grimod was exceptionally attuned to the emerging market for fine dining. A relentless critic of provisions and purveyors no less than consumers, Grimod sought to order the chaotic market of postrevolutionary dining, with its increasingly prominent elegant restaurants and their enthusiastic clientele. For that market to operate optimally—that is, with the greatest benefit to gastronomy—consumers had to be knowledgeable and purveyors had to be held to a high standard. With tests that he called "legitimations," he evaluated the quality of foods submitted to him by purveyors. Grimod took the market very seriously indeed.

Grimod had his own unmistakable voice. But his importance lies less in that voice than in the figure that he embodied and the culinary genre that he inaugurated. Our food world depends crucially on its judges. All food critics owe their existence to Grimod and his culinary adventure, which launched the modern food world.

The Analyst: Brillat-Savarin's Social Analysis

After the offbeat imaginings of Fourier, the meticulous directives of Carême, and the strict commands of Grimod de La Reynière, it is something of a relief to encounter a writer content to deal with things as they are, as opposed to how they could, should, or might be—a writer who seeks to observe the world, not change it. The unfaltering popularity of Jean Anthelme Brillat-Savarin's *Physiology of Taste* from its publication in 1826 to today owes much to this genial relationship to things culinary. Not for this amiable discussant the focused practical advice that made Carême's work so influential or the authoritative decrees of Grimod. Brillat's writing retains the quality of talk and personality of the incomparable conversationalist that the man must have been.

For Brillat as for Grimod, gastronomy was a social practice in the here and now. In contrast to Grimod's strong sense of obligation to the past and mission to promote standards of conduct rooted in that past, Brillat's concern was the present, and, on occasion, the future. Thus the *Physiology* ends with a historical elegy, in which he pities the gastronomes of the past who did not know the wonderful offerings of the food world of 1825. The same belief in culinary progress also leads him to pity these gastronomes—to whom he dedicates the *Physiology*—because they, poor souls (including himself), will never know the delights of elegant dining in 1900.

From an idiosyncratic amalgam of anecdote and empirical observation, and drawing on philosophy, medicine, and ethics, Brillat examines the fluid, modern taste community of connoisseurs who, as he takes care to point out, can be found in every social station: "Pleasure at table is for every age, every condition, every country and every day; it can be tied to all our other pleasures, and remains the last one to console us for the loss of the others" (Aphorism VII).

Brillat elevates gastronomy to the rank of a science and justifies what he calls "social gourmandise" by its exceptional social utility—like Fourier and Carême, he places food within a broader social context in which a meal is always more than food, dining more than eating. The meal is the cornerstone of "social gourmandise" because it turns a varied assortment of consumers into a community of companions.

Brillat's popularity was immediate and long-lasting. The aphorisms with which the book opens are cited endlessly. There is no resisting such gems:

Animals fill themselves; humans eat; intelligent people alone know how to eat.

At table is the only place where one is never bored for the first hour.

The discovery of a new dish does more for the happiness of mankind than the discovery of a star.

Dessert without cheese is a beautiful woman who is missing one eye.

To invite people is to take charge of their happiness the whole time they are under our roof.

Small wonder that the *Physiology* has not gone out of print in French since its publication and that English editions abound. Grimod de La Reynière has not been so fortunate. One is hard put to come up with any pithy phrase that captures Grimod's sensibility. Pedagogy does not lend itself to condensation. It is just as likely a question of temperament—the adamant traditionalist against the amiable modern commentator. Grimod established a genre; Brillat brings a sensibility to life. The food world owes more to the Critic, but it is Brillat whom we read and reread, quote and remember.

The Artists: Proust's and Woolf's Culinary Worlds
With its vision of what food does to and for us, and how it does so, art complements food talk. Visionaries of the everyday, artists fix on food to realize for the rest of us the worlds that they imagine. Among the most insightful of these artistic visionaries, Marcel Proust (1871-1922) and Virginia Woolf (1882-1941) exploited the resources of food to make larger claims. Proust is the master of sensuality, Woolf of sociability. Where Proust, in *A la recherche du temps perdu* (In search of lost time), focuses on food in all its materiality, Woolf, in *To the Lighthouse*, gives her attention to the fleeting moment of the

meal. If Proust channels Carême, Woolf bows to Brillat-Savarin. Each bends the model to different, distinctively aesthetic ends.

No reader of Proust's great novel can fail to be struck by the culinary sensibility that inflects the protagonist's everyday life. Food is everywhere, from the much-celebrated madeleine that opens the novel to the many meals of the narrator's childhood in Combray, his adolescence in Normandy, and his adulthood in Paris. The signature dish of the novel is a magnificent beef in aspic, whose construction Proust follows from beginning to end, reprising as he does so his own writing of the novel. Emblematic of the absolute centrality of cooking to Proust's conception of creativity, the episode is one that everyone concerned with food is bound to examine.

Like Michelangelo seeking "the most perfect blocks of marble for his monument to Julius II" Françoise, the cook, begins her masterpiece with a special trip to the market to procure the right cuts of meat. Just as the dish takes vast amounts of time and requires a great many procedures, so Proust's novel called for many years and much fastidious work (it was published from 1913 to 1927; the final volumes appeared posthumously). Enriched by the carefully selected meats, the stock must simmer for hours—recipes routinely stipulate twenty-five hours cooking time—for the flavors to blend into a whole that transcends the parts. That stock, the quintessence of the many and diverse ingredients, must then be purified (in culinary terms, clarified by filtering through egg white or eggshells). Only then will the cook achieve the "transparent crystals" that Proust regards as worthy of Michelangelo. The novel, like the beef in aspic, transcends its origins and bears witness to its creation.

The sculptural beef in aspic proves a compelling example of the conversion of the raw of experience into the cooked of art. Proust's narrator comes to realize that in it, or rather in its creation, he has found the novel that he is trying to write. "Why," the narrator asks himself late in the novel and late in life, "wouldn't I make my book the way Françoise made the boeuf mode . . .

where so many pieces of choice meat enriched the aspic?" The monumentality on which Proust insists with his references to Michelangelo directly opposes the ephemerality of food. *This* boeuf mode, Proust boasts, *his* boeuf mode, like Michelangelo's memorial, will endure.

This defiant challenge to the transitory nature of food ties Proust to Carême, who shared a vision of food as sculpture. Carême began his career as a pastry maker and made his mark with elaborate pastry confections. His first two books were devoted to pastry, complete with his own drawings. *Le pâtissier pittoresque* (The picturesque pastry maker, 1815) includes a history of the five orders of architecture, of which pastry, he boasted, was the last. Not for nothing did contemporaries call Carême the "pastry-architect," the "Palladio" of cuisine. Michelangelo is not so far off the culinary mark after all.

Like Proust's beef in aspic, Woolf's *boeuf en daube* in *To the Lighthouse* is a "triumph." This succulent beef stew—whose French recipe the hostess, Mrs. Ramsay, has inherited from her grandmother—centers the dinner in the first section of the novel. In contrast to Proust, who takes cooking as a model for his book, Woolf focuses on dining. Why does Mrs. Ramsay not serve grilled steak or roast beef? The least culinarily attuned of my students understands the vital connection between the slow cooking that turns the many and various ingredients into a whole that is much more than the sum of its parts and Mrs. Ramsay's creativity as a hostess. The Provençal stew of many parts figures to perfection the fleeting moment of perfect communion.

For the decidedly masculine sensibility of the professional chef and conventional host, Proust and Woolf substitute the creativity of women and women's traditional work. Proust promotes the humble cook, a woman (a peasant, to boot), to the pantheon of great artists. Woolf only mentions Mildred the cook because it is not cooking but the meal that interests her, the transformation of dining, not the metamorphosis of food. Cooking is a means to that end.

Mrs. Ramsay does not do the work of cooking. The dining room, not the kitchen, is her domain. She prepares people, not foods. She specializes in human relations. Presiding at the table and dispensing the meat in its sauce, she "put a spell on them all." She and the food that she so lovingly dispenses connect the guests over and above their many and evident differences. The beef stew is the apposite image of a transitory moment of understanding and the work that makes it happen. Like Proust's beef in aspic, Woolf's *boeuf en daube* brings together many different ingredients—the "exquisite scent of olives and oil and juice," with a "confusion of savoury brown and yellow meats and its bay leaves, and its wine," and takes much effort—three days of preparation.

Unlike Proust with the pot roast, Woolf emphasizes the parts of the stew, the separate pieces of beef that after much time and attention merge into a greater whole. The "perfect triumph" is the transformation of those parts into a whole. The cook's preparation both mirrors and prepares Mrs. Ramsay's work: "Some change at once went through them all, as if this had really happened, and they were all conscious of making a party together." With its many ingredients simmered for a long time and consumed in an instant, the stew epitomizes a precious, fleeting moment of coming together against all odds: "It partook, she felt, carefully helping Mr. Bankes to a specially tender piece, of eternity. . . . There is a coherence in things. . . . Of such moments, she thought, the thing is made that endures. . . . It could not last, she knew, but . . . the whole is held together."

In the world of perpetual change that Woolf renders so poignantly, the beef stew must disappear, and moments of communion must end: "She waited a moment longer in a scene which was vanishing even as she looked, and then, . . . it changed . . .; it had become . . . already the past." That past moment, like the dish, has become part of us.

Both Proust and Woolf write within the traditions of food writing. Proust's culinary lineage harks back to Carême and the tradition of architectural confections, while Woolf, who admired Proust, aligns her novel with Brillat's reflections on conviviality. Scrutinizing the social context of dining, Brillat proclaims gourmandise to be "one of the basic social bonds." The love of good food creates vital ties in society. It "gradually extends the spirit of conviviality which brings the different social groups together every day, melds them into a single goal, animates conversation." Although it does not eliminate social difference, the connection brought to life by gourmandise nevertheless "softens . . . the angles of ordinary inequality." The equality is no less vital for being temporary. Brillat does not dwell on the momentary nature of this conviviality. Woolf mourns the loss as she celebrates the moment. Brillat analyzes this world; Woolf envisions another one.

With all the differences that apply, Brillat's description of the conviviality stimulated by a good dinner is of a piece with Mrs. Ramsay's dinner party. Neither Brillat nor Woolf considers hunger. Pleasure at table has nothing to do with the need to eat. The meal really begins only once the first pangs of hunger are appeased. As Brillat put it, "Reflection sets in, conversation starts, another order of things is set in motion." This new order, like cooking itself, signals a radical transformation: "The guest who, until that moment, was only a consumer" turns into "a more or less convivial companion."

Proust and Woolf illuminate our dual relationship to food and art, the simultaneous sensuality and spirituality of the material. In a novel, food is never just food but it always is also food. Proust and Woolf, great food artists that they are, take the specifics of everyday life, the ordinary gestures of cooking and serving, and raise them to the level of art. The grapes, pears, and bananas that Rose Ramsay arranges so artfully, and upon which a guest "feasted his eyes," become a "trophy fetched from the bottom of the sea, . . . Neptune's banquet." Mrs. Ramsay kept "guard over the dish of fruit . . ., hoping that nobody would touch it." Contemplating the "curves and shadows" of the fruit as if it were a painting, "without knowing why . . . she felt more and more serene." In time, "a hand reached out, took a pear, and spoilt the whole thing." The Artist leaves us with memories of the culinary marvel that—like the sculptural beef, the stew, and the fruit—we accept forever. Proust and Woolf invite every reader to the table to partake of the only food that lasts—the feast laid by the Artist.

THE FOOD WORLD AS A CULTURAL FIELD

The most striking feature of all these writings about food is their affinities. They may not have been in agreement, but these writers were bound by their interest in food and in talking about it. Making use of their many personal and institutional connections, they constructed a social network around the practice of food talk and food writing. The writers all knew of one another and, more importantly, knew the others' work. Still more significant than any personal connections is the cultural resonance of their writing. Grimod de La Reynière was right about gastronomy: everyone wanted to get in the act. Its social role could not be ignored any more than the multiple functions of food in modern society that these writings analyzed, amplified, and promoted. The frenetic pace of modern society joined to accelerated social change had untold repercussions in the ways food was practiced.

These writings about food, and many others, acted in concert. They produced a discourse about gastronomy that raised culinary consciousness. That discourse, along with associated practices and institutions, formed what sociologists, following Pierre Bourdieu, call a "cultural field"—that is, an identifiable social universe endowed with distinctive institutions and operating with a certain degree of autonomy. I have claimed that the practice of gastronomy in nineteenth-century France established just such a cultural field. It was the intensity of the interrelations in this field that set nineteenth-century Paris apart from its competitors. There were food writers elsewhere, but in France alone food writing created the density of textual and social relationships that set up a cultural field.

Enthusiasts, Visionaries, Practitioners, Critics, Analysts, and Artists talk their talk today as they did in times past. Nevertheless, they do so differently, and to different effect. However much the past weighs on the present, the food world today differs markedly from food worlds past. For one, it has become incomparably more forceful. The proliferation of food talk and the sheer number of food talkers have sharpened our sense of what we are doing and make us critical of what gets done. From home cook to restaurant chef, from authoritative critic to fly-by-night blogger, participants are acutely aware of where they stand in relation to the many culinary hierarchies that rule in the twenty-first-century food world.

Today, the food world reaches further and is structured more loosely than it was a century ago. Nevertheless, today's internationalized, globalized food world operates a lot like a cultural field. Autonomy of action is a key feature. There is no denying that the food world today exerts an influence on the larger social world remarkably independent of social, economic, and political institutions and ideals. As the last two chapters of this book make clear, to a startling degree, the food world goes its own way.

As in nineteenth-century France, with the emergence of gastronomy as both practice and discourse, our latter-day cultural field draws upon new, or newly strengthened, resources: the industrialization that reconfigured the food world, the internationalization and globalization of trade, and an increase in disposable income in the developed world that encourages more people to indulge a taste for travel. The hyperdevelopment and proliferation of the media have catapulted celebrity chefs, critics, and food talkers generally into the center of the food world. Some are celebrated, most are not, but the bright lights that the media train on every corner of the food world certainly dramatize, and most likely accentuate, the culinary, economic, and social stratification of this world.

The media are all the more effective for the new forms that generate new publics and expand old ones. The free-for-all of the Internet affords immediate access to untold numbers to enthuse, preach, offer advice and critique, share recipes, and also mobilize like-minded advocates of one or another principle of conduct. Practitioners and Critics, Analysts and Artists all have multiple forums at their fingertips. Scholars set up Listservs to organize discussion groups, while newspapers and journals make space for readers' responses to articles and opinion pieces. Typing in almost any ingredient brings up recipes galore, each with readers' comments, modifications, substitute ingredients, and different proportions. Its chattiness encouraged by the new media, food talk today comes closer to a conversation than ever before. The information so readily available, from news to gossip, produces the heightened culinary consciousness that allies our food world to a cultural field.

FOOD TALK TODAY

Affinities notwithstanding, this culinary consciousness operates quite differently than in times past. The coherence, and impact, of the gastronomic field that emerged in nineteenth-century Paris was tied to a number of conditions, chief among which were size and numbers. Paris was still a French city, however cosmopolitan; the centralization of the French government and the concentration of French culture in Paris focused food talk and fixed attention all the more determinedly on gastronomy. The internationalization of the market, and later globalization, increased the numbers, the diversity of individuals and institutions, and especially the complexity of their relations. Practices and discourses once subsumed in a comprehensive cultural field multiplied and diversified so that today we can identify semi-independent fields for cooks and cookbooks, chefs and restaurants.

The social, economic, and cultural configuration of the gastronomic field has changed as the market has put a great range of foods and representations into circulation. So, too, food talk has adopted new perspectives. Along with the social roles of cooks and chefs explored in chapters 4 and 5, and the practices of new age gastronomy discussed in chapters 6 and 7, a newly prominent kind of food talk focuses on products.

To be sure, foods have always fascinated. Truffles, for one, have been emblematic in French culture for centuries. Brillat-Savarin goes on about their alleged aphrodisiacal virtues and, as the discussion of the film *Haute Cuisine* in chapter 1 indicates so dramatically if unerotically, they continue to recall a certain idea of France. The hot dogs in the competitive eating contest on the Fourth of July are just as assuredly American, and the soup that made the emperor cry in *Le Grand Chef* is the essence of Korea. The list could be extended for just about every country. A variation of pleasure talk, this new food talk promotes consumption, determines production, and identifies the culinary sensibility of our times.

Adventures in Chocolate

> Brilliant, dense, smooth, light, melt-in-the-mouth crunchy, soothing, delectable, perfect, aromatic, seductive, succulent, over-the-top . . .
>
> Tote bag logo for Jeff de Bruges Chocolates

For a sense of how food talk shapes and is shaped by today's changing food world, we can do no better than look to chocolate. As we know it today, chocolate is a modern confection. It came to Europe as an elegant drink in the late seventeenth century. Milk chocolate dates from the early nineteenth century, and the chocolate bar from later in the century. The American standard, Whitman's, proudly traces its chocolates to 1842, and its iconic sampler collection celebrated its one hundredth anniversary in 2012.

Today's chocolate world puts at our disposal amazing and unexpected kinds of chocolate. Chocolate talk circulates quickly, too. Twenty or thirty years ago, talk about chocolate was unremarkable, except, perhaps, among professionals and connoisseurs. Advertising was low key. Chocolates were tokens of affection for one's sweetheart or children's delight. Twenty-first-century chocolate has grown up. Aggressively sensual advertising stresses the eroticism of chocolate. Topics no one thought about twenty years ago, and certainly did not think to talk about, give rise to impassioned debates over the merits of Venezuelan cacao over Mexican or Brazilian. The promises of chocolate are pure pleasure talk. The film *Chocolat* shows the many sides of chocolate—its sensuality, exotic origins in South American tradition, transformational potential, and dangers as well.

Chocolate talk today insists on the link between grower, chocolate maker, and consumer. Good for the consumer no less than the artisan, chocolate now comes to us as good, too, for the environment and the producer. Today's chocolate is a "multi-cultural citizen of the world," the Paris Salon du Chocolat proclaims, and a good citizen at that. Fair trade practices ensure the well-being of developing countries rather than their exploitation.

As for the chocolatier, a veritable artisanal chocolate revolution has set chocoholics to endless discussions. Beyond the creams, nuts, and caramels of the venerable Whitman's sampler lies the land of haut chocolate. Chocolate turns up infused with everything from the familiar (vanilla, lavender), traditional (rose water, citrus) and popular (peanut butter) to the historical (chili), startling (wild Tuscan fennel pollen, sake), and frankly improbable (horseradish and lemon zest, wasabi), not excluding the pretty much unknown (aboriginal anise, myrtle). The chocolate revolution has moved lowly milk chocolate from a childhood treat to a decidedly adult pleasure. With less sugar and more cacao, this mass-market candy bids fair to vanquish the disdain of the truest chocolate devotee.

The dominant theme of the new chocolate talk is the pleasure without end that chocolate brings (there is always more chocolate to be had), not to mention the benefits to health and general well-being. We are exhorted to "discover the secret world inside this box—a place of beauty, works of art, pieces of joy." Or to choose antioxidant dark chocolate "to support lasting inner strength." Good chocolate is dark chocolate plus—high cacao content with preferably unusual fillings. Appeals to the senses are everywhere, often with not-so-subtle intimations of sexual gratification added to the mix. Food pornography pushes every image.

Chocolate frenzy? Pleasure talk without constraint? It is in any case a wonderfully apt demonstration of the way food talk takes up product and realigns the market for that product by pushing some images and obscuring others. The presence of chocolate in contemporary society has a great deal to do with chocolate talk. For an idea of how the food world got to this point of preoccupation with a product that has long been thought of as a luxury food, we need to look at the cooks who taught us how to eat and the chefs who showed us how exciting food can be.

PART II

New Cooks, New Chefs

CHAPTER FOUR

Iconic Cooks

Food talk is for every age, every society, and every person. Nevertheless, in the West, the exemplary food talkers, the most enthusiastic culinary conversationalists, the writers of cookbooks and the authors of gastronomic commentary mostly are, and certainly were, Greek and Roman, French, English, and German. Where, Americans might well ask, are we? The quick answer is that Americans were learning the language of food talk. Joining the culinary conversation meant learning to talk about food meaningfully and effectively. It meant agreeing about essentials.

And this Americans learned from our cooks. It was not the gastronome or the gourmet or the high-powered chef who taught us how to eat and talk about food knowledgeably and interestingly. It was cooks—women, not men—who translated gastronomy into the practices of everyday life and made good food a matter for discussion. Once American women took it upon themselves to talk about their cooking—and especially, to write it down— and once Americans were ready to listen, Americans could start talking about food for real.

WOMEN'S WORK AND WOMEN'S WORDS

When it comes to ranking occupations, cooking has long labored under two handicaps. First, necessity. The repetitive preparation of food—day in, day out—has to happen. Everyone has to eat, and someone has to see to the feeding. Constrained by the insistent needs of everyday life, clamoring children, hungry husbands, and, on occasion, greedy guests, domestic cooks work the ordinary. Meals are expected and noticed mostly when the expected does not occur. We mind when dinner is not ready as promised and take little notice when everything arrives on schedule. The needs that determine the cook's agenda keep cooking from existing in its own right.

Then, too, and very much an extension of the ordinariness of the expected, cooking has always been women's work. Most of the time and in most places, it still is. When men are involved, typically, cooking becomes a vocation, a profession, or a hobby—that is, a choice made at one's leisure. A woman "simply" does her job. Is it so surprising that even the most enlightened among us in the supposedly advanced twenty-first century, women no less than men, tend to see cooking as one more expression of what a woman does, must do, and should do, as wife, mother, hostess, nursemaid, housekeeper, and neighbor? This, despite the women we all know who do not do "their " job, who rely on convenience foods, on take-out and order-in, and are often clueless in the kitchen. The telephone and now the Internet have become more essential kitchen equipment than knives, spatulas, or pots and pans.

So persistent is this image of the cook subject to the whims of her family or the dictates of an employer that ambitious (male) chefs have long made it a point of honor, not to mention professional dignity, to distinguish themselves from (female) cooks. According to the military model that originated in ancien régime France, a *chef de cuisine* commands culinary operations like a general directing a battle. The cliché remains a favorite with chefs intent on calling attention to their hard work. It was entirely predictable that male chefs—not female cooks—would run the restaurants that became so characteristic a feature of the urban scene. Women ventured into the public sphere at some peril to their reputation. Like other workers aspiring to be recognized as bona fide professionals, chefs vaunted an expertise attained only through rigorous training and on which they claimed a monopoly. The nurturing female has no place in the professional kitchen, where professional norms, not individual fancy or affective ties determine the standards of excellence. It has long been axiomatic that the higher you climb on the culinary ladder, the fewer women you are likely to find on the rungs.

For cooking to attain the prestige of a "real" profession, it has to come first—before the people involved, before concerns about nutrition, before issues of health and hygiene, before both budgets and moral imperatives. Cooking must be prized for its own sake rather than for what it can do. "Good for you" is not enough: food must be good on its own terms. The preparation of food like the presentation of a meal must be more than a means. It must be an end in itself.

Clearly, this model of cooking proposes an ideal. No cook can afford to disdain the preferences of diners. Yet, without a sense of all the things that cooking can do, "women's work" will remain subject to the mundane necessities of daily life. It will be thought ordinary and unremarkable, and disregarded accordingly. At least some of the time for some cooks, cooking has to be its own reward. "The most important ingredient you can bring to [cooking]," Julia Child and her coauthors declared in the foreword of the influential *Mastering the Art of French Cooking* (1961), "is love of cooking for its own sake."

Putting this love into action is no simple matter. It means rethinking cooking and realigning the cook and the chef. Some of the prestige, rigor, and pride of chefing has to infuse ordinary, routine cooking. Something of the professional's skill has to make its way into the domestic kitchen. Some portion of the artist's pride in culinary creation has to make it to the dining table at home. Finally, at least some of the time, these aspirations must outweigh nutritional or ideological principles. Eating, in sum, needs to do more than satisfy the appetite, fill the stomach, and ward off disease. It must be regarded as a pleasure, and a higher pleasure at that. Then, and only then, will cooking become a culinary art.

The advantage that French cuisine has long enjoyed in the West owes a great deal to the close connection that it sets up between cooking and chefing. Home food and restaurant fare, everyday plain and special-occasion fancy, are not two separate worlds as they tended to be in America. Until recently—say, the past quarter century for most Americans—the public world of the professional chef scarcely intersected with the private domain of the domestic cook. For many it still doesn't. In France, by contrast, the style of cooking known as *cuisine bourgeoise* translated public chefing into private cooking, as it was meant to. Like the bourgeoisie itself, which took its cultural cues from the aristocracy, *cuisine bourgeoise* looked to its betters— that is, to the elegant dishes prepared in the kitchens of royalty and the aristocracy.

The very title of François Massialot's *Le cuisinier roïal et bourgeois* (The royal and bourgeois chef, 1691) makes the connection explicit. Where *la grande cuisine*—destined for "les grands," or "the great"—went all out for spectacle, *cuisine bourgeoise* was all discretion. If it did not disdain a bit of show now and again, on the whole the bourgeois table did not, because it could not, undertake the complex and lavish dishes prepared in the extensive kitchens of the great houses. The single household did not have the requisite human resources, from scullery maids and cooks to the aptly named "officer of the kitchen," later the *chef de cuisine* (head of the kitchen). Nor did it have easy access to the rare and exotic material ingredients required for the conspicuous consumption of *la grande cuisine*. Nevertheless, as Massialot's cookbook suggests, the two cuisines were intimately connected. *La grande cuisine* established a crucial model for the bourgeois household.

For Americans in the nineteenth and early twentieth centuries, and particularly for American women cooking at home, the idea of cooking as an art to be undertaken for its own sake would have been nothing less than revolutionary. The insistent demands of family and the equally emphatic directives of nutritionists made it unlikely that many domestic cooks thought of cooking in terms of indulgence. Overriding concern for keeping one's house in good order and one's family in good health drove the success of such cookbooks as Sarah Josepha Hale's *The Good Housekeeper* (1841), dedicated "To Every American Woman, who wishes to promote the Health, Comfort, and Prosperity of her Family."

As Hale tells her readers in the preface to the first edition, published in 1839, she intends her book "to show the rich how they may preserve their health, and yet enjoy the bounties of Providence; and to teach the poor that frugal management which will make their homes the abode of comfort." These "rational and Christian views of domestic economy," Hale asserts, have "never before been enforced in a treatise on housekeeping." For Mrs. Hale and for the readers whom she addressed, cooking was a means to these estimable ends. Pleasure for the cook was out of the question. Even though Hale did not overlook taste altogether, she placed "gratification of taste" after "the promotion of health" and "the study of economy" (preface to the second edition).

Perhaps the later disapproval by settled Americans of immigrant foods had something to do with the seemingly unseemly gusto with which these "other" women and men approached food and its preparation and the disregard they showed for the nutritional concerns that were coming to dominate mainstream American food discourse. Despite Americans' evident and often vocal pride in local produce and preparations, from corn and chicken to barbecue and chowder, little was heard about the skill of producers or the art of producing. The omnipresence of health concerns—"other" cuisines were deemed dangerous because they were not thought to be as nutritious as "real" American food—put another damper on judging cooking on its intrinsic merits. For many Americans through the mid-twentieth century, cooking remained largely instrumental, whether geared toward the health of diners or, on special celebratory occasions, justifying indulgence.

French culinary tradition looked at food, cooking, and eating quite differently. Its emphasis on the culinary arts, the political and social significance of the culinary spectacles of royal banquets, and the strong connection between *cuisine des grands* and *cuisine bourgeoise* came together to endow French cuisine with a large repertory of dishes in which both the French and outsiders recognized a tradition of excellence. "The Frenchman," explain Child and Co. in the foreword of *Mastering The Art of French Cooking,* "takes his greatest pleasure from a well-known dish impeccably cooked and served." A crucial complicity allies the cook and the diner. Metaphorically as well as literally, they sit at the same table.

New Culinary Connections

American cooking came into its own in the last two or three decades of the twentieth century, when Americans—men and women alike—embarked on a passionate, and vocal, engagement with food. Ever-greater numbers of Americans enthusiastically explored new worlds of food. They (re)discovered classic American dishes, often giving them a new twist. Local produce and erstwhile ethnic dishes moved across the country, becoming "American" in the process. Having shed their ties to the Jewish immigrants in the Lower East Side of New York City, bagels have become, in one form or another, standard items across the country (if not especially "authentic").

Like cooks everywhere, American cooks set about appropriating foods from elsewhere. Appropriation meant Americanization. Produce, ingredients, and dishes once considered impossibly exotic entered the American culinary lexicon. Who today even thinks of quiche or croissants as particularly French? Of arugula or sun-dried tomatoes or pizza as Italian in any real sense? McDonald's made (French) fries as American as the Big Mac they invariably accompany. If your local market does not yield the flavorful olive oil that you need for a particular recipe or the microbrewed root beer that you crave, the stupendous food resources of the Internet are only a click or two away.

With some exaggeration and a good deal of pride, we can nod and agree with commentator after commentator that by the new millennium America had become a gourmet nation. The change entailed nothing less than a food revolution. To judge by all the media hoopla, from newspapers and magazines to television and the Internet, Americans came alive to the sheer fun of food—cooking it, eating it, talking about it, writing about it.

Revolutions do not take place without a struggle, and this transformation in appetites was no exception. To focus on food as a source of pleasures without end, Americans had to conquer fears about food. Sensual pleasure and a sense of adventure had to prevail over concern for health and worries about indulgence. Anxious appetites had to be allayed, food fears put to rest. The ideal consumer is an Eager Eater, a consumer ever on the outlook for new taste experiences, visibly and vocally taking pleasure in food. Eager Eaters are most likely enthusiastic talkers, consumed with the urgency of sharing those pleasures with the rest of us. They know that food has to be thought about and talked about just as it must be prepared and consumed. Food talk turns food into a collective enterprise; writing turns it into a cultural text.

For this transformation to occur, for substantial numbers of Americans to consider food and its preparation as worthy of extended discussion, a great deal had to happen. And it had to happen on the home front, with the cooks who did the lioness's share of food preparation. The campaign for change had to be waged at home, and it had to be waged by women—the mothers and daughters; the wives, sisters, and aunts; in a word, the cooks who feed family and friends, who shop for the food, set the table, and run the kitchen. In the best of all possible worlds, these cooks made the comforting favorites that evoked an earlier, simpler time when food solved most problems. Precisely because cooking is so closely connected to women's work, women had to be the revolutionaries.

Domestic cooks tend toward the culinarily conservative, and understandably so. If the tried and true works—that is, makes the family happy, or at least peaceful—why risk change? At the same time, anxiety—the concern to do the right thing by their families—prompted attention to issues of health. Understandably, cooks in the early twentieth century were highly attuned to the discoveries and doctrines of domestic science, or what school programs came to classify as "home economics." The gendered world of mid-twentieth-century American secondary schools sent girls to "home ec" for cooking and sewing and boys to "shop" for work with tools. The "science" of feeding was a crucial part of the larger project of household management. Vitamins trumped taste, and foods were ranked on the culinary stratification system according to the goodness—not the taste—that they promised to deliver.

CULINARY TRANSLATIONS
Fannie Farmer

> Food is anything which nourishes the body. Cookery is the art of preparing food for the nourishment of the body.
>
> Fannie Farmer, *The Boston Cooking-School Cookbook* (1896)

Cooking became modern in the twentieth century under the tutelage of instructors such as Fannie Merritt Farmer. The many editions printed and copies sold of the *Boston Cooking-School Cook Book* (1896) for over a century (and counting) testify to Farmer's status as both culinary icon and household name. My copy, probably the 1930 edition, belonged to my mother and was inscribed as a wedding gift from her mother-in-law. She, in her turn, likely started her own marriage with the original edition of the *Boston Cooking-School Cook Book* at hand. Mothers and mothers-in-law across the country passed Fannie Farmer on to the next generation.

The importance accorded science in the American food world at the end of the nineteenth century shows up in Farmer's dedication of the *Boston Cooking-School Cook Book* to "the President of the Cooking-School" in gratitude for her "untiring efforts in promoting the work of scientific cookery." This was no small matter. Scientific cookery, Farmer claims, means nothing less than "the elevation of the human race." In the preface, which expands on the dedication, she acknowledges the time and effort that scientists have devoted to the study of foods. The world will be better for it: "Then mankind will eat to live, will be able to do better mental and physical work, and disease will be less frequent." Her "tried and tested recipes," Farmer hopes, will "awaken an interest through . . . condensed scientific knowledge which will lead to deeper thought and broader study of what to eat."

Putting culinary science into action, Farmer opens with a minimalist, physiological definition of food as "anything which nourishes the body." Food is "necessary for growth, repair, and energy." She reviews the digestive system and examines water, salts, starch, sugar, gum, pectose, and cellulose, plus the familiar milk, butter, cheese, fruits, vegetable acids, condiments, and flavoring extracts, specifying the chemical formula or the composition of the food where appropriate.

But Farmer says nary a word about food as an agricultural, much less a culinary, product. Although the second chapter acknowledges that cookery is the "art of preparing food," that art is at the service of "the nourishment of the body." Food is cooked "to develop new flavors," and especially "to make it more palatable and digestible," and also, by the 1918 edition, "to destroy micro-organisms." The third chapter, on beverages—"any drink"— details uses that are entirely physiological. Beverages quench thirst, introduce water into the circulatory system, regulate body temperature, carry off waste, nourish, and stimulate the nervous system and other organs. However useful, the information Farmer supplies is unlikely to inspire the cook in search of something to prepare for the next meal.

Nowhere do these pages bring up taste as an attribute to be valued or even much considered. The quality of the products with which the cook works, the flavor of the dish that the cook makes—the scientific cook, apparently, pays them no heed. Can we say that Farmer assumed the importance of flavor and quality? Chapter 4, on bread and bread making, holds French bread up as a model: "Who does not appreciate the loaf produced by the French baker, who has worked months to learn the art of bread making?" Still, even though Farmer values the bread and the skill that went into it, this is not an appropriate model for her students and her readers. French practice may supply a reference for the "art" of cooking, but it is of little matter for the home cook. French bakers, after all, are professionals.

Other than a desire to learn how to cook, Farmer assumes little on the part of her readers. Whence the importance of the exact measurements so often cited as an innovation of this cookbook: "Correct measurements are absolutely necessary to ensure the best results." If some cooks will eventually be able to measure by sight, "the majority need definite guides." Here, as in every chapter, Farmer teaches the basics, quite as she must have instructed her students at the Boston Cooking-School. To a modern denizen of the wondrous world of food, much of this food talk seems dreary. No narrative lightens the instructions. The words *pleasure* and *joy* appear nowhere in the (searchable) 1918 edition. Discussion never engages eating as a personal experience. Cooking is reduced to gestures and acts. No sensibility comes into play, no attachment to the food makes us want to cook.

And yet even this culinary world—shaped by the imperatives of nutritional science, household management, and relentless measurement—offers a glimpse of a different vision of what cooking is and can do. Sandwiched between the dedication and preface that make so much of scientific cooking, Farmer inserts an epigraph with nothing scientific about it taken from lectures of the English cultural critic John Ruskin to (fictional) future "Little Housewives."

In a startling statement, Farmer places her cookbook under the sign of an astonishing quartet of women, none of whom is known to have spent time in a kitchen and all of whom were noted in the arts of seduction. "Cookery," Farmer tells us, "means the knowledge of Medea and of Circe and of Helen and of the Queen of Sheba." Surely these legendary figures were perverse models for Ruskin's young girls. They were perhaps stranger still for the Boston housewives who were Farmer's students and first public. These women were hardly model cooks. They cast spells and dispense charms (Circe) and make use of opiates (Helen) and poison (Medea). The Queen of Sheba seems to have been all about display and seduction. Cooking is transformative, of course, but such practices do not fulfill Farmer's agenda of scientific cookery.

Even so, these characters suggest just how seriously Farmer took her culinary instruction—more seriously, perhaps, than she recognized. The passage must have been in general circulation in culinary circles. It is doubtful that Fannie Farmer spent her leisure hours reading John Ruskin, even a putative lecture to housewives in training. But because it is enchantment and art, cookery is power, and that is why women should not skip over the epigraph. It takes the power of cooking seriously. It looks beyond the demands of nutrition, budgets, and household management. Whatever the hesitations as to their moral stature, Medea, Circe, Helen, and the Queen of Sheba make cooking all about the power of food properly prepared.

The rest of the passage quoted from Ruskin brings cooking somewhat back to the kitchen and recognizable culinary practice. Even so, cooking subsumes a set of contraries: practicality and innovation, medicine and science, tradition and modernity: "It [cookery] means the knowledge of all herbs and fruits and balms and spices, and all that is healing and sweet in the fields and groves and savory in meats. It means carefulness and inventiveness and willingness and readiness of appliances. It means the economy of your grandmothers and the science of the modern chemist; it means much testing and no wasting." Farmer draws on Ruskin to expand the horizons of cookery beyond what mere recipes can convey. At its best, cooking draws on a striking trio: "English thoroughness and French art and Arabian hospitality." (One wonders what proper Bostonians made of "Arabian hospitality.") For the final flourish, Farmer, still quoting Ruskin, calls on the long tradition of women as providers. By the etymology of the word, a *lady* is tied to—indeed defined by—the food that she provides. In households that revolved around bread, as the *Oxford English Dictionary* tells us, *lady* designated the "loaf-giver" (or "kneader"), in contrast to the lord, who was loaf, or bread, "keeper," and the servant, who was "bread-eater." "In fine, [cookery] means that you are to be perfectly and always ladies—loaf givers."

What do we make of Fannie Farmer's food talk? There is, most prominently, her commitment to scientific cookery. Yet a number of her recipes propose elaborate dishes heavy on decorative detail. The epigraph strikes a still more discordant note, for it suggests that cookery is more than measurement and decoration. It offers a mysterious power. To take the exhortation to culinary enchantment seriously, to count French art, English thoroughness, and Arabian hospitality among American culinary virtues, in sum, to unite the many contraries in this epigraph, a different state of mind was wanted.

A MODERN CULINARY EDUCATION

To turn cooking into an adventure as wondrous, satisfying, and empowering for the cook as for those to whom she offers her ladylike loaves of bread, American cooks in the early twentieth century needed more than the directives of scientific cookery. Exact measurements had their place. They also had their limitations. Although they undoubtedly reduced anxiety, the measuring spoons and cups did little to promote culinary exploration. American cooks needed a different kind of food talk. They needed to hear about sensual pleasure.

Such food talk existed, and in some quarters flourished. Few will be surprised to learn that women did not move in those circles. In America as elsewhere, men wrote gastronomic commentary. To women, the cooking and writing of cookbooks; to men, the culinary interpretation, analysis, and judgments. The term *gourmet* in America, like *gastronome* in France, invariably referred to a man. While women took care of the kitchen, men acted in the public sphere that was so inhospitable to women. Men were deemed, as they deemed themselves, proper judges of fine food as of the even more heavily masculinized world of wine.

Empowerment of the cook could not come from the world of male gastronomic consumption and commentary. Change in the usual attitudes and familiar practices could come only through the women who served most of the food most of the time. For women to put cooking first and to consider cooking its own reward, they needed models. They found these models in three women who cast their spell on American cooks, who charmed American kitchens and inspired American diners.

Across more than thirty years, three women wrote the cook out of the kitchen: Irma Rombauer, whose *Joy of Cooking* (1931) broadcast by its very title that if cooking was work, it was also pleasure; M. F. K. Fisher, whose gastronomic writings beginning in the 1930s made the case for refined sensuality; and Julia Child, who starting in the 1960s taught American cooks how to make that sensuality a reality in their own kitchens.

However different their culinary perspectives, these three domestic enchantresses taught American cooks that cooking could, and should, be valued for its own sake. Although these women had considerable company in redirecting the American food world—James Beard immediately comes to mind—it is to them that we return again and again. Together and separately, they pushed American cooking and eating into new territory. As M. F. K. Fisher put it, a taste "missionary" brings "flavour and light to the taste blind." Which, she added, "is a destiny not too despicable." Although many people have written on the culinary contributions of these three women, my aim is to see how each "talked" American cooking into a different state of affairs and, in so doing, set the stage for the food world of the twenty-first century.

Irma Rombauer

> An index isn't literature, but a careful perusal of it will sometimes produce a poem.
>
> Irma Rombauer, *The Joy of Cooking* (1943)

The Joy of Cooking made Irma Rombauer one such missionary. By any standard, this cookbook was a rousing success, and it continues to sell a sufficient number of copies to warrant regular revisions. According to her publisher, over twenty-six million copies of *The Joy of Cooking* (not counting the knock-offs) had been sold by Rombauer's death in 1962.

Key to the success of *The Joy of Cooking* was the voice that spoke from the pages. Rombauer did not just provide ingredients, instructions, and measurements or explain what to do and how to do it. She established a personal relationship with her readers, and she did so by embedding her recipes in stories and anecdotes. Like the many cookbooks today that have followed Rombauer's narrative lead (whether they recognize the connection or not), *The Joy of Cooking* makes much of stories and anecdotes to frame the recipes— so much so that at times the instructions get lost in the narrative.

The subtitle of the original *Joy of Cooking* presented what could be reasonably expected of a cookbook, namely, a "Compilation of Reliable Recipes." But that is not all. Readers are also promised a "Casual Culinary Chat"—food talk that binds the recipes together and makes them the expression of a personality. With what would soon be recognized as characteristically Rombauerian chattiness, this food talk articulates the joy in cooking that Rombauer thought so important for the cook. Even as dependable recipes reassure the reader in her kitchen, culinary conversation integrates her into

Figure 4. FIGHTING THE GOOD FIGHT IN THE KITCHEN. The cover of the original edition of *The Joy of Cooking* shows Marion Rombauer's illustration of St. Martha of Bethany, the patron saint of cooking, slaying a dragon—the dragon of kitchen drudgery. The jacket blurb stresses the connection between the saint and the modern woman, "faced with tasks almost as diversified as St. Martha's, and cooking is not the least of the problems she must meet with intelligence and understanding." Reprinted with the permission of Scribner Publishing Group from THE JOY OF COOKING 1931 FASCIMILE EDITION by Irma S. Rombauer. Copyright ©1931 by Simon & Schuster, Inc. Copyright renewed ©1959 by Simon & Schuster, Inc. All rights reserved.

a community of like-minded cooks. Rombauer was the friendly guide that servantless middle-class American housewives needed. Where earlier generations might have worked together in the kitchen, sharing culinary lore and techniques, modern homemakers were much more likely, as Rombauer herself put it, to face the stove on their own. A friend in the kitchen was a friend indeed, and Irma Rombauer meant to be that friend. By the 1943 edition, and despite the downgrading of the culinary chat to an occasional aside, the conversation was well under way. Readers frequently sent in their own recipes to continue the conversation. Because she knew how central culinary conversation was to her success, Rombauer steadfastly opposed those who wanted her to drop the chats.

Joy negotiates the different imperatives of a cookbook. Like her predecessors, Rombauer makes claims for utility. The table for weights and measures at the beginning of the original *Joy* pays her dues to scientific cookery. Practicality comes to the fore with "Suggestions for Left Over Food" as well as both luncheon and dinner menus at the end. The much-enlarged 1943 edition expands the charts for health, vitamins, calories, equivalents, and proportions, along with the original weights and measures. For a wartime food world, Rombauer rushed to include "emergency chapters" on "Sugarless and Sugar-saving Recipes," "Meat Stretching and Substitutes," "Wartime Emergency Soups," and "Suggestions for the Use of Soybeans" (as a protein substitute).

Along with recipes, Rombauer offers whimsy. "The spice of life," she observed in a chapter entitled "Miscellany," "is also to be found in cook books." As proof, she offers some foreign cooking instructions that English translation makes wonderfully wacky. A characteristically French culinary personification conjures up raw materials with preferences of their own: "The hare demands to be flayed alive, the rabbit prefers waiting." Or the humor of the entirely unhelpful instruction from a German recipe: "Take twelve eggs, if you have them." Rombauer cites these sayings with glee, convinced that her readers will find them as amusing as she does. The sense of fun must explain the section on "Favors for Children's Parties," with its directions and drawings for a "Fig and Raisin Cat" and other figures.

How can you not warm to a woman who, in the midst of Prohibition, opens her cookbook with a section on cocktails and the disarming contention that "most cocktails containing liquor are made today with gin and ingenuity." The single concoction containing liquor (gin and orange juice) that she offers should not constrain the cook because all that anyone needs, really, is "an ample supply" of gin and "your imagination."

Times changed and Rombauer's advice with them. So, the 1943 edition relegated alcoholic cocktails to a chapter on beverages at the end of the book where "they may blush unseen by those who disapprove of them," yet "may be readily found . . . by those who do not." The children's recipes had disappeared by this edition, pushed out, presumably, by the increase in the number of recipes along with the sobering exigencies of wartime.

Following the usual instrumental conception of a cookbook, Rombauer tells her first readers that she aimed at making "palatable dishes with simple means." The second half of the sentence points to the future. She makes much of a larger purpose. For she wants to "lift everyday cooking out of the commonplace." Raising cooking out of the ordinary, the humdrum, and the routine takes the first step to the joy promised in the title.

Cooking, Irma Rombauer tells her readers again and again, is a joy. Even if, like the author, readers have to keep "one eye on the family purse and the other on the bathroom scale," there is room, the confident author assures one and all, for "indulgence." A run-through of *The Joy of Cooking* reveals the extent of that indulgence in the disproportionate number of recipes for cookies, cakes, and candy from Rombauer's vast storehouse of German baking recipes. My mother, who was a very good cook, had little tolerance for baking, so I was especially moved when I opened her well-worn copy of *The Joy of Cooking* and found a note on the cover page directing the reader to page 595 for "Cilla Cookies"—my favorite sugar cookies, now as then.

Rombauer turned her readers into collaborators. The original edition notes the contributions of "good cooks at home and abroad." She remembers friends through their recipes, and later editions include contributions from readers whom she knows only through the recipes that they send. The foreword to the 1943 edition notes that the book began as "a private record" of family preferences and friends' recommendations, along with exotic dishes "made familiar by foreign travel" and given "an acceptable Americanization."

The voice that Rombauer gives to others ends up merging with her own. Lobster Newburg Barbarini, for an example taken pretty much at random from the 1943 edition, a "good recipe" from "an English woman living in Massachusetts," is provided "as nearly as possible in her own words." The narrative allegedly supplied by Rombauer's (unnamed) informant makes the dish a far more extensive presentation than the recipe for Lobster Newburg reprinted from the original edition that immediately precedes it. The proportions, guaranteed by someone who has obviously made this dish many times, will satisfy "two rather greedy people," though doubling the quantities will take care of "five very average servings."

Rombauer exudes self-assurance. Her narratives pass that confidence on to her readers: "I always mess with my sauces and add as I go by rule of palate." An asterisk refers to a note at the end of the recipe that warns the reader not to expect an explanation for the two tablespoons of cold water added at the next-to-last minute: "It may be lunacy on my part," her English correspondent admits, "but I firmly believe that it gives a special smoothness." If cooking can accommodate a bit of lunacy from one cook, surely it can make room for a bit of folly from others. The imaginative gesture stamps the cook's signature on the cocktails and the dishes as well.

Enveloping and giving sense to the chatty narratives in the book is Rombauer's own story. As she relates in the preface to the 1943 edition, her children first suggested putting together a cookbook to alleviate the loneliness of the widow and the middle-aged empty nester to whom "many familiar doors seemed closed." Much to her surprise, "suddenly a new one flew open" with the "multitude of human contacts, experiences and gratifications" that *The Joy of Cooking* gave her. No wonder Rombauer feels "*useful*" (emphasis hers) once more, "far more useful than [she] ever expected to be."

Sales transformed the self-published venture of 1931 into a (revised) trade edition five years later. Yet, as Rombauer makes clear in the preface to the second edition of 1936, the encouragement that mattered came from the readers who followed her instructions and took her stories to heart, like the eloping bride who telegraphed her parents to send her a Rombauer cookbook at once, the man who sighed with pleasure that "at last" he could eat spinach, and the maid who swiped her mistress's copy!

Irma Rombauer was no Queen of Sheba or Circe. Nevertheless, *The Joy of Cooking* tells a story of culinary empowerment. In 1931, after "thirty odd years" of cooking as an "avocation," from a reader of cookbooks she became "a writer—of a kind." Like other women who take to writing cookbooks, Rombauer reinforced the domestic association of cooking even as she took cooking into the public sphere. The book lived up to the promise of its title. No wonder so many American women looked to the woman whom Julia Child affectionately called "Mrs. Joy."

Irma Rombauer baked her cake and published it, too.

Highly conscious of cooking for an American audience and with American products, Rombauer ardently advocated the conveniences of modern American technology. She delighted in canned soups. But the American food revolution of the late twentieth century needed more than canned soups, reliable recipes, or even a culinary chat. It needed inspiration and example from a different source. And that is where France and French cooking come in.

Neither was unknown. But for most Americans, French meant fancy. It meant complicated, rich sauces and elaborate table settings—the more forks, the better. It meant the exceptional occasion celebrated in upscale restaurants, in private clubs, or at meetings of the gourmet societies founded in the 1930s. French food meant indulgence. It meant the sophisticated cooking of the professional chef. Women had little or no access to either the men's gatherings or the professional organizations. The absence of any substantial population of French immigrants made things French all the more foreign, a sampling of odd if appealing ideas and strange practices brought back from trips abroad by the lucky few. As far as daily cooking practices were concerned, and unlike many other so-called ethnic cuisines—Italian offers the most striking example— French cuisine was never really "naturalized." Middle-class America continued to consider French products and practices as other.

For all the foreignness of French cuisine, *The Joy of Cooking* included some of its standard preparations—from "omelette aux confitures" to "sautéed fillets of sole"—in the index of the 1943 edition. The proper accent on *sautéed* emphasized the foreign quality of the dish in contrast to the orthographically Americanized, and simplified, *omelets*. Still, *omelets* or *omelettes* stood out against the far more numerous baked goods from Rombauer's German culinary storehouse, which scarcely seem exotic at all. Given the significant presence of German immigrants in the United States, particularly in the Midwest (Rombauer came from an old Saint Louis family), the Americanization announced in *The Joy of Cooking* was already well under way in shops, restaurants, and homes.

Americanizing the dishes of French cuisine required a greater and more conscious effort. It required articulation of principles and justification of practices. French cooking needed translation into the culinary terms of ordinary American life. For French food to become familiar rather than fancy, it had to move out of the rarified atmosphere of restaurant kitchens into the domestic kitchen.

M. F. K. Fisher and Julia Child made just that move from public to private culinary space. Irma Rombauer proclaimed the delights of cooking, and a little later M. F. K. Fisher made the case for eating. A generation later, Julia

Child taught American cooks how to make that sensuality a reality in their own kitchens. Both talked about the difference that French food could make in daily life—American life. Fisher and Child translated French ways of doing food into American terms. For it was in France that both women learned to cultivate a sense of flavor, to savor food, and to appreciate the pleasures of preparation and consumption. Each also had high hopes for American food. They did not preach; they proposed and suggested. Most of all they showed what could be done. Together and separately, Fisher and Child set America on a great culinary adventure.

For Americans, such exploration represented a real shift in cultural priorities, especially when we consider the models that Americans have so often turned to for a sense of national identity. The quasi-iconic status of Benjamin Franklin's *Autobiography* gives it more than individual interest. Americans, Franklin lets us know in no uncertain terms, were meant to serve their country. Meals were not for the enjoyment of food; they were a pedagogical opportunity. Franklin cites his own father's practice: "At his table he liked to have . . . some sensible friend . . ., and always took care to start some ingenious or useful topic for discourse which might tend to improve the minds of his children. . . . [L]ittle or no notice was ever taken of what related to the victuals on the table." Given their associations with France and with the aristocratic society that the young United States worked diligently not to emulate, sensual pleasures came across as vaguely un-American.

Other Americans, particularly those with experience of France, bemoaned the consequences of this disdain. James Fenimore Cooper, the immensely popular author of the *Last of the Mohicans* who lived in France from 1826 to 1833, had little good to say about his compatriots' foodways: "There is a familiar and too much despised branch of civilization, of which the population of this country is singularly and unhappily ignorant: that of cookery. . . . The Americans are the grossest feeders of any civilized nation known. As a nation, their food is heavy, coarse, ill prepared and indigestible."

M. F. K. Fisher

> Truly a man is not a gourmand, much less a *fin gourmet*, by wishing to be so.
>
> M. F. K. Fisher, "To End," *Serve It Forth* (1937)

For M. F. K. Fisher, writing a century after Cooper, the state of culinary affairs had not improved. To the contrary, with mass production of food-stuffs, from canned goods to breakfast cereals, the quality of what Americans ate had suffered. Why, she wondered in *How to Cook a Wolf* (1942), is America so ungastronomic as a nation? Fisher lays the burden on the condemnation of pleasure, which she had experienced firsthand. Her redoubtable grandmother made sure that the dining table in California celebrated food even less than the Franklin dinner table did. Food talk, the assertion of the pleasures of taste, was strictly forbidden: "We and almost all American Anglo-Saxon children of the second generation [Fisher was born in 1908], have been taught when we were young not to mention food or enjoy it publicly. . . . We have not been allowed to cry out with pleasure but instead have been pressed down, frowned at, weighted with a heavy adult reasoning that such display was unseemly, and vulgar, and almost 'foreign.' "

In short, no food talk, no resavoring of foods through fond memories, no sharpening of taste by comparison. Fisher's example points to a conspicu-ously strict Protestant—"Anglo-Saxon"—distrust of food. She sees her own grandmother in the story that Walter Scott tells about his antigastro-nomic training in early nineteenth-century, very Protestant Scotland. Taking pleasure in food endangered one's soul. Once when he was very hungry, the young Scott forgot the obligatory reticence. " 'Oh, what a fine soup!' he exclaimed. 'Is it not a fine soup, dear Papa?' " No sooner had he voiced his pleasure than his father poured a pint of cold water into what Fisher surmises was already a pretty watery broth. Why? "To drown the devil."

Drowning the devil is hardly an invitation to enjoyment, and such invitations were M. F. K. Fisher's special province. Fisher's writings on food, cooking, and eating celebrated the sheer sensual pleasure of food to counter American notions that make us "taste-blind." In America, she tells us, "we eat, collectively, with a glum urge for food to fill us. We are ignorant of flavour." If butter dominates French cuisine, olive oil and lard define Italian and German cooking, and sour cream Russian foods, so the dominant flavor of English cuisine may be, "unfortunately," water or drippings. As for American cooking, "perhaps," Fisher ventures, the reigning flavor can be traced to "innumerable tin cans." Hardly a promising forecast for culinary satisfaction. The canned soups that so often come to the rescue in *The Joy of Cooking* have no place in M. F. K. Fisher's kitchen of earthly delights.

Here, as usual for the time, Fisher masculinizes generalities, but in this case she specifically addresses American men caught in their routine. It was her job to convince the "ten million men [who] rush every noontime for their ham-on-white and cherry coke" that they ought to "experiment." Otherwise, they "may die taste-blind as well as stomach-ulcered." What they need is to be "shocked into recognition of their own powers of enjoyment." The rewards are great. For the man who learns to savor and to taste, "life itself has . . . more flavour, more zest." Forget so-called "balanced meals." They only bully the diner. Better that we should aim to balance the day. Then, and only then, following Fisher's instructions, "palates will awaken to new pleasures or remember old ones. All those things are devoutly to be wished for, now especially" (she is writing in 1942).

The joys of eating are the joys of living. They engage body, soul, and mind. About her pleasure in drinking the right wine with the right food, Fisher writes, "Nobody knew it except my own exhilarated senses and my pleased mind, all of which must enter into any true gastronomic experience." Only when eating engages the intellect as well as the senses will the taste-blind "eat with their minds for the first time." Then, and only then, will they know what they are doing.

Fisher takes her place in a venerable tradition of culinary commentators and champions of gastronomic pleasure. Who were, by tradition, men. To women, the practical side of domestic culinary production headed for the family dinner table; to men, the refinements of gastronomy, possible only in the dedicated sanctuary of the upscale restaurant or exclusive club. Women were thought to have no notion of true gastronomic appreciation. Fisher's food writing moved into male territory. Her ambiguous signature—initials rather than a gender-revealing name—intrigued.

Fisher was aware of breaking new ground. Recipes might appear, she warned at outset in her first book, but only perched "like birds in a tree—if there is a comfortable branch." What counted was the gastronomical moment. Like Brillat-Savarin, whom she took as a model and whose work she translated, Fisher analyzed and honored the pleasures of consumption. Like him, she writes "about eating and about what to eat and about people who eat." James Beard puts Fisher in this illustrious company. America has produced "quantities" of cookbook writers, Beard acknowledges, but few gastronomic writers anything like Brillat-Savarin. Until Fisher. Until this incomparable writer came along, Beard claims, the field was empty. New York super chef David Bouley paid tribute to Fisher's redefinition of food: "If more people read M. F. K. Fisher this country would be a much better country! She was a pioneer, she made food sound sensuous, which was probably something I had no idea existed." That a woman could be worthy of a place in the (male) pantheon of gastronomy—as opposed to the culinary commentary found in women's magazines and cookbooks—was little short of revolutionary.

Julia Child

> To La Belle France
> whose peasants, fishermen, housewives, and princes—not to mention
> her chefs—through generations of inventive and loving concentration
> have created one of the world's great arts.
>
> Julia Child, et al., *Mastering the Art of French Cooking* (1961,
> dedication)

Some twenty-five years after M. F. K. Fisher started writing, beginning with the publication of *Mastering the Art of French Cooking* in 1961, Julia Child laid out the techniques that made those pleasures possible. It was she who put American cooks working in American kitchens with American ingredients and serving American diners in a position to "cook in the French manner."

The dedication of *Mastering* says a lot about how Child and her coauthors saw both America and France. Like Fisher's France, the France of Les Trois Gourmandes (The Three Gourmands), as the three authors called their Paris cooking school, was the country that produced French cooking. It was the country of those who made that cooking part of daily life—the peasants who cultivated the earth, the fishermen who harvested the rivers and seas, and the women at home who transformed these wonders into the even greater wonder of the French meal. Though the authors pay homage to the princes and chefs who put French gastronomy on the world stage, *Mastering* celebrates above all the toilers in the vineyard and in the kitchen. They are the ones who create the art of the everyday that is French cooking.

Mastering the Art of French Cooking is profoundly traditional. With something of a sideswipe at all the odd marshmallow-jello dishes that American cooking of the 1950s doted on, the foreword declares that "the French are seldom interested in unusual combinations or surprise presentations." Because their tradition is so strong and reaches so far—remember the "generations" in the dedication—the French prize above all "a well-known dish impeccably cooked and served."

The Three Gourmands were writing for Americans, and specifically for "the servantless American cook" who must rely on readily available American products. The foreword at once reassures and raises hopes. The cook need not worry about finding "out-of-the ordinary ingredients." In any case, neither produce nor ingredients make the French difference. For it is "more to cooking techniques than to anything else" that "French cooking, and good cooking in general" owes its excellence. And techniques travel, far more readily than ingredients.

"Cooking is not a particularly difficult art," the authors of *Mastering* encourage us. Still, it has its requirements. First of all, cooking, as this cookbook understands it, takes time. Lots of time. Cutting corners will lead to "pseudo-French cooking." Skipping steps and skimping on ingredients (Child is notoriously lavish with butter and cream) are surefire recipes for disaster. Asking, or even thinking, "Who will know the difference?" sounds the "death knell for good food."

The authors know full well that Americans are not going to become French. Too much stands in the way—tradition, the pressures of modern life, the harried housewife's schedule. Even so, "on occasion," the would-be French cook must be able to forget about "budgets, waistlines, time schedules, children's meals, the parent-chauffeur-den-mother syndrome." Nothing should get in the way of "the enjoyment of producing something wonderful to eat."

That enjoyment is key to the enthusiasm of Child's fans. For a time—the time, say, it takes to prepare an especially elaborate recipe—not only is the cook able to indulge herself; it is incumbent upon her to do so. The cook's pleasure turns out to be a culinary imperative. The Three Gourmands wrote for "those who love to cook." To be sure, every cook hopes for an appreciative audience. More important still, she herself must have a "love of cooking for its own sake." The foreword ends with the injunction to "above all, have a good time."

There will be work. There are no short recipes in *Mastering* and many are very long. Here and in subsequent books by Child, there is an emphasis on details that other cookbooks pass over as unnecessary or unworthy. The insistence on homemade stock for stews, for example, puts these dishes in the company of restaurant fare—certainly not something for a pickup meal. For "precision in small details can make the difference between passable cooking and fine food." Child and her collaborators explain at length why detail matters so much—why, for instance, butter has to be beaten slowly into egg yolks for hollandaise or béarnaise sauce.

Much time, effort, and research went into getting the right translation from French techniques to American home practice. Those acknowledged range from the Agricultural Research Service of the U.S. Department of Agriculture to the Meat Institute of Chicago and, for their help with French meat cuts and French fish, the École Professionnelle de la Boucherie de Paris and the Office Scientifique et Technique de la Pêche Maritime. That research was crucial to the book's success. Even if almost no one makes the French bread in volume two of *Mastering*, the complexity of the immensely time-consuming recipe makes the reader appreciate the wonder that is good French bread. I made the recipe only once, but I am a better cook because of it. I remember how, after I spent the night at the Child home in southern France one time, Julia spent an entire morning turning gazpacho soup into a salad in a glass bowl. Each layer of vegetable had its specific weight and therefore its particular place in the sequence of brightly colored layers. Do the tomatoes go on top of or underneath the green peppers? Where do the onions fit? The cucumbers? Getting a recipe right takes many tries.

Cooking involves the mind, as M. F. K. Fisher emphasized. It also works the body. One attraction of Julia Child's cooking has to do with her exuberant physicality. She exhorts readers to use the "wonderful instruments" of their hands and fingers and to learn to handle hot foods. Although in the days before the food processor, a pastry blender was undeniably useful,

Mastering stresses that there is no substitute for getting "the feel of the dough in your fingers. Il faut mettre la main à la pâte!" The television shows brought that physicality to the fore. On the cover of *The French Chef*, the cookbook based on the television show, Julia, wooden mallet raised high, stands ready to clobber something on the cutting board.

Fisher and Child did not effect a food revolution alone. There is no overlooking the work of James Beard, the first American TV cook, or Craig Claiborne, the influential restaurant critic for the *New York Times* beginning in the 1960s. They, too, educated culinary America. And there were others. Alice B. Toklas, who had lived long years in France, wrote a cookbook in 1954 to render French food into terms that Americans could understand and use, devoting a section to French dishes that are most suitable for American and British kitchens. (There was also a recipe for marijuana brownies that made the cookbook a favorite with countercultural cooks in the 1960s.) Predecessors notwithstanding, Julia Child was America's first celebrity cook. Her evident love of anything to do with food captured the public, their enthusiasm and their love.

COOKS WATCHING COOKS COOKING

Who were the readers of this cookbook that made the exotic doable and the "fancy" familiar? It is important to have a sense of this public, the readers of *Mastering the Art of French Cooking* who turned into a devoted television audience for *The French Chef*, scarcely noticing (and not caring if they did notice) that the star was neither French nor a chef. It was these readers and spectators—these fans, ultimately—who put Julia Child on the cover of *Time* magazine in 1966. Finally, it was these readers-turned-spectators who turned this woman into the cult culinary figure of the American food world who set the stage, and the conditions, for the many who have followed in her footsteps.

These readers—originally, at any rate, and like most readers of cookbooks—were women. More than that, these women had already absorbed

Irma Rombauer's lesson that cooking should be joyful. Many already knew something about cooking, even French cooking. Of the factors usually cited as incentives to food adventurism (increase in disposable income, rise in education, more leisure time), travel is the most immediate. The grand tour of American elites at the end of the nineteenth century turned into a middle-class possibility, especially with travel guides such as Frommer's landmark *Europe on 5 Dollars a Day*, which told Americans how to tour inexpensively. For all kinds of reasons, Americans crossed the Atlantic in increasing numbers, and since travel in Europe was cheap for Americans, eating well was more than possible on a limited budget.

To be sure, not everyone had M. F. K. Fisher's sensuous revelations or experienced a culinary epiphany comparable to Julia Child's first encounter with butter-drenched *sole meunière* rendered so memorably in the film *Julie and Julia* (2009). But many had their own epiphanies, and they will tell you about them at a moment's notice. More and more Americans found that French food was to their liking. It was, they realized, more than fancy fare for fancy people. French food was for them, and it was for every day.

French cuisine was no longer the exclusive province of the nobs in first class. Middle-class Americans filled cabin class and tourist class, with a heavy contingent of students. Many knew something about French fare, and their travels convinced them that they wanted more of it. Moreover, they wanted that French fare at home. What drew them to French cuisine—the dishes that they had found so much to their liking—was *cuisine bourgeoise*, the tried and true classics of French cooking, from roast chicken and lamb stew to profiteroles and soufflés, dishes served in homes and neighborhood restaurants.

Mastering the Art of French Cooking brought this French food home. I first encountered the cookbook in Paris, where I was working after college. I was fond of steak with gobs of béarnaise sauce and regularly repaired to a neighborhood restaurant for my fix. After the *Herald Tribune* published an article on *Mastering* with béarnaise as a representative recipe, making this favorite sauce became a snap. Steak with béarnaise became home cooking, and I trotted off to Brentano's for my very own copy of *Mastering* so I could expand my repertory. It was crucial to the success of the book that the first readers of *Mastering* already knew enough about cooking to make the most of its lessons.

Consider me and my friends Barbara, Susan, and Lois. I had taken cooking lessons in Paris when I was a student in college a couple of years earlier, so I was not a complete neophyte. Barbara had been cooking for her husband and children for some time when she discovered *Mastering*. Since they were living outside Paris at the time, she already knew firsthand many of the dishes in the recipes. Like me, she rushed to Brentano's for a copy, and then to Dehillerin (the fabled cooking supply store still in operation) to stock up on the proper equipment, which she eventually lugged home to Chicago. Barbara was the quintessential reader targeted by *Mastering*, the cook who already knew how to cook, loved cooking, and was eager for culinary adventure.

As a teenager, Susan started reading cookbooks for fun and regularly cooked complete meals for her parents—her mother would do the shopping. Her parents' Southern roots meant that they knew good food, and a trip to France opened her eyes to French cooking. Once she had her own apartment, she started cooking recipes from James Beard's books and the recently published *Mastering*. She soon became an inveterate cookbook collector and experimenter. Reinforcement came, because she lived in Cambridge, Massachusetts, where Julia Child had become a local celebrity. There were Julia sightings around town. When he learned that Susan and her husband were there because of Julia, the local butcher of (Julia's) choice took them into the meat locker for a tutorial on cuts of beef. The seafood purveyor, too, was primed for Julia's fans. It was, as Susan says nostalgically, "all very small town and personal."

It is perhaps Lois who best sums up what Julia Child meant to cooks across America in these years before the Food Network and the blogosphere created so much culinary conversation. Like Barbara and Susan, Lois was prepared to make the most of Julia's lessons. Her mother had cooked out of Dione Lucas's Cordon Bleu cookbook "long before anyone was thinking of French cooking." A grand tour of Europe as a teenager, then living with her army officer husband stationed in Europe for two years, gave her tastes of new worlds. Back in the United States, she "was a stay-at-home mom who loved to cook (and to eat)." Julia's books and television program gave Lois a lifeline out of the small town where she lived: "Julia filled a huge gap in my knowledge of how to reproduce some of the things I had fond memories of . . . and introduced me to many I had neither tasted nor heard of." Lois's children knew that *The French Chef* program was "mother's time," and that she was not to be disturbed while watching it. No pesky kids need knock (though a couple stayed to watch.) The lessons were put to good use. Her husband's business visitors, many from abroad, gave Lois plenty of occasions to try things out, "and try them out I did."

Cooking turned into a lifelong avocation. Like thousands of others across the country, all four of us were fixated on food. Members of the younger generations, like my colleague Amy, got to the same spot watching *The French Chef* with their mothers. Some of my recent students, their parents fired up by the film *Julie and Julia*, received copies of the newly reissued *Mastering* to take to college for another sort of higher education. Whatever the generation, everyone read, and continues to read, voraciously about food, from M. F. K. Fisher and Craig Claiborne's columns in the *New York Times* to that great home of French food enthusiasts, the late, lamented *Gourmet* magazine.

Julia Child was by no means the first to cook on television. But she was made for the small screen. She brought into the home an outsize person (at six feet, she topped almost everyone else) and an outsize personality. Her enthusiasm was infectious. She was, as Lois remembers fondly, "a hoot!" No wonder that her fans never refer to her as anything other than "Julia." She was a totally reliable friend in the kitchen. She did not recognize disaster; she redefined it. The upside-down tarte tatin did not hold together? Well, then you have a lovely applesauce cake. When something "did not go very well," and she knew that it often did not, recovery was always possible. After all, in the oft-repeated mantra, "Who is there to see?"

An appearance on the *David Letterman Show* in 1987 offers an exemplary performance. Child has everything set up to make hamburger, but then the hot plate does not heat. So, in the spirit of improvisation that every follower of hers will recognize, she turns the failed hamburger into a triumphant steak tartare, which she finishes off with a grated cheese topping. Fortunately, she never travels without her trusty blowtorch and melts the cheese for the now-rebaptized "steak tartare gratiné Letterman." Letterman is comically wary of the blowtorch and cautious when faced with the prospect of eating raw meat. It's the first time he's tried it, and it's scary, as it no doubt was for a good many of the viewers at the time. He worries about disease. "What do you get from eating raw meat?" Letterman wants to know. "You get healthy," responds Julia. The whole wheat pita bread makes it even healthier. Julia digs in; Letterman makes a game attempt and pronounces his steak tartare "very interesting" (subsequently revised to "not bad at all.")

The show is hilarious—Child gives Letterman as good as she gets. As on her cooking shows, her slapdash manner belies her serious intent. Education was the name of the game. Even in the unpromising venue, with its non-functioning hot plate, she is teaching, working hard to bring the audience up to (her) speed and showing viewers how to come out on top in any situation. Like Julia, her readers learned how to cook and taught their families and friends how to eat. She taught them how to make the best of culinary mishaps, cheerfully admitting to some "really awful" dishes. When Letterman asks what she does with them, she even more cheerfully owns up, "I feed them to my husband." Her repartee is as integral to her performance as the spectacle of torching the grated cheese on the raw meat.

The performance is just what we expect. But it is momentous as well as fun. This appearance on a national television talk show with a hugely popular star anchorman testifies not only to Julia Child's personal stature but also to the status of food talk in American popular culture. There can be no more perfect spot for food talk than a talk show, and talk Julia does. Wonderful as her performance is, it is notable most of all simply because it took place. Letterman bestowed the ultimate legitimation of food, cooking, and eating as topics worth the attention of millions of spectators and the investment of the sponsors. Food talk, the talk show proposes, is talk for our times.

+ + + +

Culinary experiments caught on. American cooks by the score followed Irma Rombauer, communed with M. F. K. Fisher, and emulated Julia Child. Erstwhile unimaginable culinary ventures became the stuff of ordinary living. Knowledge that was once arcane became common parlance for cooks and consumers alike. We do not talk about food the way we used to not so long ago, and we do not at least in part because of cuisines that most Americans did not, and could not, imagine—much less consume—thirty years ago. The steak tartare that Julia Child introduced to a fearful David Letterman twenty-five years ago is no longer unthinkable, and sushi seems to be everywhere.

Julia Child was an innovator because she was the first to grasp that culinary television was all about entertainment. Food was a means to that end. Viewers can learn food preparation, and many no doubt do. It is far more important that every viewer, however kitchen averse, come to understand food as a whole world of adventure.

To get to this understanding, to think of cooking in terms of culinary adventurism, Americans needed more than accessible foods, the joy of cooking, and a love of eating. Food had to become more than pleasurable and appeal to more than the senses. Food had to become exciting. That excitement, that exhilaration, is the most striking feature of food talk today, and it is due, in large part, to high-profile chefing, to the celebrity chefs who impressed upon American culture that not only could cooking be fun, it could be—indeed, it was—a whole world that called for exploration. Cooks opened up the domestic kitchen by bringing in the outside world. Chefs brought the kitchen and cooking to that outside world.

CHAPTER FIVE

Chefs and Chefing

> A restaurant is a really terrific place for sociological study. . . . When you take the trouble to look, our profession lets us see wonderful things.
>
> Gilbert LeCoze, chef-restaurateur

Cooks cook. Chefs cook in public. They cook for show. They perform. Unquestionably artisans, perhaps artists, and definitely experts, chefs today are also entrepreneurs subject to the vagaries of the market, the inconstancy of diners, and the changing nature of their own visions of excellence.

These conditions of uncertainty give chefs a good deal in common with artists. More imperatively than for painters and writers, though, creativity for the chef means not just making a product, no matter how great or how grand. In today's media-saturated food world, creativity demands performance. Where the elaborate table settings and extravagant pastry constructions of the aristocratic table showed off the food, chefing makes cooking part of the show. Production becomes as conspicuous as consumption.

A full performance of any sort needs conversation, commentary, and criticism, on judgments rendered, disputed, and defended, in a continuous round of talk and response. In this respect, the public cooking of the early nineteenth century not only redefined the chef as expert but also recognized cooking as chefing. In our own times, food talk has transformed chefing from an established profession into a fluctuating, unstable expertise that covers an increasingly broad and continually renewed set of players. The excitement is palpable, the anxiety as well.

THE DRAMAS OF CHEFING

If the discussions, directions, and dramas of cooks on the home front induced Americans into cooking for its own sake and for their own joy, the exhibitions of chefing set the food revolution on a fast track. The media— television most prominently—accelerate the pace of change, and they do so by putting chefing within everyone's reach. No one need take a bite of anything to take in the celebrity chef's dazzle, thrill, and exhilaration.

Chefs have always been high-stakes players in the game of conspicuous consumption. The lavish royal banquets of centuries past strutted their stuff, as do upscale restaurants today, with their luxurious dining rooms, elaborate floral arrangements, and ever-more-refined, remarkable culinary creations. The more celebrated the chef and dramatic the culinary spectacle, the more conspicuous the consumption. For attention seekers, the more conspicuous the consumption, the more people are likely to take notice. The elegance of the dining table exhibits the standing of the host. The elaborate array of dishes, silver, and linens, not to mention the prodigious sugar constructions that dominate the table itself, say that this is a person to reckon with. The product counts, not the producer. The host has nothing to do with the actual meal, and the kitchen and its workers remain well out of sight. Production is invisible.

Today's culinary spectacles differ from those of the past. The restaurant makes the difference. Starting in earnest in the nineteenth century, and becoming absolutely essential in the twenty-first, the restaurant set up another game—the game of conspicuous production. Restaurants brought cooking out of the kitchen, the better to bring diners into the restaurant. Display focused attention on the visible manifestations of the owner-host-impresario's prestige, from the décor to the dishes. No wonder that so many chefs want to be restaurateurs. Or that when asked what they wanted to be doing in five or ten years, so many—from maîtres d'hôtel to captains down to waiters—talk about the restaurant that they dream of opening. Production competes with the product. It is not enough for diners to ooh and aah over the dishes set before them. They must see the chef at work. The now-common open kitchen puts the whole kitchen brigade on parade. An individually prepared dinner at a reserved table in the kitchen brings guests closer still to production. Conspicuous cooking transforms the sensual into the aesthetic and intellectual. In short, eating becomes consumption.

The forceful entrance of the media into the food world turned the spotlight on chefs. In the modern food world of restaurants and hotels that showed up in gastronomic commentary and cookbooks, chefs join forces with the media to astound and amaze on the spot and at a distance. Then there are all the television personalities, whose advice may be less useful because they are more intimidating. Surely it is the food world centered in restaurants that bears the most obvious mark of the media-defined culinary game. For chefs along with the rest of us, the media domination of the food world is a simple matter of fact.

Every chef plays the game differently. Family dynamics define domestic cooking; power struggles, both in and out of the kitchen, shape chefing. The chef must cope with the conflicting demands of customers, staff, and the media—not to mention investors. It is no surprise that as they become entrepreneurs, chefs contend with forces only dimly perceived by their predecessors not so long ago.

Making Meals Matter

> Persons who in no way share any special interest can gather together at the common meal—in this possibility, associated with the primitiveness and hence universal nature of material, there lies the immeasurable sociological significance of the meal.
>
> Georg Simmel, "The Sociology of the Meal" (1910)

"We've come to spoil the broth."

Figure 5. A CROWD IN THE KITCHEN. The domestic kitchen, too, shows the effects of media chefing. In an update of the adage that too many cooks spoil the broth, culinary media mavens stand ready to overrun the hapless homemaker's kitchen. In contrast to the friend that Irma Rombauer and Julia Child promised to bring to the home kitchen, the squadron of chefs in signature toques and aprons threatens invasion. Ken Krimstein, The New Yorker Collection / www.cartoonbank.com.

Fascinated by the markers of modern social life, the sociologist Georg Simmel pointed out the paradoxical situation whereby the most general social behavior, the activity in which every human being must engage—eating—gives rise to immensely complex systems of social differentiation that at once generate and promote invidious distinctions. Eating rituals throughout recorded history and across many cultures show this differentiation of dining in action. Royal dining put the social stratification system on view. The king sat apart from other diners on a raised dais—sometimes with the royal family, sometimes in solitary splendor. Along with other consumption goods, rare foods and elaborate preparations imposed as they affirmed the monarch's dominion. Beyond expressing preexisting power relations, the sumptuous banquets at court brought them into existence. Diners incorporated the stratification system with every mouthful. Like the great fountains at Versailles, the magnificent gardens, and the château itself, these culinary spectacles produced as they represented the power of the monarch.

Public consumption governed culinary presentation. Viewing trumped eating, presentation prevailed over consumption, and extravagance preempted taste. Dishes were to be contemplated and admired. There was much to look at, from the profusion of silverware and porcelain (an important French industry since the late seventeenth century) to candles and crystal. Manuals offered detailed instructions on the intricacies of folding napkins. Of the many elements that set the magnificent scene, none was more important than the French sequence of service. *Service à la française* set all the many dishes for each course on the banquet table at the same time. There was no distraction from the centerpiece, which was typically an outsized architectural pastry construction. Presentation favored the collective aesthetic experience, which can be shared, over the individual act of consumption, which remains idiosyncratic. Aesthetics topped taste.

The individual nature of consumption restricted those directly involved in the culinary enterprise. To turn such a transitory good to greater social account, one strategy was to include spectators. Consumption became more emphatically a matter of spectacle rather than taste, though gastro-voyeurs did not always go hungry. At the French court, once the king and his favored courtiers had decamped, the leftovers went to anyone still around. Such delayed consumption altered the meaning of the meal because it abolished the social connection between host and guest. The bystanders may have eaten the same foods as the diners of first instance, and they may have been seated at the same table, but in no way did they share a meal—a salutary reminder that every meal excludes as much as it includes. First come, first served—on the condition of being invited in the first place. Nor has the culinary spectator disappeared. Anyone who has looked at diners through a café window or watched others eating at a restaurant has been in the same position of nondining spectator—simultaneously at but not of the occasion.

Every era puts status on the table. The more conspicuous the consumption, the stronger the statement and the greater the prestige. For spectacle to operate most effectively, for conspicuous consumption to confer distinction on the host, production had to be out of sight. Deliberate inattention to cooking was the necessary counterpart of attention to dining. Because invisibility was so basic an element of traditional production, kitchens were located far from the site of culinary consumption. As so many historical television dramas have shown, the kitchen was "below stairs," in a world of little consequence to those seated at the banquet tables above.

The military model that governed aristocratic kitchens in ancien régime France gave the *chef de cuisine* command of the kitchen. Ultimately, what mattered was the commander-in-chief, that is, the employer-patron. The low social origins of chefs—artisans from families of artisans—made the social difference between patron and cook both apparent and "natural." Any other kind of relationship would have been unthinkable. The chef reigned in the kitchen on the condition that he stay there.

MODERN CHEFING

No matter that they made the meals that mattered; in the highly scripted world of spectacular dining, chefs got none of the glory. The combination of inconspicuous production and conspicuous consumption kept the dirty work of cooking out of sight and the producers out of mind. Notwithstanding his culinary authority, the chef was woefully outclassed by his employer-patron on every social and economic measure. In time, with the expansion of print culture, chefs began to insist on their authority and press their claims—for their cuisine as well as for themselves.

Their first bids for public notice trumpeted their elite connections. The fulsome dedications in cookery books that appeared in a steady stream beginning in mid-seventeenth-century France testify to an uneasy compromise between pride in authorship and consciousness of reaching beyond the cook's lowly station. The dedication of *Le cuisinier françois* (The French cook, 1651) stresses the unbridgeable social gap between the chef and the "very high and powerful lord." Yet that same chef expresses confidence in the work that he does not hesitate to call a masterpiece: "Consider that after all, this is a masterpiece that appears from the hand of he who will be all his life, My Lord, your very humble, very obedient and much obliged Servant François Pierre, known as Varenne."

The great chef Marie-Antoine Carême most dramatically marks the turning point in the chef's quest for social status. With his tireless campaign to advance his own culinary practice, and recognizing the crucial role played by the nobility in the past and the new nobility in the present, Carême insisted upon the artistic and professional status of the chef. The chef might not be on an equal footing with his patron, and he worked below stairs. Yet Carême saw patron and chef as a true culinary couple, united by a common commitment to gastronomic excellence. The extreme social distance that once separated chefs and their patrons belonged, he proclaimed time and again, to another era.

Carême sidestepped the problem of recognizing social distance by dedicating his first book not to a patron—Talleyrand would have been a logical choice—but to a colleague: M. Boucher, the comptroller of Talleyrand's household, with whom Carême worked and from whom he had learned much (*Le pâtissier royal parisien*, 1815). That same year Carême dedicated *Le pâtissier pittoresque* to M. Mueller, the steward to the Russian Tsar, and *Le maître d'hôtel français* to the Robert brothers, chefs who had cooked in the most illustrious households in Europe. Carême returned to the older pattern with the dedication of his summum, *L'Art de la cuisine française,* to Mme. Rothschild, the wife of his last patron, who could be put on a pedestal without compromising the authority of the chef.

Symptomatic of the professional status that he sought, Carême demanded that the chef and his staff not eat with the servants. Later he made much of being driven to the Rothschild château in his own carriage. Of course, he knew full well that this social promotion remained an ideal since "cooks today are not always appreciated in France." Aligning himself with other creators devoted to their calling, Carême made sure that his readers were aware that, like these great men, he sacrificed health, happiness, and his own funds to further the science, art, and profession of cooking. Absent support, "the love of knowledge alone" sustains the chef.

Carême's prominence in the world of French cuisine, as he was well aware, rested on his writing. More than any other figure, this chef understood the power of the written word in turning French cuisine into a true profession—a repository of socially organized expert knowledge that codified, produced, and transmitted a body of knowledge and set of practices. The greater the competition and more numerous the competitors, the more crucial culinary writings of every sort became. These books established the individual chef and the profession as well. It is no wonder that Carême wrote so much. His authority was a function of words, words, and more words.

With this culinary system Carême set chefs on the path to modernity. He firmly believed that the principles he laid down would serve generations to come, and he was right. At the same time, he was mindful of continuing a glorious tradition. His first cookbooks on pastry recreated the spectacular dining of the past—a recreation made all the more striking by the images of his elaborate architectural creations that filled them. He could not boast enough about the detailed engravings of pastry confections made from his own drawings.

Carême never forgot what he owed the great chefs of the past. Like them, he put dining on display. Consumption had to be conspicuous, which is why he had no sympathy for the Russian-style service—*service à la russe*—that served the dishes of each course to diners individually. Carême would have none of it. Nothing could compare in elegance to the French service, which focused on the spectacle of the banquet table with many dishes laid out together. As it had for Louis XIV, the culinary space of the table counted more than the diner's plate. The spectacle, Carême proclaims time and again, is his doing. With these many bids for recognition, the king of chefs laid claim to his kingdom. The "other" kings, lesser mortals in the new world of conspicuous production, sat on the sidelines. Production was becoming part of the show.

Competitive Dining

> As soon as experience taught us that a single new dish made with care was enough to make the inventor's fortune, self-interest . . . set every imagination on fire and every cook to work.
>
> Jean Anthelme Brillat-Savarin, *The Physiology of Taste* (1826)

The restaurant redefined consumption no less than production. Though restaurants first appeared in late eighteenth-century Paris, the rapidly urbanizing city of the early nineteenth century made the restaurant the quintessential urban institution. Although the chef continued as a subordinate in the restaurant kitchen, he was now an employee in a commercial enterprise. Rather than cooking for a patron whose tastes he knew well, the restaurant chef had to please a public that was largely unknown and shifted constantly. In contrast to the closed world of private dining, the restaurant, in principle, took all comers. This new institution turned guests into customers, the host into a businessman, and, in the best-known restaurants, the chef into a star employee. Expenses counted. Not surprisingly, given the grandeur of his conception of French cuisine, so uncongenial were the exigencies of the bottom line that Carême soon gave up the pastry shop that he opened in Paris in the early years of the century.

Cities have always been known for their great range of eating possibilities. Starting in the fourteenth century, visitors singled out Paris for the variety and abundance of foods available—in inns and a great range of specialty vendors on the streets. The exclusive banquets of the wealthy were another world altogether. In the rapidly urbanizing city of the nineteenth century, high-class restaurants pushed that once-closed world into the open. As Brillat-Savarin recognized, the slightest chance that a new preparation might capture the public's fancy set every cook to thinking up new dishes.

It was a whole new media-saturated world of competitive dining. With his journal, *L'almanach des gourmands* (1803-1812), A. B. L. Grimod de La Reynière brought gastronomic criticism into the food world. As food talk expanded exponentially, consumers grew to include readers as well as diners, and consumption focused on immaterial as well as material goods. The reputation of a restaurant, and therefore its ability to attract customers and compete, rested on the food talk that it generated.

The restaurant shaped the food world that we recognize today, not least by ensuring a steady supply of trained personnel. It was the prime mover in the professionalization of cooking. Until culinary schools came on the scene later in the century, restaurants were the only training grounds. They train chefs today as well, despite the numbers of cooking and hotel schools, in the United States, France, and elsewhere.

By the middle of the century, in urban centers in Europe and America, the spread of hotels catering to affluent travelers depended on an extensive network of trained service personnel. The exemplary culinary couple was no longer the chef and his patron—Carême and Talleyrand—but the partnership between the chef and the hotel magnate—Auguste Escoffier and César Ritz.

The primary impact of the restaurant—that is, the fashionable restaurant that catered to the well-to-do—lay in its power to confer prestige in a society that was noticeably, blatantly mobile, both geographically and socially. Although by no means absolute, the clearly defined social hierarchy of pre-Revolutionary France had the advantage of marking place. By the nineteenth century, labels meant less. The exclusions of the private dinner or banquet gave way to the ostensible openness of the restaurant.

The grand ceremony of aristocratic dining moved into public space. Hotel dining rooms could be breathtaking, the individual servings sumptuous. The flames of crêpes Suzette—those superthin pancakes cooked in orange-flavored butter and orange liqueur set alight at table—epitomize the new aesthetic that made the individual diner the center of attention. The modern chef performs in the restaurant in order to reach beyond. Indeed, with its luxurious décor and stunning flower arrangements, the restaurant itself becomes a stage, with the consumers on view along with the menus commonly posted outside—both so much publicity for the restaurant.

Media Matters

The many developments that thrust the restaurant onto the urban scene occasioned a good deal of commentary intensified by the competition. Grimod de La Reynière inaugurated a vibrant tradition and turned judging restaurants into a recognized professional enterprise. Reviews are more than an advice column on where to dine next. To be sure, we pounce on a review to find out about a restaurant, but that is half the story at best. For reviews also tell us about the changing food world, new foods, new preparations, new venues, and new modes of production and consumption. We want to know what a particular critic has to say about the food world today. In short, the personality of the reviewer counts for a great deal. A restaurant reviewer for the *New York Times* put it clearly: His readers from all over the world were curious about the food scene in New York, which they might or might not explore personally. Some look to the quality of the writing. Others enjoy a good polemic. In the best case scenario, restaurant reviews merge into food writing as such—the reviews turn into mini essays on food and dining.

Personality is not without its drawbacks. Opinions can be too personal, too idiosyncratic, too opinionated. Readers in search of guidance will turn elsewhere. And one place that they turned to early on was the purportedly impersonal standards of a select few highly trained anonymous assessors. In 1900, Michelin, the French tire company, launched the first of these "tribunals," where a formalized rating system determines the ratings. Anonymous inspectors replaced opinionated critics. The more recent "plebiscite" guides—Zagat's is the best known—replaces the critic-judge with popular acclaim. Anyone who logs onto the website and fills out the survey has a say. The blogs that multiply by the hour do not, at the outset, dispose of any particular culinary authority, though in time some acquire a following that reinforces the sense of random selection with the commentary.

The resulting dialogue of readers virtually excludes chefs who must counter as best they can with their own media campaigns to circumvent the "outsiders." With their cookbooks and memoirs, their television shows and lecture circuit appearances, savvy chefs make their appeal directly to the public beyond the restaurant. Today's celebrity chef is a media master. To stay competitive, he has to be.

Mastery of the media is part of what a chef must do in order to be the chef that he (and, less often in the upper reaches of haute cuisine, she) wants to be. Again and again, in interviews conducted with a sample of prominent chefs in Manhattan in 1990 and 1991, and confirmed by many of them in public interviews since then, the emphasis falls on the sheer sensual pleasure of working with food, on the satisfaction of transforming the raw into the cooked and the cooked into something eminently, palpably, gloriously sensual. There is also the differently sensual pleasure of eating—chefs, my informants told me, have to really love food; they have to want to work with the material. They also have to revel in the primal sensual experience of eating. This is what food exploration is all about—the newest and freshest ingredients, locally raised food—and making sure that the food world knows about it.

All of these enhance the possibility of turning the instrumental goal of eating—food is, after all, fuel—into a higher pleasure. As French chef Joël Robuchon put it, chefs are in the business of selling happiness—and that means their own happiness along with that of their customers, the first dependent on and a function of the second.

Such are the pleasures of creation. Like every enterprise that prides itself on rewards beyond the immediate, chefing makes greater claims. Chefing turns the material to aesthetic and intellectual account, precisely the transformation that food talk is all about. The body takes humans on a privileged path to the spirit. This is also the search for culinary perfection, a perfection that is illusory and elusive. It is just this illusion that keeps chefs chefing.

From Culinary Connection to Social Tie

> To invite people to dine is to take charge of their happiness the whole time they are under our roof.
>
> Jean Anthelme Brillat-Savarin, *The Physiology of Taste* (1826)

No matter how tempting the dishes created, chefs must communicate beyond the kitchen and with more than the culinary product that they make. The restaurateur's pleasure in receiving guests mirrors the chef's pleasure in preparing food. The meal counts—not the food, not the individual diner, and not the chef. The important personage, then, is the host-impresario. When Chef Robuchon says that chefs sell happiness, he is thinking of the chef-restaurateur—the host who, for the time you are under his roof, is responsible for your well-being. The pleasure of the meal is a social pleasure. Food is a means to that end. As Brillat-Savarin recognized, the meal socializes dining by turning individual appetite into a collective enterprise.

The chef-restaurateurs whom I interviewed some twenty years ago, and most especially the French chefs in my sample, concurred on this point. Brillat was, I now see, the model that they followed. Better than anyone else, he articulated the meal as a primal social phenomenon. Anyone in charge of a meal bears the responsibility for the gathering. More than one contemporary chef was all but channeling Brillat. When asked what he most liked about being a chef, New York superstar Jean-Georges Vongerichten cited the animation, the crackling atmosphere, and the diners' evident enjoyment in one another and the moment. What he likes best of all, he told me, is "a room that's full to bursting." So in a dining room far too noisy for my tastes, this chef-restaurateur saw "a party" where "people talk, . . . have a good time. That's what a restaurant is."

Another New York–based French chef made the point more emphatically. Jean-Michel Bergougnoux "really love[d] cooking," but, he said, it's not cooking but people that make the chef, the people you work with: "And then, in the kitchen, you spend a lot of time with your cooks. . . . We get along well, and it's good to work with people you get along with. I couldn't take working in an office." For him, cooking is also about the people you serve: "Being a cook-chef-restaurateur is fantastic in the sense that you receive people, give them pleasure, see them leave happy, see them come back. . . . And you have permanent connection with people, and that's something I like. . . " Personal connections are vital: this same chef reiterated that generosity is the key to running a restaurant, and giving of one's self is essential. The chef has to like and want what the customer wants: "One thing that I want to say. A chef-restaurateur, a chef-owner has to be generous. It's very important. For this work you have to want to live well, you have to love to eat and to drink. You have to love to take care of people."

Not for nothing are restaurants included in the hospitality industry. Talking about food trends—Meyer lemons this year, who knows what will be hot next—Danny Meyer, one of the most successful restaurateurs in New York City in the past twenty years, made sure to add that "the only ingredient that does not go out of style is hospitality."

Sociability is the goal of meals, no matter how astonishing the food. If the French chefs among my interviewees had a criticism of their American colleagues, it was their intellectualization of pleasure—quite the opposite of Vongerichten's craving for the excitement of vibrant interaction. "Jumping around the kitchen like crazy, that's exciting. . . . In a restaurant where there are fifteen bored tables and you're spinning your wheels in the kitchen, you're not producing, and there's no pleasure." The social element is what's important: "Everyone forgets that people don't go to a restaurant just for the food. Eating out is a social occasion. If the cooking is good, fine, but . . . eating is not just focusing on your plate. And eating is not reflecting on what you're eating, it's taking pleasure in what you're eating. . . . They eat, it's good, that's great. That's what a restaurant is for. . . . It should be good, it shouldn't be too intellectual." For New York French chef Daniel Boulud, cooking should protect the product and make the most of it without adding too much. "I don't like an unknown cuisine with lots of things in it. It's fun but you don't know what you're eating." Was the cooking too intellectual, then, I asked? Boulud agreed that sometimes it was "too cerebral, too analytical." Everything needs trial by stove.

The more outspoken Gilbert LeCoze, chef of the restaurant Le Bernardin, denounced culinary analysis in no uncertain, and somewhat vulgar, terms: "I don't want to start acting like Rodin's 'Thinker' looking for discoveries. That's intellectual masturbation and you never find anything. You never find anything on intellectual bases. You have to be calmer, more yourself, more spontaneous. Everybody . . . intellectualizes everything." Intellectualization gets in the way of enjoying food, of taking the proper pleasure in one's self: "After all, we're animals, we do the same thing every morning, we get up, we brush our teeth, and we pee. There are a few small differences, but on the whole there are not a lot of people who can claim to have touched you strongly in your life. There are one or two, a few writers, a few great musicians. Cooks are nice guys [and that's it]."

This charismatic chef was by no means lacking in ego and worked at making an impression. Yet he balked at the hyperpromotion of chefing. As exacting as he was about his food, cultivating purveyors to get the freshest and best fish available, LeCoze believed that a culinary connection was a human connection. That's why waiters had to be psychologists. They had to know what diners wanted. The businessmen intent on a deal cannot be treated like the couple on a first date or a quartet of old-time friends. It is up to the waiter to figure out whether "Monsieur" has, or has not yet, "made it with Madame," and adjust the service accordingly.

The meal is an experience of conviviality, to be judged as much by the company kept as the food consumed. The home meal reaffirms the family; the outside meal creates, if momentarily, another collectivity. The strength of this model, and in particular its hold in French culture, has to do with its articulation. In contrast to the aristocratic banquet-spectacle that both assumed and confirmed hierarchy, Brillat-Savarin's ideal meal as convivial moment suited the everyday life of lesser mortals, and above all, those mortals who frequented restaurants. Each table made its own community.

Where the opulence of dishes and decor at great banquets paraded hierarchy, the restaurant meal created its own, ostensibly coherent and egalitarian community. Brillat recognized that the equality of eating together—commensality—was temporary, lasting only as long as the meal. It was, as well, a fiction, a story that a group tells about itself. The success of a meal hinged upon just such a construct of participation in a common venture.

This is the lesson that M. F. K. Fisher learned in France. It is hardly surprising that she chose to translate Brillat-Savarin's *Physiology of Taste* as the primary text through and with which she sought to awaken American taste buds and transform American eating. For Fisher, as for her genial nine-teenth-century guide, food supplies only one ingredient of a meal. The foods served contribute to a larger, and incomparably greater, whole. "The Perfect Dinner" that Fisher thought so carefully about put into practice Brillat's rec-ipe for a good dinner—fairly good food (probably more than that for Fisher), good wine, guests chosen with care, and time to savor both the food and the conversation. We would do well to pay attention to the implications of the French word for "guest"—a *convive* is someone we live with for the moment of a meal. The community is temporary, but it exists.

This model meal is, of course, utopian. Brillat makes every effort to con-vince his readers to act in accordance with the standard that he somewhat disingenuously holds up as a norm. As for making this ideal a reality, the challenges have never been greater than in today's postmodern food world. Foggy though our notion of "postmodern" may be, the term has the virtue of recognizing that our food world is different in fundamental respects from anything history has to offer. Our food world continually reinvents itself in search of the new. The equanimity and settled quality of Brillat's convivial meal seem long ago and far away in the increasingly strident brouhaha that surrounds celebrity chefs and the new culinary constructs that they con-stantly urge upon us.

More destructive of the ideal of conviviality is the culinary practice referred to, variously, as "modernist cuisine" or "molecular gastronomy," or that is, more simply and more personally, associated with the cuisine of the Spanish chef Ferran Adrià. What these approaches to cooking share is an emphasis on the intellectual and the technological. On the "culinary pyra-mid" elaborated by Ferran Adrià, "conceptual creativity" is at the very top, the summum of what cooking should aim for.

The culinary ideal has shifted. Not that "intellectual cuisine" is really new. Whenever food becomes an end in and of itself, whenever the culinary creation dominates the context, whenever the culinary spectacle supersedes taste, we confront an intellectual or aesthetic conception of cuisine. Whenever authors of cookbooks take a stand, whenever they make a point of defining what is characteristic or new or different about their cuisine—as cookbook writers tend to do in conditions of escalating competition—they turn cuisine into an intellectual construct.

These new foods work against "comfort food." Television and print media alike set before us culinary options unknown only a short while ago. Although the expansion of culinary choices has much to recommend it—there is no more certain remedy for culinary boredom—the plethora of choices unsettles the meal. From the perspective of sociability, the further the consumer moves into unfamiliar culinary territory, the greater the anxiety that eating will generate. It is difficult to keep up your end of the conversation when you are confronted with an unknown brew that may be unappetizing and perhaps downright unpalatable. An unrelenting focus on food as an end in and of itself undermines the meal as a social occasion.

The vast majority of restaurateurs, like those whom I interviewed and have cited, place the pleasure of the meal ahead of the perfection of the food. The most driven of culinary artists, the most concerned with creativity, recognize the primordial importance of pleasure. Because hospitality never goes out of style, for these restaurateurs as for the rest of us and as it was for Brillat-Savarin, a meal is not just about food. Notwithstanding his multiple Michelin stars—three in California, three in New York—and his constant seeking after perfection, chef Thomas Keller puts his customers first. Whatever Keller's views of what he must regard as massacred meat, which he would never serve on his own, a customer will get the steak well done as ordered.

Competitive cooking has no place in the restaurant dining room, where the goal is—as it has to be—the pleasure and satisfaction of the diner. Surely one reason that American chefs have not fared particularly well in international cooking competitions such as the Bocuse d'Or is the dominance of restaurant cooking in their training. A restaurant, ultimately, is a business enterprise. It focuses on the customer. Competitive cooking bypasses the customer, or, more accurately, turns the consumer into a judge. Pleasure is not a factor.

Exploration and Experimentation

> We have transformed elBulli into a place of reflection through cooking.
> Ferran Adrià

If a modern scientific perspective can be traced at least to Brillat-Savarin, not until the late twentieth century was there much concern with the physiological transformations brought about by cooking. Although Carême spent some time on the molecular basis of a good beef bouillon, like professional chefs now as then, he was an empiricist, with menus to think up, supplies to order, a staff to deploy, and dishes to serve. Restaurant chefs cannot afford to spend time on analyses of theoretical interest if limited application in a kitchen primed to turn out meal upon meal.

Ferran Adrià is one chef who thinks very differently. Although the celebrated Spanish chef and restaurateur was not alone in shaking up the food world in the 1990s, his cooking was the most notorious for its disdain of convention. More than that, Adrià sought a new culinary mode altogether. His restaurant, elBulli, had received all the conventional recognition that the food world has to offer—three Michelin stars and nomination five years in a row as the world's best restaurant. From 2001 to 2011, elBulli satisfied only eight thousand of the over two million requests for reservations. More significant for the impact of this restaurant on the food world as a whole, some three thousand experienced chefs competed every season for one of the thirty-two intern slots in the elBulli kitchens. ElBulli was *the* go-to place for adventurous chefs. Those who did not get to the restaurant read Adrià's books, heard him talk, and themselves interned with the lucky few who had passed through his kitchens.

Ferran Adrià's saga is extraordinary and, at the same time, representative of the ambitions for change. There is, first of all, the emphasis on unconventional culinary techniques. Technology has long intrigued professional cooks, from the low-tech pastry bag acclaimed by Carême to the nouvelle cuisine of the 1970s that made much of food processors and microwave ovens. Adrià's technological savvy is something else again. For Adrià, technology brings much more than convenience to cooking. It does more than allow cooks to do faster, more easily, or better what they already do. To this chef, technology offers the means to be a totally different kind of chef.

The changes effected by cooking—transformations from raw to endless permutations of cooked—became veritable metamorphoses. Many testify to Adrià's "liberation" of cooking, his pushing of the limits of what is possible. As a young chef put it, more than simply throw a few new techniques into the mixing bowl, "Ferran changed how people think about cooking. What Ferran said is that anything is possible. What . . . all those guys [leading lights of French cuisine] said is that you can expand, while Ferran said you can take every structure and explode it and start from the beginning." The foams now on restaurant menus all over the world testify to Adrià's reach. These are not ordinary foams, made from the cream or eggs that chocolate mousse lovers count on. They are incomparably lighter than any ordinary mousse, made from the natural flavors of vegetables and meats and served from a whipped cream canister powered by nitrous oxide. Then there are the hot gelatins, frozen air, and spherified foods (small caviar-like spheres of liquids) that makes the lowly olive unrecognizable even as the spheres retain the very essence of oliveness. Rice Krispies make a highly untraditional paella, a cage of gold-tinted caramel encloses quail eggs, foie gras becomes frozen dust, gazpacho turns into popsicles . . .

Such culinary inventions challenge consumption, as of course they are meant to. The pleasure of the diner that is so central to Brillat-Savarin's conception of the meal does not concern Adrià. He is a committed explorer, fixated on expanding the universe of taste experience, pushing foods into new taste territories. Whether the diner likes the dish or not is of little concern. Adrià rejects the privilege accorded the customer. ElBulli replaced the traditional à la carte menu with a tasting menu of at least thirty courses. Prodigious variety and no choice whatsoever.

Such a radical move raised questions in high places. It broke one of the rules of the Michelin Guide. A member of the elBulli team remembers the switch: "Suddenly, customers were not allowed to choose anymore. . . . We had to keep the menu for three years, because Michelin could not decide whether this was a positive thing or a negative thing. . . . But the moment came when Ferran said: 'We are going to take the menu out because when a client asks for the menu it breaks the rhythm of the kitchen and this is not my way of cooking. This is not what we want to show clients.'" ElBulli had no monopoly on tasting menus. More and more restaurants in recent years ask diners to put their meal in the hands of the chef, who essentially asks them to abdicate control over their the culinary experience. The tasting menu abolishes the great innovation of the modern restaurant—the menu that allowed diners to put together their own meal. The tasting menu gives that power to the chef. In a gesture to the customer, to restore some sense of diner control and blunt the latent antagonism of chef and customer, neighborhood bistro and fashionable eatery alike more often than not hedge their bets by offering two or three options for each course as well as a few selections à la carte.

Ferran Adrià appreciates just how different his approach is. In an interview in 2010 he drew the line between his attitude and style and that of every other restaurant, from every other cuisine: "In high-end cuisine, the big difference that elBulli has made is that before people cooked for others to like what you do; we . . . cook to create." Pleasure takes a back seat to experimentation: "[We cook] for you to have an experience, regardless of whether you would like what you eat or not. It is an experience; the incorporation of provocation, of sense of humor, all these in the meal, is something that is not normal in cuisine. . . . We have transformed elBulli in[to] a place of reflection through cooking."

Adrià is hyperconscious of his status as an outlier in the food world, a phenomenon off the charts, out of range. To further his program of experimentation, elBulli regularly closed six months out of each year. In July 2011 it closed altogether, replaced by a nonprofit research center of creativity under the name "elBulli Foundation." Adrià is convinced that the "concept of a restaurant will die." Guests will be fed *very* differently: "It is a foundation, it is a creative center, there will be no reservations, and nobody will pay. So you might ask . . . and who will come?—It doesn't matter." Ferran Adrià has replaced the high-end restaurant with a tasting think tank. Creativity is conceptual. Reflection, intellectuality, and high-tech experimentation all but define the social relationship of chef-consumer out of existence. Predictably, opinions are mixed, though Adrià has an impressive record of garnering funding from external sources, from the communication multinational Telefónica to a course on the science of cooking at Harvard University. If Adrià is the chef's chef, he is also very much the academic's chef.

EXTREME CUISINES

It isn't given to every man to season a sea-lizard nicely.

Athenaeus, *The Deipnosophists*

What, you may ask, and diners at elBulli often did, does all this turmoil mean? Although experimentation does not engage the vast majority of diners, cooks, or chefs, avant-garde cuisines redefine the possible. Through the food talk that they generate, modernist cuisine, molecular gastronomy, and constructivist cuisine reconfigure the food world. Though their practices filter into conventional preparations, the principle of perpetual experimentation to which they adhere keeps these cuisines on the edges of the food world. Like other avant-gardes, avant-garde cuisine remains a specialized world.

Partly this is a simple question of finances. All basic research, meaning experimentation with no identifiable payoff, requires infusion of resources from external sources that need to be convinced to invest. Scholars and chefs alike must sell themselves in one way or another to reach publics outside the academy and legitimating institutions beyond the restaurant. Four stars from the *New York Times* or three from the Michelin Guide increase bankability exponentially. Celebrity escalates opportunities for consulting along with product lines, connections to other parts of the food world, new restaurants, and, for the experimental chef, culinary research.

Ferran Adrià's three Michelin stars, which proclaimed his mastery of classic cuisine, translated into backing for his experimental cuisine. Then, too, and however much such a move would seem to run against his principles, he has not been shy about promoting mass-market products such as the lowly potato chip. In this venture Adrià follows a well-established pattern that makes top chefs heads of their often multinational empire. A cadre of committed staff trained to further the enterprise is the scarcest commodity of all. For a chef as self-consciously experimental as Adrià, these researcher-disciples must share a vision of a new food world with cuisines unknown and undreamt.

Such is the remarkable territory of what I call extreme cuisine, whose practitioners deliberately position themselves on the edges of the food world. The new makes sense only in contrast to the familiar, so that, to counter current practices, a Ferran Adrià must have them in mind. As in all the arts, communication requires commonality. The parallels with high fashion are inescapable. The clothes that come down the runways of the seasonal fashion shows in Paris, New York, Milan, or London are not for the woman on the street. Expense is one reason, of course; straight wearability is another. Extreme cuisine, like extreme fashion, does not wear easily, having as much to do with food as high fashion has to do with clothing.

Because it strives to astonish and reveal, extreme cuisine negates the very idea of comfort food. To understand how comfort food works its magic, there is no better example than the Proustian madeleine. One dismal autumn afternoon, Proust's narrator dips the familiar, ordinary cookie into tea. The taste so intimately connected to time and place immediately transports the disheartened and dispirited older man to his childhood. One bite of this wafer dipped in tea, rather than Communion wine, revives the narrator, brings him back to life. Comfort food joins self and setting. The food need not, should not, be exceptional. The food counts not for itself but for the culinary connections that it makes.

Extreme cuisine will have none of this. It faces the future, not the past, looks to the unknown, not the familiar. The research chef disdains comfort and wants to shake things up. A chef of a high-end restaurant in New York City (not connected to elBulli) was grateful for the push: "Because food has been around for so long, it was difficult to consider something new. . . . It helped us, woke us up a little bit . . . 'cause to be quite honest nothing has really changed that dramatically. . . . But to, like, shake us a little bit and say: there are newer ways or different ways of bringing this medium that we have always had and bringing it to the customer in a new kind of form." The more extreme the cuisine, the more inappropriate a model it offers restaurant chefs. Research risks alienating customers. A restaurant must innovate, to be sure, and top chefs feel the pressure to do so. Culinary boredom is deadly, and the most faithful diner wants variety. But innovation must be balanced by food that resonates with diners. The insistence on the chef's singular discovery of the moment abstracts food from dining and eliminates the diner from the meal.

Avant-garde cuisines have minimal impact where affective relations govern the meal. Such situations have little place for the intellectuality or the determined search for the untoward and the unknown. Cooks flout the preferences of their privileged consumers at their own peril, whether these be families at home or regular diners in the restaurant. The chefs who succeed in challenging their clientele and holding on to it as well are, as they have to be, in the minority. Creativity is a luxury that few chefs can afford. They are aware how far is too far, and many admit as much. Extreme cuisine is not for everyone, and it is not for every day—not even, as he concedes, for Ferran Adrià.

How Far Is Too Far?
Extreme cuisines remain extreme for a number of reasons—expense and lack of trained personnel among them. Still, it is not an absence that sidelines avant-garde cuisines. Rather, it is the presence, and the authority, of a different culinary model. This model, articulated in particular detail by French writers and put into practice most notably by French chefs, insists on the meal—that is, on the social context of food. As the chefs cited above say over and over again, the complete culinary act is not cooking, it is dining. Consumption in the dining room, not production in the kitchen, centers culinary interest. In contrast to extreme cuisines controlled by the chef, this model meal includes the diner in the culinary equation.

Cuisine, then, does not exist on its own. It is part of a social exchange, a means to an end. Extreme cuisines do not look for the proof in the pudding of eating, in the pleasure of tasting dense chocolate or smooth custard sliding down the throat. Rather, they look to the pudding program, the concept of pudding, the exploration of pudding-ness, the extension of pudding possibilities into heretofore nonpudding territory. The intellectual excitement is patent, the pleasure payoff debatable.

The goal of the meal, and therefore of cooking, is satisfaction, well-being, happiness. While culinary discoveries may be made in the course of a meal, discovery is neither the purpose nor the aim of dining. Generations of French chefs and restaurateurs have practiced this culinary model, most recently reiterated by the identification by UNESCO of the French "gastronomic meal." The meal, not the cuisine, is taken to embody an identifiably French conception of culinary creativity—a conception that is incompatible with extreme cuisine of any sort.

+ + + +

Chefs, cooks—these are types, ideal types in sociological parlance, that concentrate traits, features, and characteristics distributed unequally in the real world over individuals and institutions. No cook is The Cook and no chef, not Ferran Adrià himself, is The Chef. The ideal type is an analytical tool that helps make reality less muddled and more intelligible.

I suggest that it is more useful to think in terms of the activity in which individuals engage. "Cooking" has a counterpart in the "chefing" that emphasizes the variability of these activities over time, place, and mood. The greatest chefs must also cook, and the most unadventurous cook in the everyday work of running a kitchen and producing dishes to entice family and friends takes on a good bit of chefing. One of the striking characteristics of our twenty-first-century food world is the degree to which food talk blurs the lines between these two analytically different attitudes toward food. That same food talk obscures other fundamental divisions in the food world, in particular the lines between dining in and dining out. It is to this culinary confusion that the next chapter turns.

PART III

The Culinary Landscape in the Twenty-First Century

CHAPTER SIX

Dining on the Edge

Like cooks and chefs, diners today find themselves in an exhilarating world of inventive dishes, exciting new ways of thinking about food, and unusual modes of dining. No more than cooking or chefing is dining what it was even a half century ago. Largely responsible for many of these myriad changes at table is the loosening of the forms that structured dining in the past. "Informalization" marks a democratization that exemplifies contemporary aspirations. By modifying the dynamics of dining and redefining the relationship between consumer and chef, informalization alters the meaning of the meal no less than the setting.

Once confined to carefully defined and delimited occasions, such as breakfast and picnics, the relaxed attitude and absence of obvious ceremony that now impinge on dining across the board bring new publics into the culinary equation. Not even the loftiest of restaurants is exempt from the need to cater to culinary preferences that would not have been noticed, say, thirty years ago.

On the whole, the twenty-first-century food world disdains, disregards, and largely dispenses with many of the forms that once made dining—whether at home or outside—both a distinctive experience and a regulated one. Meals were scripted and governed by an array of rules, conventions, and norms, both explicit and implicit. More often today, diners sit down at table with no script at all. The rise of culinary individualism, the loss of the communal forms that once presided over meals, and the substitution of familiarity for formality have unsettled contemporary dining. The excitement of adventure triumphs over the security of the known (or, for outsiders, the anxiety of the unknown). This is the new world of competitive dining.

GOING "OUT," STAYING "IN"

EAT IN 1 TALL LATTE

> receipt from Starbucks Plattekill Travel Plaza,
> New York State Thruway

The "tall latte" is a dead giveaway for Starbucks. In what sense do we "eat in" at Starbucks, as the receipt proclaims? Classification becomes more problematic still in this particular instance since the Starbucks in question is located on the New York State Thruway. To be sure, there are tables where one can sit to imbibe the coffee and ingest a muffin, though none is connected to Starbucks. Perhaps, as a colleague suggested, "eat in" points us back to the car, where so much food is consumed. Truly, then, eating turns the automobile into a mobile home. Other Starbucks venues on the thruway evince a conventional conception of eating in and eating out. The receipt from the New Baltimore Plaza a mere two stops away makes it clear that the order is "to go."

A few years ago, my culinary ventures hampered by a broken wrist, an exceptionally thoughtful friend had a number of dinners catered for me and my husband. We didn't think of the meal as "eating out." On the other hand, neither was it "eating in" as usual. It was not a "home-cooked meal," though we were dining at home, at our table with our cutlery and our china. I reheated the various dishes on our stove and in our microwave, which the culinarily challenged in our heat-and-eat culture may well consider cooking. With all that, it seems cheating to claim that we were either "eating in" or "eating out." We were in culinary limbo. I have since come to think of these meals as a combination of "dining in" and "eating out," the former because we followed relatively formal dining procedures at home, the latter because the food came almost fully prepared from outside.

So what is eating out? Every measure in today's food world shows that we are doing it more and more. Every reader can duplicate a hundred times over the permutations of crossover consumption that I experienced on the highway and at home. Because understandings of "in" and "out" shift over time and place, in the end eating out and eating in are a function of each other. It is a sliding scale.

Because what counts as eating out varies over time, place, and people, any one of us will construct "in" and "out" differently. For the contemporary Western food world, eating in a hospital is not eating at home for either patients or staff. Is it eating out? Most of us would probably say no, primarily because we associate eating out with choice. Settings as unalike as a school cafeteria, prison, industrial canteen, or airplane are characterized by minimal choice, if any.

Other situations are less obvious. Different standards apply to the food, setting, and service. Ideally, company get the elaborate recipe, the tidied-up dining and living room, the extensive menu, and the good china (if there is any). The hosts sport "company best" and spruce up their table manners—no boardinghouse reach across the neighbor, no gulping or scarfing, and a likely injunction to FHB (family hold back). Guests take priority.

The restaurant that evolved over the nineteenth century made the most of the disparities and contrasts between private and public dining. That difference turned the restaurant into a crucial public space where it was possible to escape the restrictions of home and the banality of the everyday. As a public site outside the home for the consumption of prepared food, the restaurant was, as it remains, a characteristic urban institution. With space at a premium in the rapidly expanding nineteenth-century city, the archetypal metropolitan meal was a meal outside the home in a specially designated space. Those meals might be taken in any number of places, from the fanciest of high-end restaurants for the favored few to the most ordinary plain fare and bare-bones eatery frequented by the less-fortunate famished. The best of all possible culinary worlds allows us to fix on haute cuisine or revel in the grubbiest of everyday fare and every variation in between.

Eateries of all sorts respond to the needs of different populations, all of them growing. The nineteenth-century city boasted, in addition to restaurants proper, a wealth of options for eating and imbibing outside the home. Paris had a vast array of cafés, *estaminets, guinguettes, auberges, gargotes,* cabarets, *bouchons,* and *bouillons.* London boasted its hotels, taverns, inns, pubs, coffeehouses, and bars, as well as that characteristically English institution, the club. Despite the fact that clubs were closed to the public at large, they provided a key model for meals outside the home as well as a standard of masculinity. From the masculine sociability to the elaborate cuisine, the club set itself against the domestic world of women, family, and ordinary cooking.

If today's restaurant differs from its predecessors, the difference has mostly to do with the many connections that now tie dining in and dining out. Chefs, cooks, and consumers obscure singular features as they move between shifting spaces of food consumption and proceed to talk about the experience. Food talk has made a new food world.

MOVEABLE FEASTS

To say anything useful about dining, out or in, we need to know what we eat. We also need to know when we eat. Where? Why? And with whom? We need to know about the meal because its changing configuration allows us to figure out what, in fact, we mean by dining.

The *Oxford English Dictionary* comes to the rescue. I will surely not be the only one surprised that, unlike the French *repas,* which comes from Latin (and leads to *repast*),the Old English word *meal* has no necessary connection with food. The original sense offers a salutary reminder that the meal is a social enterprise situated in time and bounded in space, for until the thirteenth century, *meal* designated a unit of measure and a unit of time. The particulars of time, space, and social setting give the meal rules, and those rules in turn give it form. Because rules vary according to the purpose and occasion of the meal and differ across cultures, every group has its own notions of a proper meal—the correct sequence of courses, the appropriate content of dishes, and the right times and suitable places for consumption.

The development of the restaurant over the nineteenth century diffused a specific model of the meal. Working off the elaborate rituals inherited from the dining practices of seventeenth- and eighteenth-century elites, especially at one court or another, the restaurant determined dining out. Like the city, the restaurant gave unprecedented scope to individual initiative. No longer centered on the (private) host, dining did not yet fix on the (professional) chef. It was the individual diner, metamorphosed into a paying customer, who focused the meal and the restaurant.

Reading Meals
Still, however much the restaurant can be said to have liberated the consumer-guest from the tyranny of the host, it is an institution, and like every other institution, it places constrictions on the individual. Despite the choice of foods and services that it offers every comer, restaurants are no culinary free-for-all. Whether visibly or not, restaurants regulate meals.

The restaurant exercises this control by guiding the diner through the presentation of foods. In the nineteenth and twentieth centuries, the patterns of the restaurant meal framed the dishes proposed. In principle, diners pick whatever they want in whatever order they fancy. But to do so, they must get past the menu, and menus are decidedly instrumental texts. Every menu seeks to guide the reader to a "good" reading, which is, in effect, a "good" meal. Choice is neither random nor free. No restaurant presents an accidental menu. Every menu enforces categories that, by implication, promise a "proper" meal. All of which means that reading a menu is no idle occupation. To understand a menu and use it correctly requires reading the culture behind the text. The categories in which the menu places dishes must be meaningful, and the dishes themselves must make sense, not simply to the chef but also, crucially, to the potential customer.

Variable over time and cultures, meals always follow some sort of succession. There is, ideally, a sense of the whole of which the menu lists the parts. It makes no difference whether the entrée is the main course, as is usual in American dining, or is served before the main course, as in France. Whenever it comes, the entrée has its place in the model meal proposed by the menu. It is, as the term tells us, the entry into that meal. The French model—hors d'oeuvres, soup, fish, and meat followed by salad, cheese, and dessert—often strikes Americans as excessive, quite possibly decadent, and definitely very French. It is not all that far-fetched to invoke Americans' sense of themselves as "plain" rather than "fancy" folks when they think about the restriction of courses to appetizer, entrée, and dessert. Or more plainly still, starter, main course, dessert. That Italian menus list pasta as a separate course reminds the diner, should a reminder be needed, just how basic pasta is to any Italian meal.

Cultural attitudes are encoded in both the order of the meal and the culinary terminology—that is, the words used to identify dishes. Thus Americans find it appropriate to tease their appetite with "appetizers"; the French prefer to "amuse" the mouth with *amuse-bouches;* and Italians organize the meal around pasta, with antipasti, which situate the opening of the meal in Italian American cuisine, existing in relation to the pasta course. The French *hors d'oeuvres*—meaning "outside the work"—tells the diner that the most important part of the meal is yet to come. *Entrée* indicates the place of the dish in a sequence, while *dessert* comes from the word to clear the table (*desservir*). Anything that does not fit in the sequence is linguistically relegated to the sidelines: *entremets* (foods that come "between" other foods) for the French, *contorni* (things "around" the main dish) for Italians, or *sides* for Americans.

Like menu order, the pantheon of classic dishes is one of the striking features of French cuisine. Both are conceived in terms of a culinary code. The names of dishes place them in a system in relation to one another. A hollandaise or béarnaise sauce, or any other of the many French sauces, is fixed. Variations mandate new names. Orange-flavored hollandaise is rebaptized *sauce maltaise*, and tomato turns *sauce béarnaise* into *sauce Choron* while meat glaze makes it *sauce Colbert*. And so on, through the impressive repertoire of French sauces.

Such is the culinary code that defined what came to be known as "classic" French cuisine, which emphasizes less the ingredients—seldom specified—than the finished preparation. The name—an epithet, really—places the dish beyond the contingencies of preparation. The necessity of decoding the dishes turns reading a traditional French menu into an exercise in translation. To figure out what you are eating, you have to crack the code.

Every menu comes between the diner and the dinner. It speaks to those familiar with the language, code, and customs these express. French cuisine is notable for the density and intricacy of interconnections in that code. To understand, say, what you are getting with a BLT, all you need to know, really, are the ingredients, and the name tells you: bacon, lettuce, and tomato, and you get to specify the kind of toast. *Sauce Choron* is another matter. If you want to know what *sauce Choron* is, you need to know that it is *sauce béarnaise* with tomato and, more fundamentally still, that *sauce béarnaise* is a sort of hollandaise transformed by wine. The name is no help.

The diner confronting a French menu, especially one heavy on the sauces ("à la" whatever) needs specialized cultural knowledge. The basic component foods in *steak frites* with béarnaise sauce gets you to the steak. To figure out what will turn up on your plate—or, even more dramatically, what is already on your plate—culinary literacy is essential. Menu French is its own language, not to be confused with the French language from which it derives. Béarnaise requires at least beginners Menu French, *sauce Choron* an intermediate level. Knowing the works and career of the nineteenth-century writer François-René de Chateaubriand will not give you any clue as to what "Chateaubriand" on the menu will put on your plate (a beef tenderloin served with a reduction of white wine, shallots, tarragon, and butter, allegedly invented by Chateaubriand's cook).

Menus, then, resemble all food talk in that they both help eating and hinder it. Why, outsiders understandably feel, must the menu stand in the way of enjoyment? Why, plain-food Americans may query resentfully, cannot the menu just list what's in a dish? Ingredients ought to suffice.

The answer is that ingredients—nature—are only part of what French cuisine is about, and often a small part at that. French cuisine appreciates dishes less as food than as culinary creations. All cooking transforms. The question is how much. French cuisine puts a premium on transformation and on the words that talk about it. The cook in *Haute Cuisine* takes palpable pleasure in reciting the menu that she will prepare. The litany of named dishes on French menus encodes those transformations and formalizes their connections. No food stands on its own. The code supersedes the dish. The whole is greater than the sum of its parts.

The coherence of its codes and the formalization of its practice early on gave French cuisine a decided advantage in the bid for culinary authority. Easy to teach, the French culinary system traveled well. Travel among the upper classes extended the French model still further. Menu French came to be a lingua franca of elites, none of whom had trouble reading menus at any banquet or in any restaurant where they were likely to dine. It made no difference if they massacred the French language. Menu French sufficed.

Given the distinction conferred by fluency in Menu French, a cuisinologist might wonder why Thorstein Veblen did not include dining in *The Theory of the Leisure Class* (1899). The use of food by those whom he skewered as the "leisure class" would have given him a terrific instance of what he saw as their trademark conspicuous consumption. With its formal order of consumption, dining in an identifiably French mode illuminates the contrast that Veblen draws between luxury and necessity. The forms of dining correspond perfectly to the distance that Veblen's leisure class strove to put between their cultural practices and everyone else's worlds of work. The obstacles that French menus put in the way of readers give the insiders who have mastered the culinary code and forms of dining yet another means of distinguishing themselves from outsiders. The formal restaurant offered a superlative setting for the display of dining distinction.

Reading Restaurants

Before consumption venues multiplied so dramatically in kind and number, the differences between public and private dining spoke pretty much for themselves. The more self-sufficient a community, the more traditional its food culture and the fewer the dining opportunities. In the early modern period in Europe, roughly before the nineteenth century, dining out as we understand it today was a relatively rare occurrence. Except for someone else's home, there were few places to go, and those that did exist drew a limited clientele. Middle- and upper-class women in the seventeenth and eighteenth centuries, for instance, did not generally frequent public eating establishments. Barring extraordinary circumstances, no respectable woman would have thought of dining in a tavern or an inn or a café. Restaurants, too, were suspect. If we go no further than nineteenth-century French and English novels, the women who frequented restaurants were certainly thought to be ladies of good appetite and easy virtue.

The marked social, economic, and geographic mobility of modern society brought into being a social order in which the boundaries between dining in and dining out cross and recross. Women move about more freely, if not without risk. This permeability created considerable insecurity. The spread of dining venues of every sort and on every level, from the neighborhood diner to the destination restaurant, has produced a remarkably mixed and often chaotic food world.

Today the staggering array of possibilities complicates dining decisions immensely. Zagat's guide to any city offers features that we might never have thought of: BYO; Child Friendly; Chef's Table; Fireplaces; Historic; Gluten-free; Offbeat. The 2012 New York City Zagat's guide showcases fifty-two special features, jumbling food, décor, and ambiance. Then there is the type of cuisine—Zagat offers one hundred choices, from Afghan to Vietnamese, French (regular, bistro, brasserie) to South African, and we surely must not pass over Health Food and Tea Rooms.

Still more unsettling, fixing on a restaurant does not end the insecurity. Customers looking for elegance used to be able to count on finding a familiar mode of dining. Many restaurants today, notably the more ambitious ones, pride themselves on the unconventional. From the nineteenth century on, stylish dining followed French norms. Formal dining, stylish or not, "did" French almost by definition, for modes of consumption as well as cooking. The restaurant spread this archetype of dining throughout elite and, eventually, middle-class culture.

This model of production and consumption depended upon a relatively fixed social canvas. In much of contemporary society, where that stability no longer holds, the very conceptions of dining in and dining out became manifestly variable and perceptibly unstable. One of the most striking developments over the past hundred years is the blurring of the distinctions between the two, between what is considered eating in and what is deemed eating out. The more mobile a culture, the more it and everything in it will "move." All that movement puts norms and conventions, culinary and otherwise, up for grabs.

CULINARY INDIVIDUALISM

Culinary individualism sets the tone and the rules of today's culinary game. Endlessly amplified by the media, insistence on the priority of individual preferences has created a contemporary dining landscape of quite another order of complexity than its counterpart a century ago. One word sums up the differences: informalization. In the strict sense of losing or rejecting the forms that structure how we conduct ourselves, informalization has realigned the contemporary food world.

The forms that once characterized restaurant dining—the food terminology, prescribed order of the meal, and expectations of behavior and dress—no longer restrict consumers as they once did. They no longer shape expectations to the same extent. Chefs go their own way, and often, so do diners. The paradigmatic example of such culinary deregulation is undoubtedly Ferran Adrià's restaurant, elBulli, where diners knew only to expect the unexpected. Ironically, it was the restaurant as a modern institution—the prime instrument in transmitting the norms of elegant dining out—that gave culinary individualism its base.

The differences show up everywhere. Meals parade their experimental intent. At every point in self-consciously avant-garde restaurants—in the food prepared, the service, and the setting—and for all participants—chef, servers, and customers—there prevails a sense of thumbing one's nose at the conventional. There is a conspicuous ambition for something that does more than tweak standard dishes. New is not enough; "beyond new" is the aspiration for the truly unusual and defines this dining. Partly, the reorientation has to do with a culture that prizes novelty. The new has virtually become a tradition in itself. The greater the premium placed on innovation, the more powerful the push for every sector of the food world to seek new products and new markets.

As part of the process of muddling the distinctions between dining in and dining out, today's culinary customs defy the boundaries of the meal. To puzzle what is eating out and what is eating in, we need to figure out what counts as a meal—a "real" meal. Think of the many modifications of the compartmentalization of meals over the day. More and more, the individual decides, leaving restaurants scrambling to feed the importunate customer at the odd hour. The power relation between customer and restaurateur has shifted accordingly. The dynamic has become all the more unpredictable in view of the spectrum of prospects for eating out and the radical individualization of food consumption. The distance could scarcely be further from the standard forms and behavior that went with restaurant meals a century ago.

First, consider the sequence of meals over the day. While it is true that the times of meals vary greatly over period, place, and milieu, a common sequence of meals tends to hold for any given sector within the larger culture. The middle classes had one order, and the working classes had another, which started early in the day, like their work, with meal breaks taken accordingly. For both classes, the work schedule determined the eating schedule. Factories might have cafeterias for all personnel, and the upper reaches of the corporate world make much of the executive dining room. Other institutions—such as schools, hospitals, the armed forces, and prisons—similarly impose an externally driven meal schedule. The more restrictive the institution, the more rigid the meal schedule and the less individual the selection.

Today, outside such institutions, the ceaseless movement of urban populations makes it harder and harder to pinpoint meals. Despite the strong association of breakfast with the beginning of the day, many restaurants now serve "breakfast" all day long. Fried eggs and bacon dished up at 6 P.M.

in an American setting definitely disrupt dinner. A venerable and elegant Michelin-starred Parisian restaurant serves scrambled eggs as a first course at lunch, thereby transporting the humble everyday egg dish routinely made at home with the unequivocally unhumble setting. Decidedly, traditional culinary associations are disappearing. Scrambled eggs at high noon it may well be.

Informalization

As many commentators have noted, sometimes with approval and often without, the shift in late twentieth-century dining that brought this question to the fore is the increasingly conspicuous "informalization" of eating out. The formal complexity of the food served no longer requires a formal setting. The elaborate food preparations of avant-garde or "creative" cuisine are no longer obligatorily consumed in an elegant setting marked by specialization of silver, table, and glassware. And whereas customers once "dressed up" to meet the difference of the restaurant experience, today anything that seems formal looms as an obstacle to enjoyment for most. Diners dress down, or rather they refuse to dress up, most noticeably younger generations and those who have not mastered, or not found it worthwhile to master, the codes that allow the production of an egalitarian dining space.

The flip side of Brillat-Savarin's egalitarian dining utopia exposes the meal as a battleground of insiders against intruders. As public establishments dependent upon a renewable clientele, most restaurants in the twenty-first century cannot exercise blatant discrimination. Yet every restaurant reaches towards new customers whom it hopes to attract and discourages others. The posting of menus, once outside the restaurant and now on its obligatory website, puts customers on notice about the financial resources required. There are many other indicators of exclusivity, some obvious, some subtle: menus that list dishes in another language, a waiter visibly impatient with questions that betray the neophyte, a bewildering assortment of knives, forks, and glasses. The same principle applies to every dining establishment, no matter how downscale.

This informalization skews the hierarchy of eating out. It was once relatively clear that the opposition of informality versus formality concerned both food and place. No one expected either soufflés or tuxedos in a bistro, and everyone would expect both at a formal dining occasion. This is no longer the case. Strict dress codes are not invoked as they once were. Few establishments today require men to wear ties, and if some expect a jacket at dinner, they keep the attire on hand for unadorned customers. Women no longer think about wearing trousers, whereas not so long ago the "better" spots turned away any woman not in a skirt, elegant designer pantsuit notwithstanding.

Even so, the awareness of forms lingers in a sense of transgression. Top New York chef Daniel Boulud put transgression to use when he invited guests to attend a fundraiser at his restaurant Daniel with an injunction to wear their . . . jeans: "We realized [guests] love the slightly forbidden-fruit idea of coming to one of the city's most elegant restaurants and feasting on a sumptuous meal . . . in their blue jeans." Without doubt, the jeans that showed up were designer jeans, and there was no shortage of bling, but jeans it was—as much a dress code as any other and fulfilling the same function of designating insiders.

Informality is not without its disadvantages. On the one hand, the diminishing distance between the everyday and the special dining experience would seem to make eating out more welcoming to a broader range of individuals. On the other hand, that same informality may reduce the incentive to eat out in the first place. There is little inducement to go out if it's just like home. Take-out or order-in would do as well. Ultimately, every diner has to determine how much value the restaurant adds, and every restaurant has to work at adding that value.

Responses to this dilemma vary greatly from one end of the eating-out spectrum to the other. Some businesses stress the connection with the good side of "home cooking" by serving comfort food at an affordable price and cultivating a convivial atmosphere. This is the standard for diners, bistros, coffee shops, and neighborhood delis, eating establishments that opt for the familiar.

New Menus, New Meals

Out with the old forms, in with the new. In many restaurants today, above all those where a celebrity chef is in charge, the tasting menu has replaced the free choice of à la carte dining. The foods served likely differ as well, especially for restaurants seeking to make their mark as culinary hot spots. In place of the classic dishes encoded in the repertory of French cuisine, the quest for the new leads to unfamiliar ingredients, from yuzu to yak—the more exotic, the more exciting. Different principles organize the menu. In place of the formal menu, with its predictable progression from appetizer to dessert, avant-garde restaurants put together their menus to guide the diner through the distinctive cooking of the chef.

Thus, at Le Bernardin, perhaps the premier fish restaurant in Manhattan (three stars from Michelin, four from the *New York Times*), the dinner menu proceeds from "almost raw" to "barely touched" to "lightly cooked." (The lunch menu provides more direction, perhaps to accommodate a less sophisticated clientele, specifying that the dishes in the first two groups comprise the first course and those in the last group the main course.) Dessert has its own menu and chef, a difference that the menu marks graphically as well as culinarily. Only at the end of the meal proper (as designated by the menu) does the waiter hand out the separate dessert menu (the website lists the dessert menu separately). Dessert follows its own norms. As the term suggests, it clears the table—*desservir*—and the palate. The menu makes clear that the "real" meal is another category altogether.

Le Bernardin replaces conventional categories and dishes with terms that delineate the ideal meal of this restaurant and this chef. Meals elsewhere are something else again since they may well have their own code. Insofar as the menu at Le Bernardin speaks a language all its own, experience in other restaurants is of little help with dining there, just as Le Bernardin provides little guidance for dining elsewhere. Standard Menu French, which it would be reasonable to expect in a restaurant with the strong French inflection of Le Bernardin, or even Advanced Menu French, gets the diner only so far.

True, Menu French recognizes *en papillotte, sauce tartare,* crème fraîche, mousseline, *verjus sabayon, "en salade," nage, sauce vierge,* and *pomme gaufrette.* Still, Menu Japanese would be equally useful (hamachi, "sashimi," yuzo, sake-miso sauce, edamame, wasabi, shiso broth) while Spanish (adobo sauce, sofrito sauce, fideos, "ceviche," *chicha* sauce, jalapeño broth, *a la plancha*) and a nodding acquaintance with Indian (basmati, tamarind) would be a big help. From still other culinary traditions, tabbouleh, bacalao, and "carpaccio" drive home the need for Advanced Avant-garde menu-speak.

LE BERNARDIN DINNER MENU (summer 2012) CHEF: ERIC RIPERT

almost raw

    OYSTERS Single Variety or Assortment of Oysters (Six Pieces)

    CAVIAR Organically Grown Farm-Raised *Osetra Caviar* ($120 Supplement per ounce)

        Farm-Raised Golden Osetra Caviar ($135 Supplement per ounce)

    GEODUCK Shaved *Geoduck* Clam; Smoked *Edamame Mousseline, Wasabi*-Citrus Emulsion

    TUNA Layers of Thinly Pounded Yellowfin Tuna, Foie Gras and Toasted Baguette

        Shaved Chives and Extra Virgin Olive Oil

    STRIPED BASS Wild Striped Bass *Tartare*; Baby Fennel, Crispy Artichoke, Black Olive Oil and Lemon

SALMON Cured Wild Salmon; Pickled Sunchoke and Heart of Palm,
Cardamom-Ginger Vinaigrette

FLUKE Fluke "*Sashimi*"; Micro Watercress, Avocado, *Jalapeño*-Lime
Broth

SEA SCALLOP Flash Marinated Sea Scallop; Sweet and Sour Grapes,
Extra Virgin Olive Oil-*Yuzu* Vinaigrette

HAMACHI *Hamachi "Sashimi"*; Mint, Cucumber and Apple, Sweet
and Sour Carrot Vinaigrette

CAVIAR-WAGYU ($45 Supplement) Nebraska *Wagyu Beef*, Langous-
tine and Osetra Caviar *Tartare*

Black Pepper-Vodka Crème Fraîche, Pomme Gaufrette

MESCLUN SALAD Salad of the Day's Market Herbs and Vegetables
with Balsamic-Shallot Vinaigrette

barely touched

CRAB Chilled Peekytoe Crab Salad; Baby Radish and Avocado,
Green Apple-Lemongrass *Nage*

YELLOWFIN TUNA Ultra Rare Seared Tuna; Marinated Fennel, Basil
and Capers

LOBSTER Warm Lobster "*Carpaccio*"; Ruby Red Grapefruit and
Heart of Palm, *Verjus Sabayon*

BACALAO Grilled Salted Cod; Hearts of Baby Romaine, "*Caesar
Vinaigrette*"

ALBACORE Seared Albacore Tuna Confit "*En Salade*," Bibb Lettuce,
Deviled Quail Egg, Liquid Black Olive, Preserved Tomato and Pepper

SEPIA Grilled Baby *Sepia*; Sweet Pepper Jam, Red Wine-Squid Ink
Sauce

COBIA Curry Crusted *Cobia*; Roasted Pepper Vinaigrette, Coconut
Lime Broth

SEA MEDLEY Caviar and Shellfish Medley; *Yuzu* Scented Custard,
Smoked *Bonito* Broth

OCTOPUS Charred Octopus *"a la plancha"*; Green Olive and *Black Garlic* Emulsion, Sundried Tomato *Sauce Vierge*

VEGETABLES "Summer Vegetables"; Israeli Couscous *"Tabbouleh"*, Herb Vinaigrette

LANGOUSTINE Sautéed Langoustine; Summer Truffle and Chanterelle, Aged Balsamic Vinaigrette

SCALLOP Warm Scallop *"Carpaccio"*; Snowpeas and Shiitake, Lime-*Shiso* Broth

lightly cooked

DOVER SOLE Sautéed Sole; "Almond-Pistachio-Barberry" Golden *Basmati*, Brown-Butter *Tamarind* Vinaigrette ($18 Supplement)

RED SNAPPER Bread Crusted Red Snapper; Saffron *"Fideos"* Smoked Sweet Paprika Sauce

STRIPED BASS Lacquered Striped Bass; *Chayote Squash, Sofrito Broth*

SKATE Baked Skate *"En Papillote"*; Pickled Chanterelles, Baby Turnips, *"Green Marinière"*

BLACK BASS Crispy Black Bass; Roasted *Shishitos* and Acorn Squash *"Ceviche,"* Peruvian *Chicha* Sauce

MONKFISH Roasted Monkfish; Wilted Mustard Greens-*Daikon* "Sandwich," *Adobo* Sauce

ARCTIC CHAR "Ultra-Rare" Arctic Char; Truffled Peas and Favas Butter Lettuce-Tarragon Emulsion

SALMON Barely Cooked Wild Salmon; Asparagus, *Wasabi*-Bean Purée, *Yuzu* Emulsion

HALIBUT Poached Halibut; Glazed Baby Bok Choy, Bergamot-Basil Emulsion

CODFISH Baked Cod; Baby Octopus and Sea Bean Salad, Cumin-Red Wine Sauce

LOBSTER Baked Lobster; Stuffed Zucchini Flower, *Sake-Miso Sauce*

RED SNAPPER Whole Red Snapper Baked with Lemon and Rose-
mary; *Byaldi Natural Jus* (Please Allow 24 Hours Notice; For Two)
DUCK Roasted Duck Magret; Turnip, Walnut, Red Wine-Grape
Mostarda Sauce
LAMB Pistachio Crusted Rack of Lamb; Grilled Spiced Eggplant, *Jus*
PASTA Black Truffle-Buffalo Mozzarella Stuffed Ravioli, "Summer
Vegetables", Parmesan Sauce
FILET MIGNON Beef Filet au Poivre; Medley of Seasonal Market
Vegetables

The diner confronted with this menu needs to know the jargon of Le
Bernardin—that is, the specialized language of this particular group. Le Bernardin regulars will understand Bernardin-speak; everyone else will resign
themselves to peppering the waiters with questions. Yet, fluent though we
may be in this novel language, the ingredients and preparations tell us little
about what we might be ordering. Because the eclectic menu, of which Le
Bernardin offers a splendid example, is combinatory, it must be descriptive.

The only solution—description—is a partial one. Every dish stands on its
own. Unlike the standard French repertory, it is not part of a code. You will
not find the "Almond-Pistachio-Barberry" Golden *Basmati* [rice] and Brown-
Butter Tamarind Vinaigrette anywhere else (unless, it is to be hoped, it is
credited to Le Bernardin). Though you may recognize the sole in the Dover
sole dish, Menu French will not tell you anything about its preparation. It is
not *sole normande* (mussels, shrimp, crème fraîche) or *amandine* (with
almonds) or *meunière* (drowned in butter). Nor is it any of the more than one
hundred coded preparations for sole listed in the *Larousse Gastronomique*,
from *sole à l'américaine* to *sole Saint-Germain*. This menu offers Le Bernardin's
sole. More disconcerting, you will not find this dish two months hence,
when the menu will have changed. The menu will no doubt feature sole—but
a different sole.

The capital letters fix the dish, and the quotation marks brand the combination. "Sashimi," the quotation marks let us know, is not sashimi as Japanese cuisine understands the dish (lobster does not traditionally figure as sashimi) just as "carpaccio" is assuredly not the paper-thin sliced meat that is a staple of Italian cuisine. If *ratatouille* sounds too plebeian and too much like everyday fare, then call it *byaldi natural jus*, with a tip of the toque for those really in the know to French chef Michel Guérard, who first turned ratatouille into this dish worthy of haute cuisine.

This liberation of the menu from standard categories is not new. Over two decades ago, Georges Briguet, a prominent French restaurateur in New York was already complaining that when he went out to restaurants in New York, he could no longer read the menu. In contrast to a French menu typical of what we may now see as the "classic" era of restaurant cuisine—roughly from the mid-nineteenth through the end of the twentieth century—menus were already going in every direction, joyfully disregarding the cultural and culinary forms that once dictated the sequence and the content. "Any French restaurant in France or here had only culinary terms. The same dish had to be exactly the same . . . everywhere. Now, the interpretation of the food has changed. No longer gastronomical terms, but tuna with cucumbers, etc. Every chef is like his own master, cooks what he likes. When I go out to restaurants in the city, I don't understand the menu, I have to ask questions."

I had my own comeuppance when my reading of the menu at Le Bernardin required more than one Google search. Advanced Menu French did me little good. Without a doubt, I need to frequent the restaurant more assiduously if I am to have any hope of raising my proficiency in Bernardin-speak. Fortunately, waiters now routinely ask diners, "Are there any questions?"

In this age of competitive dining, the setting also needs to be distinctive. It has to identify the restaurant and distinguish it from competitors. Given the slipperiness of taste and the stress of new dishes, visuals play a vital role in translating the newness that the ambitious restaurant needs to convey.

Any restaurant aiming for the top has to "refresh" the décor as well as the cuisine, and do so regularly. One French restaurateur in New York whom I interviewed contended that Americans insist upon new things. He'd just redone his restaurant in soft peach tones to get as far as possible from the deep reds that screamed old-style French restaurant.

It was not enough to change the menu and hire, at first, an American chef, and then, at the time of our interview, a Japanese chef. The setting had to display a unique newness. The décor had to proclaim that the restaurant in question—La Caravelle—was beyond the same old, same old. Undoubtedly because there was no question of doing away with their traditional specialties—dropping quenelles and duck would alienate too many regular customers—the décor shared the burden of keeping the restaurant up with the times.

Stylization celebrates the difference of eating out. Flowers are a case in point. Floral arrangements have taken on enormous significance as markers of difference, whether in a large bouquet on the bar (long a hallmark of the French bistro) or exquisitely artful blossoms in spectacular, and, it goes without saying, extraordinarily expensive arrangements. The greater the competition—in large urban centers with a high density of restaurants—the greater the need to be up to date in every domain, flowers along with food.

Whether customers like the décor or not is, in the end, of little consequence. The point is to make the new visible. Whatever one thinks of the renovated Le Bernardin, its bid for originality is unmistakable. Over the previous twenty-five years the décor had been modified so subtly that no one, apparently, paid much attention. And so Le Bernardin celebrated its silver anniversary in 2011 with an emphatically up-to-date, radically sleek postmodern look that one could not fail to notice.

BETWEEN CHARISMA AND ROUTINE

Culinary individualism works two ways. Diners feel at ease—"at home"—with the informality of dining; chefs take advantage of the loosening of convention. If the interests of the two coincide—both want a "good restaurant"—they also collide. A power struggle is inevitable because production and consumption have different priorities. Each claims to define the meal, each defines it differently, and each seeks to impose that definition. Today's food world has liberated diners and chefs alike from once-strong cultural and culinary constraints. Few restaurants pursue an idiosyncratic, unconventional cuisine as singlemindedly as Ferran Adrià did at elBulli. If this restaurant epitomizes extreme cuisine, many more make much of the audacity of "their" cuisine and "their" preparations in "their" restaurant. Chefs work hard to turn their individual authority into a brand that transcends the everyday of the restaurant.

Culinary Authority: Big Night

The à la carte menu promotes choice and encourages choosiness. Diners today range across the menu as their fancy dictates—two hors d'oeuvres and no main course, perhaps an appetizer taken for the dessert course, even two desserts! As the wonderful film *Big Night* (1996) shows, diners may carry indulgence to the point of disgust. The customer who wants spaghetti and meatballs along with risotto outrages Primo, the chef. She is, he exclaims, nothing less than a "criminal" and a "philistine." Nor does she understand that spaghetti need not come with meatballs. "Sometimes," Secundo, the manager–waiter, tries to explain, "spaghetti likes to be alone."

Everything turns on culinary authority. For the meal to proceed smoothly the diner must accept the chef's authority. In *Big Night*, Primo's customer did not acknowledge his expertise. She was, moreover, affronted that the chef had the temerity to question her taste. It was the customer's culinary preference against the chef's authority, and the customer won. A fabulous cook, Primo lacked the charisma and therefore the cultural legitimacy to impose his culinary vision. His disgruntled customer left, and others never came. Predictably, the restaurant failed.

The culinary landscape today is very different from the 1950s New Jersey of *Big Night*. Yet the question of culinary authority remains as critical as ever. The tasting menu is designed to showcase the chef as much as, perhaps more than, to please the customer. That customer may well want to control the meal and requests (demands?) substitutions. Ordering a meal launches a series of delicate negotiations between the customer and the chef relayed by the waiter-buffer. Waiters need to make customers happy, but they work for the chef-restaurateur.

The more upmarket audience for this movie, which appeared some forty years after the incident, accepts Primo's culinary authority because it has learned the lesson that Primo was trying to teach. It is easy for contemporary sophisticates to dismiss the New Jersey matron who wanted risotto and spaghetti in the same meal. We moderns agree with Primo that she is a culinary ignoramus, and we agree because we recognize the dishes that Primo prepares so lovingly. The spaghetti bolognese that sends him into raptures just thinking about it—"You have to kill yourself, you can't live" after tasting the dish—has become part of a broad culinary lexicon. If anything, it is old hat. We culinarily savvy viewers appreciate Primo's vision of authentic Italian cuisine because we believe in it as he does. We assent to his declaration of faith that "to eat good food is to be close to God," though most of us would likely not put it that way. If, like Primo, we cannot say why "the knowledge of God is the bread of angels," we take the proverb on faith. Then, too, we would never, *ever* think of mixing risotto and spaghetti.

Beyond the Kitchen

Primo was no celebrity chef. He had no right to tell customers what they should and should not eat. Such a position of legitimacy depends on external reputation, which is why, to maintain their authority, celebrity chefs must look beyond cuisine and kitchen. The chef needs food talk to amplify charisma: in cookbooks and television shows; in critiques from established dining guides and blogs; and in commercial ventures from potato chips to kitchen equipment. Then there are the memoirs that profile already prominent chefs, along with films and documentaries that portray the chef in heroic terms. Inconspicuous production ended long ago.

All this food talk, you might assume, gives the chef the upper hand in the culinary discussions that go on in every restaurant. Diners at table have in effect signed an unwritten contract to accept the chef's definition of the situation by consuming the meal on the menu. At the same time that chefs have become public figures as well as aggressively experimental, consumers know more about food. They are more experienced in the food world, and highly attuned to the new—products and personalities no less than preparations. The consumer may know a good deal about individual chefs, their cuisines, and their culinary philosophies.

For the knowledgeable consumer, once-exotic ingredients have become familiar, available in specialty markets and often in supermarkets as well. A click opens the cornucopia of the Internet, where cybersurfers can find specialty items from appetizer olives to postprandial nuts. The more culinarily sophisticated consumers become, the more likely they are to have their own opinions. Contesting the chef's choices is the next logical step. The old-school professional gastronome took it upon himself to critique the chef. Today a sizable public feels free to do so.

The culinary proficiency of the experienced diner recalibrates the relationship between consumer and chef. The importance of regular customers for the continued existence of so many restaurants gives special weight to these diners, whose presence will be noted so that the staff may act accordingly.

Take the jargon at a smattering of New York restaurants: Del Posto ensures that "Always," a super-regular customer, always gets a table and that "Neighbor," who lives nearby, receives extra attention; Le Cirque tags its guests as "Pesce Grosso" (big fish), "Frittura" (fried fish, "small fry"), and

"Vergini" (newcomers); Annisa and Daniel identify their finest customers as "B. G. E." (Best Guest Ever) and "The O. G.'s" (Original Gangstas), respectively. Union Square Café has a finely calibrated system of classification, beginning with "f. t. d" (first time diner), moving to "reg" (a regular), "soi" (soigné, a very special guest), and not forgetting special occasion diners with "H. B." (Happy Birthday), "H. A." (Happy Anniversary), and "N. L.," for the guest who needs love. There will be no overlooking "K1" (who will be proposing) and certainly not the guest who "drops coin" (spends a lot on wine). And so on. No doubt every restaurant, low-end as well as high, evolves a code that allows the restaurant to control the meal.

Culinary sophisticates join forces with the regulars to up the ante for innovation, all the more so if they overlap. Both push for new dishes, and both look for the unexpected delight. The more conversant diners are with the chef's fare, the more they will eventually want something different, something beyond what has become ordinary.

The other side of the coin of creativity is the comfort that a restaurant provides. The more regular a customer, the more surely the staff—computer files at the ready—will make a point of knowing personal preferences or quirks, foods to avoid and to offer. Allergies, intolerances, or just plain dislikes figure along with the foibles of the gentleman who regularly requests a side order of mashed potatoes or has a special vinaigrette in the restaurant refrigerator.

Small attentions have large implications. Personalization transforms the chef into a host and the customer into a guest, making it clear that the connection between the customer-consumer and the chef is more than a purely commercial exchange. Restaurants are commercial affairs, but the hospitality business is not—and cannot be—an "ordinary" business focused on a discrete product. However necessary a component, food is not hospitality.

No ordinary business enjoins its staff to show special care to special customers—remember N. L.? Personalization is by no means confined to high-end restaurants. Short-order diners and food-cart proprietors also know the preferences of regular customers in the daily offerings. Just hang around a neighborhood restaurant for a bit. Where the chef is intent on making a mark in the food world, personalization costs more because it requires complex monitoring. Every guest cannot receive an extra glass of champagne if champagne is to remain something special. Should "extra" champagne become expected, the restaurant will need to devise other means of pampering that special customer.

On the one hand, it is hardly an overstatement to see the constant stream of culinary innovations as so many miracles—unexpected by definition—that manifest the extraordinary, that is, charismatic, status of the chef. These menu miracles maintain the chef's charisma, celebrity, and authority. On the other hand, miracles do not provide a solid basis for a commercial enterprise like the restaurant. As Max Weber argued long ago in his analysis of charisma, this "gift of god" that confers extraordinary powers lays an unstable foundation for authority. The necessary unpredictability disqualifies miracles as a foundation for durable success, which requires repetition and routine reproduction.

To retain the power and effect that charisma confers, to follow Weber, a leader has to remain aloof from the mundane and the everyday. The restaurateur-chef is caught between the exigencies of creativity and the demands of a viable service establishment concerned with profitability, product reliability, customer base, and staff performance. The chef has to stand apart from and manage the world of work. Whether in the great kitchens of the present or the past, "Chef" designates the head officer who tells others what to do, decides on the battle plan, deploys the troops, and brooks no questioning of authority. In the kitchen, "Yes, Chef" is the only possible response to any order.

Precisely because of its ambitions for creativity and innovation, the adventurous restaurant is subject to contrary claims. The requirements of creativity vie with appeals for comfort, the exceptional confronts the familiar. Culinary creativity seeks the distinctive and the unique. Running a restaurant requires the capacity to reproduce the (unique) creations of the chef. As one New York chef put it, he knew how to make an amazing meal. The success of the restaurant depended on his ability to train a staff of twenty to reproduce that same meal for diners night after night.

Organization and structure channel creativity, and that channeling, in Weberian terms, entails the routinization of the chef's charisma. Here is all the work of setting standards, procedures, making the singular a matter of routine, and turning the exceptional into the everyday. This is the chef's predicament. Routine destroys charisma by making the extraordinary ordinary. Routine turns the remarkable into the mundane. It leaves no room for miracles. Yet without mini miracles or breaks in the routine to legitimate the chef's authority, no restaurant can claim distinction. Absent consistent procedures and a basic repertory of predictable dishes, it cannot survive.

Every chef answers these questions differently. At one end of the spectrum is extreme cuisine, illustrated most dramatically by Ferran Adrià. As chapter 5 explained, Adrià essentially disregards the customer. At elBulli, the gargantuan tasting menu—all thirty-five courses in sequence—was the only option. It is the experience of tasting that counts for Ferran Adrià, not the pleasure of consumption. The logic of creativity and concomitant disinterest in the consumer have a lot to do with Adrià's closing of his restaurant in 2011 to concentrate on experimentation.

The opposite end of this continuum is occupied exemplarily by the Swiss-born New York chef Daniel Humm, co-owner and executive chef, who is intent on marrying creativity with collaboration. His Manhattan restaurant, Eleven Madison Park—EMP in the blogosphere—works at doing away with the distinction between dining out and eating in: "We're really trying to blend coming home and going out. When you walk into this room, the high ceilings, the china . . ., the silverware . . .: everything feels like 'going out.'

But the human interaction should feel like coming home." The integration of the "back of the house" with the kitchen brigade and the "front of the house" with the waitstaff is such that the cooks come to the table and explain the food. Diners choose from sixteen ingredients (four meats, four vegetables, four fish, and four desserts) and convey their food likes and dislikes. "We want it to be a dialogue," the chef explains, "We want to get a little bit of feedback from our diners, and based on that, we create the menu."

MENU—ELEVEN MADISON PARK (SUMMER 2012)

Hamachi	Radicchio	Langoustine	Foie Gras
Carrot	Black truffle	Skate	Lobster
Chicken	Pork	Lamb	Veal
Hobelchäs	Coconut	Lemon	Chocolate

Tasting Menu: $195

Four Courses: $125

Wine Pairings: $95/$145

NEXT

Where does the food world go from here? Meals loom large in the social landscape not because humans need to eat but because they need to connect. Meals orchestrate the distinctive rhythms of our lives. Food is fuel in any circumstance. The meal acquires meaning in a cultural space and time for performance of social relations. Eating together is an event, and it is an experience, which is why, as every one of us can attest from our own food encounters, a stellar meal satisfies soul and body alike.

Such a meal depends on the confluence of several factors. No matter how splendid the food, whether traditional fare or experimental, or innovative the culinary preparation, the material does not create the experience. Primo, the chef in *Big Night*, is in good company when he asserts that people ought to come to his restaurant for the food alone. Alas, as his brother reminds him, "they do not." Every restaurateur must decide how much the food will count. The range is enormous, from elBulli to the restaurants that the Zagat guide put in a class of their own—the "Teflon" establishments whose astonishing popularity renders them impervious to devastating critiques from all sides.

Eating out in today's food world makes production and consumption conspicuous. Cooking is a public endeavor, consumption a public occasion. The great value of the restaurant meal is the luxury that it proclaims in taking food beyond necessity to the land of liberty. The very fact of eating in public shows the world that our relationship with food is of our own making—from the fundamental decision to eat out to the subsequent selection of where and what to eat. Because we are what we eat, it is crucial to our sense of self that we, not someone else, determine what we eat; that we, not someone else, control our body, and our self. Eating out parades those choices, and food talk makes sure that everyone "out there" knows what those choices are.

CHAPTER SEVEN

Haute Food

What one chef dubbed "endless reinvention" drives everyone in these culinary conversations, from the principal players—chefs, cooks, and consumers—to the vast network of support figures—investors, promoters, consultants, suppliers, and media mavens—without whom the food world would not do what it does the way that it does. The new and the novel are no longer the exception. Thanks to the unprecedented availability of foodstuffs from all over the world, the consequent sophistication about food, and the relentless push for innovation, reinvention has become the rule. The singular and the exceptional, contemporary culture tells us, are very good things indeed, toward which every one of us should strive.

This clamorous urgency for the new reaches deep and far. When revolution is the stuff of the everyday and innovation becomes banal, everyone—diners, chefs, and cooks—understands cooking and dining differently. They understand themselves differently. They even understand food differently. Diners become connoisseurs, chefs turn into hosts, and haute cuisine competes with haute food, which jettisons convention to create its own tradition. All of these pressures, separately and in concert, assure that every one of us talks about food differently.

NEW FOOD IN NEW PLACES

Because innovation is identifiable only in the context of the known, the most striking culinary experiment makes sense only in relationship to a recognizable setting. Thus, the familiar frame of the menu reassures potentially anxious diners. At a loss when confronted with strange dishes, the neophyte diner looks for something—anything—known. The menu offers familiarity, less in the particulars of the dishes than in the order of their presentation. The menu at Le Bernardin, discussed in the previous chapter, is replete with out-of-the-ordinary ingredients, in unusual combinations, with little-used identifications. Not to fear. This menu guides the diner through what turns out to be a conventional order, beginning with light fare—"almost raw"—and proceeding to more substantial dishes. "Barely touched" leads to "lightly cooked," with (sweet) desserts last. Despite the nonstandard labels and descriptions, the order is apparent, and it is familiar.

MENUS Restaurant Jean-Georges, New York City

TASTING MENU - LUNCH $128

    Caviar Meyer lemon gelée and crème fraîche

    Hamachi Sashimi avocado, yuzu and radish

    Green Asparagus and Avocado Salad sorrel dressing and sesame

    Steamed Skate with new onion vinaigrette and spring vegetables

    Rack of Lamb smoked chili glaze and spring onion compote

    Rhubarb Dessert Tasting

TASTING MENUS - DINNER

VONGERICHTEN'S ASSORTMENT OF SIGNATURE DISHES $168

    Egg caviar

    Sea Scallops caramelized cauliflower and caper-raisin emulsion

    Young Garlic Soup with thyme and sautéed frogs legs

    Turbot with Château Chalon sauce

    Lobster Tartine lemongrass and fenugreek broth, pea shoots

    Broiled Squab onion compote, corn pancake with foie gras

    Chocolate Dessert Tasting

SPRING MENU $168

> Caviar, Meyer Lemon Gelée and Crème Fraîche, Scallop Carpaccio
> with rhubarb, ginger and olive oil
> Green Asparagus with morels and asparagus jus
> Halibut steamed with Kaffir lime, herbal lemongrass sauce and white
> asparagus
> Sautéed Maine Lobster, ramp butter, fava beans and potato
> gnocchi
> Rack of Lamb smoked chili glaze, spring onion compote and
> fiddlehead ferns

A few blocks uptown, another French-inflected restaurant, Jean-Georges, boasts another chef whose innovative cuisine has captured three stars in the Michelin Guide and four from the *New York Times*. Restaurant Jean-Georges, too, arranges the dishes starting with the lightest at the top of the menu. Beginning with sea trout, oyster tartare, and scallop carpaccio, the dishes on the regular menu become progressively more robust. Prospective diners read their way through two soups, two salads, a pasta, and several fish preparations, ending with the most substantial dishes—in this case, grilled beef tenderloin with cherry mustard, mustard greens, and purple potato chips. The tasting menus (above) keep to the same structure, reproducing (without making the categories explicit) the conventional sequence of hors d'oeuvres, first course, fish course, and entrée (traditionally meat). As is usual in high-end restaurants that stress elegance, dessert has its own menu.

Diners may order a meal out of order. Yet, although it is *possible* to start with dessert and end with raw fish, the scenario is not really probable. The authority of the chef, together with cultural habit, disinclines diners from rejecting the conventional order or testing the chef. After all, the chef's reputation for creativity presumably led them to the restaurant in the first place. Few are likely to undermine their own choice.

The relative formality of the dining experience reinforces the structure of the meal put forward by the menu. The abundance of knives, forks, spoons, plates, and glasses—the costly material support of culinary creativity on which the chef has lavished much time, thought, and money—further reminds the diner that a higher culinary authority is at work creating a meal that realizes his vision (and we are typically dealing with men). Not yours.

The authority of the chef weighs most heavily in the diner's acceptance or rejection of the suggested order of the meal. The menu, the order of dishes, the loving descriptions, the style of the restaurant—these elements realize the chef's image of dining. The diner must deal with this construction, with this definition of interesting food, and with this conception of a meal worthy of this restaurant. The greater the culinary authority, the easier it is for a chef to insist on a total dining experience.

Off the menu, small touches proclaim the chef's definition of what the meal should be—the appetizer or *amuse-bouche* at the beginning (sometimes more than one), the selection of special breads, the unexpected palate-cleansing sorbet somewhere in the middle, the miniature chocolates at the end of the meal, or the little cake presented in a tasteful signature shopping bag as you leave the restaurant. Each of these extras brings one more building block to the construction of the total dining experience.

More is going on in this gift economy than meets the eye. Each unheralded dish, unexpected taste treat, or off-menu indulgence impresses on the customer that the chef is more than a skilled cook or even a creative artist. The chef, these extras let us know, is our host. These gifts are tangible tokens of the generosity that so many chefs see as integral to their sense of self and their mission as restaurateurs. Like the elaborate culinary productions that place these restaurants squarely in the tradition of aristocratic dining, the inconsequential extras offered to diners are not extra at all. They redefine the chef.

In this gift economy, the extras transform the chef into a host and the customer into a guest—with all the obligations that being a guest entails and with the decommercialization an invited dinner implies. The generosity of the host shows off the chef's originality. Each extra offers another opportunity for the chef to perform, another vehicle to show off culinary expertise and demonstrate professional authority. The hors d'oeuvres introduce a "signature" dish, the unusual pretzel roll displays the latest bread experiments in the kitchen, and the miniature chocolates propose a taste of dessert for those benighted souls who unaccountably forgo it.

What is striking is the way that these extras, along with the tasting menu, subtly though unmistakably negate the choice that made the restaurant modern. The great innovations of the restaurant and its grand luxury were choices—among restaurants, among dishes, the basic choice of ordering anything at all. Eliminating these choices—any choices—redefines the restaurant and redistributes the roles of its players.

Of course, any customer may disdain the signature *amuse-bouche*, disregard the rolls, or leave the chocolates on the plate untouched. Yet no gift is without obligations, and no rejection is without consequences. Gifts oblige the receiver and the giver alike. Refusal has costs. Those who turn down these gifts may sense that they are not living up to what is expected of guests. In declining the food offered, they are acting like the customers that they are rather than the guests that the chef's gifts suggest. To refuse these offerings is to reject the chef-host's claims to authority.

Between personal preference and duties as a guest, most diners, it is safe to say, do not perceive the dilemma. They either reject redefinition as a guest with obligations to the host and do not taste the food offered or, in the more probable scenario, take pleasure in the transformation and consume the offerings with gusto. Regular customers likely come to expect these gifts.

The quandary of the diner torn between preferences as a customer and duties as a guest seldom comes out in the open. When it does, the resulting discomfiture, confusion, and potential embarrassment affect the entire dining experience. I remember my own distress at the very upscale (three Michelin stars) Paris restaurant of Guy Savoy. For reasons that I cannot recall, after a conversation about a previous meal, the chef sent out a special creation of lentils that was not on the menu. My allergies meant that I could not consume the lentils and therefore could not do my duty as the guest that the chef's gift had turned me into. Sending clean plates back to the kitchen masked what I hoped was a surreptitious exchanging of plates with my luncheon companions, who were pressed into what was, given the extensive meal, certifiably heroic consumption duty. In the confrontation between chef and diner, this chef came out ahead (of which he was no doubt blissfully unaware).

The conflict can become a matter of principle. One of the cardinal rules of sociological research is to avoid close connections to the subjects of the research. It is drummed into the researcher's head that the objectivity of the research must not be compromised. This is a sound principle in general that I had to jettison in my interviews with chefs. In an early interview with a New York chef, my colleague and I reluctantly accepted cappuccinos. It would have been especially awkward to abstain since the chef we were interviewing ordered one for himself. When we moved into the kitchen to talk to the *sous chef,* after a few minutes two mini raspberry-pear ganache soufflés suddenly appeared in front of us, sent by the pastry chef across the kitchen. After all, he reasoned, "you can't very well cook in front of them without giving them anything to eat." Subsequently, when two of our interviewees invited us to meals, we knew that we could not refuse, research protocol or not.

In all of these instances, the generosity of the chef-restaurateur came to the fore, and that is how we took these gestures. (The soufflé was lovely and my lunch exquisite.) For a moment, the chef took over, transforming us from social scientists at work to guests under his command. We had our interviews—and I had a (belated) insight into the dynamics of dining.

HAUTE FOOD AND EVERYDAY LIFE

No matter how opulent the setting, spectacular the décor, or attentive the service, celebrity chefs and their restaurants are all about food, and the food in these establishments is made to astonish. To be sure, every restaurant exists for the food that it serves. Even so, celebrity cuisine stands apart. The dishes that come out of the kitchen likely do not fit into any traditional culinary context. Celebrity cuisine does not reproduce the familiar. The food brought to table is the chef's food, defined and designed by the chef, its flavors discovered by the chef, its dishes invented by the chef. Ideally, the cuisine is, as the chef intends it to be, uncommon and distinctive.

The requirement of singularity explains the crucial importance of the signature dish for the high-powered chef. Any dish identified with a chef launches a brand with which that chef competes in a restaurant world that is ever more competitive. As any diner would expect, Jean-Georges Vongerichten's brand—his "Asian-French fusion" cuisine—is all over his menu (see above). Nowhere is the chef's pride more evident than in the tasting menu that is defined by dishes that encapsulate the chef's career. "Vongerichten's Assortment of Signature Dishes" offers the diner a culinary biography along with dinner. In a culinary world where one original dish is an achievement, this master chef signs seven.

Welcome to the world of haute food: the world of the celebrity chef and celebrity cuisine. The vast majority of restaurants seeking fame and fortune in the culinary stratosphere offer most of the features associated with haute cuisine—a sumptuous setting, extravagant floral arrangements, service that caters to every whim, elegant presentation, and an extensive wine list. Today, as in the past, the regular diner knows and the newcomer learns what to expect.

The world of haute food is something else again. Haute food is not haute cuisine, though it cannot be understood without haute cuisine. Haute food need not come in a fancy setting, and increasingly, with informalization

"Bad news, Sam, we're going haute and you have to take off your cap."

Figure 6. GOING HAUTE. Haute food turns up in the most improbable places, and when it does, the lingering associations with haute cuisine raise the stakes. Charles Barsotti, The New Yorker Collection / www.cartoonbank.com.

setting the tone, it does not. Creativity is the watchword, innovation the goal, endless reinvention the motto. Haute food chefs do not set their sights on the familiar classics. They want, and the restaurant needs, to come up with the unexpected. Ferran Adrià at elBulli manifested this phenomenon at its most extreme, but every ambitious chef thinks along these same lines.

One of the clearest expressions of the old mentality that prizes tradition turns up in Julia Child's characterization of French cuisine. The Frenchman, the foreword of *Mastering the Art of French Cooking* explains, derives the greatest pleasure from a "well-known dish impeccably cooked and served." This was the tradition that Julia Child dedicated her entire career to making available to Americans. The cuisine in question was not haute cuisine. It was not the fancy food of restaurant extravaganzas. Nonetheless, there were connections. The domestic French cuisine—*cuisine bourgeoise*—that Child lay before Americans drew on time-honored traditions and practices that also shaped haute cuisine. As she was neither the first nor the last to observe, French cuisine draws much of its strength from this connection.

Haute food, to the contrary, turns from the treasured past to an uncertain, potentially exciting future. Haute food is eclectic, and its practitioners dedicate themselves to hunting out new flavors, new culinary idioms, and new ingredients. The recent memoir by Ethiopia-born, Swedish-raised, and French-trained New York chef Marcus Samuelsson makes clear how driven a chef can and indeed *must* be—to learn more, do more, and find more. The increasingly international reach of the food world and the opportunities for short-term internships in kitchens around the world bring chefs into contact with vibrant culinary traditions of which their basic training had no notion.

Given this perspective, it is scarcely surprising that chefs in exploration mode experience traditional cuisines as constraining, an obstacle hampering initiatives to find something unusual. In her goal of translating French cuisine into an American culinary idiom, Julia Child lamented her French coauthors' insistence that there was only one way to proceed: the way they had learned at home. That version of French cuisine had ruled the luxury restaurant world for over a century. French chefs sent to work in luxury hotels around the world cooked French no matter where they were. Local ingredients were banished from the kitchen, which catered to an international clientele accustomed to French cuisine and uninterested in exploring indigenous fare.

From the late nineteenth century on, the ideal in upscale culinary venues around the world was a kitchen that produced recognizably, certifiably French cuisine. Escoffier's modernization of Carême dominated professional training. In the 1970s, a determined culinary explorer such as Jean-Georges Vongerichten could learn about local cuisines in international hotels in Bangkok, Singapore, and Hong Kong, and then only because he was determined to break the mold. Vongerichten took his meals with the local staff and learned their cuisines. The cuisine that he has fashioned from these

European-Asian encounters in the kitchen, the preparations that became his signature dishes, infuse an Asian sensibility and Asian ingredients into a French base.

In our twenty-first century of unbridled culinary exploration, it is difficult to imagine how problematic such culinary fusion originally appeared. As Vongerichten noted in our interview, in the 1980s sophisticated New York thought (fresh) ginger—the very ginger now found in supermarkets across the country—a big deal. A decade or so later, Marcus Samuelsson experienced the same culinary insularity in hotels and restaurants that clung to French cuisine. To satisfy his hunger for knowledge about new culinary worlds, Samuelsson signed on to cook for cruises in Asia. Like Vongerichten at the staff dining tables of international hotels, aboard ship Samuelsson cooked standard international, basically French fare. His culinary explorations had to be relegated to time off in the Asian ports of call.

Ordinary Luxury

> In the U.S., Wendy's serves such signature items as fresh, square ground-beef patties and the Frosty. In Japan, . . . it's adding decidedly more upscale fare to its menu—namely, lobster and caviar.
>
> The Lobster Surf & Turf Burger and the Premium Caviar & Lobster Sandwich will be offered for a limited time at Wendy's Tokyo locations. . . . "Each sandwich is priced at ¥1,280 or approximately US$16.28," reports Burger Business. "Or go big (¥1,580/$20.11) for the Garden Sensation salad with lobster and caviar." The dishes use Omar lobster meat imported from Canada. . . .
>
> There are no plans to introduce a similar sandwich line in the U.S., where Wendy's entrées don't tend to top $5 or $6. Wendy's left Japan in 2009, and reentered in December 2011 with a new slate of ritzy offerings, including a $16 burger topped with foie gras and truffle sauce.
>
> dailyfinance.com (August 2012)

A caviar and lobster sandwich at a fast food outlet? A hamburger with lobster, or with foie gras and truffle sauce to go? Wendy's was not the first to ratchet its burgers into the realm of haute food. When New York–based French chef Daniel Boulud opened db Bistro Moderne in midtown Manhattan in 2008, the much-ballyhooed signature dish was—as it still is—a very upscale burger by any standard.

THE ORIGINAL db BURGER

Sirloin Burger Filled with Braised Short Ribs

Foie Gras and Black Truffle, Served on a Parmesan Bun

Pommes Frites or Pommes Soufflées

With a price tag of thirty-two dollars (in 2012), Boulud's incarnation of carnivorous excess (short ribs in addition to ground beef and foie gras), luxury ingredients (sirloin steak, foie gras, black truffle, parmesan cheese), and familiar foods (bun, French fries) is unlikely to be mistaken for run-of-the-mill fast food fare. The customers at Wendy's and dB Bistro Moderne would be equally unlikely to connect, and the eateries still less likely to compete.

It was only to be expected that Wendy's culinary promotion should make press in industry journals such as *Burger News*. Or that it would turn up in the business section of the *Wall Street Journal*. But Wendy's initiative caught attention beyond specialized outlets. Ordinary consumers like me found out about the boosted burger from reports in general news media around the world. Tabloids and television commentators alike found the pairing of lobster and hamburger incongruous, bizarre, wacky, and—for all these reasons—newsworthy.

The ingredients in the lobster-hamburger combination were not remarkable on their own. Both are familiar main-course foods. Nor was it their pairing that captured attention. "Surf and turf" is standard fare across America, and that is exactly how Wendy's presented the menu in Tokyo. It was the combination of these foods in this place that caused the uproar. "Surf and turf" may be a regular menu item in steakhouses and other, mostly mid-level restaurants—but not in fast food chains. In crossing these food worlds, Wendy's amplified its hamburgers into haute food—that is, foods conceived and presented outside their ordinary context. In the fast food world, lobster, caviar, and burgers are a contradiction in terms.

The promotion at Wendy's shows how deeply haute food has penetrated everyday life. Foods once almost entirely associated with luxury dishes and upscale dining are becoming common coin. Foie gras in a fast food outlet pushes the informalization of dining to new limits. The restaurants that are becoming more casual and the diners who dress and act with increasing informality together erode the boundaries that were once fairly clear between plain and fancy. The specialty food trucks turning up in more places—at various times of the day and year there are at least five within five blocks of the main entrance to my university—are poised to do away with the fixed eating establishment altogether. At the same time, in these places, the food often demands more attention. The food truck with lobster sandwiches is selling food only. It is a luxury, though at $15, it is an affordable one. Haute food has become part of everyday life.

Blurring once-fixed boundaries redefines the paradigm of distinction that identified foie gras as fancy food consumed by fancy people in fancy places. Foie gras now also turns up on hamburgers and has on occasion replaced (or joined) mozzarella, tomato, garlic, and a host of other everyday ingredients as a topping for pizza. These are so many instances of a pervasive banalization of the exotic, a diffusion of the exclusive, the metamorphosis of plain into fancy.

The 2006 ban on the sale of foie gras by the City Council of Chicago raised protests from unexpected quarters. As one might have expected, a few prominent Chicago chefs continued to serve foie gras as they always had— only now under the table, so to speak. But one would not have expected to find a pizza parlor on Chicago's South Side (not known as a gastronomic haven) adding foie gras as a topping to pizza or a hot dog shop that slapped foie gras on the bun. The chefs at these more casual joints were not defending the superior delights of gastronomy. They were standing up for their right to serve what they wished. Similarly, the run on foie gras immediately before the bans in Chicago (and now California) went into effect—there were reports of requests for foie gras on sushi—had little to do with gastronomy. Consumers were vocal about their right to choose. In the same way, the opposition to Mayor Michael Bloomberg's campaign to restrict the size of soda containers sold in New York City is all about choice.

Whatever the arguments in support of food legislation of almost any sort, protest invariably focuses on the elimination of choice in a domain—namely taste—that individuals feel belongs to them and to them alone. Arguments that invoke a collective good have a hard time convincing consumers who place their preferences above the common good. The conflict surfaces in practices ranging from fluoridation of municipal water supplies to innoculations against disease. Even among such conflicts, food preferences stand out as especially intractable.

The Ethos of Haute Cuisine

Haute food would not be nearly so significant if it turned up only in fancy—or, in the case of Wendy's—not so fancy restaurants. For one, the food talk that spills over from this high-pressure world of dining out makes haute food a general concern, whether we dine at the eateries in question or not. Haute food reaches beyond restaurant dining to home dining. The radical shift in priorities and the consequent reconfiguration of dining have turned haute food into a characteristic culinary phenomenon of the twenty-first-century food world.

Haute food reconfigures the links between producer and product and redirects those between eating and the foods eaten. The ordered world of haute cuisine, with its rules and regulations and its reverence for the whole over the part, gives way before the often chaotic, mobile world of haute food. In the culture of haute food, culinary individualism trumps established authority, innovation takes precedence over tradition, and experimentation has priority over formality. Haute food reconstrues the very meaning of consumption.

As haute cuisine is a manifestation of early modern aristocratic society, so haute food is the product of the more loosely connected and more various twenty-first-century food world—from the increasingly global reach of jet-setting chefs, consumers, and produce to the seemingly infinite numbers of television programs, movies, websites, and mobile apps devoted to food of some sort. Then there is the vast amount of food talk generated by all of these activities, which complexifies the food world still further. Finally, the most conspicuous indicator—the priority given to change—invests all the others with uncommon urgency. Separately and together, these transformations have produced an aggressively up-to-the-minute food world.

Haute cuisine stands for a cultural ideal. This ideal of culinary perfection is what makes competitive cooking in France so unsparing of competitors and its verdicts so absolute. The contenders in the Meilleur Ouvrier de France (MOF) and the Bocuse d'Or competitions discussed in chapter 1 do not test the other contestants as much as they confront the idea of Great Cuisine. No individual can hope to attain the ideal. In this way, and supported by institutions such as the MOF and the Bocuse d'Or, French cuisine looms larger than any of its parts. In this world of Great (French) Cuisine, haute cuisine as redefined for a modern food world, judgment takes into account all of the established rules, traditions, and principles. At once sign and symptom of culinary individualism, haute food alters our sense of food and our experience of eating.

CULINARY INDIVIDUALISM

Culinary individualism surfaces in many areas. There is, for one, the increasing emphasis on identifying the provenance of the foods that we consume. Such identification is not new. The value accorded sources elaborates

"And exactly how is the peanut–butter–and–jelly prepared?"

Figure 7. HAUTE FOOD AND EVERYDAY LIFE. Culinary individualism redefines the most ordinary fare. The consumer cannot be too wary when the chef's creativity knows no preordained bounds. Ed Koren, The New Yorker Collection / www.cartoonbank.com.

the long-honored French tradition of *terroir*—the association of the taste of a product, most often wine, with the soil in which it originated. On the level of practice, this tradition extends the "market cuisine"—*la cuisine du marché*—that megachef Paul Bocuse and others less media savvy began touting in the 1970s. That the freshest food comes from known producers has led some chefs and a good many diners today to make something of a cult out of situating the food that we consume. The "locavore" has become an exigent consumer, who insists that the foods consumed be of local origin.

There is no end to the disputes over what counts as "local." René Redzepi, the chef of the famed Copenhagen restaurant Noma, certainly believes that foraging is the epitome of local, and he has his followers. The priority accorded local, and preferably foraged, products inevitably conflicts with the goal of serving a wide range of the best possible foods to satisfy diners who have come to expect variety. For Chicago chef Charlie Trotter, freshness came down to sources of supply and networks of transportation: "What's regional? What's local? It's irrelevant. . . . I defy anyone from Maine to serve better swordfish from Maine than we can. I don't care if they're right there. We get the stuff twenty-four hours out of the water." Gilbert LeCoze, chef and co-owner of Le Bernardin, similarly called attention to the contacts that he cultivated at the Fulton Fish Market in Lower Manhattan, which at the time of our interview was the longtime wholesale site for fresh fish in New York City. Black bass from North Carolina that arrived in New York in four or five hours after being caught for the lunch that we were eating—it doesn't get fresher than that. LeCoze took justifiable pride that he could get such fish. He may not have known English when he arrived in New York, but he knew fish. Freshness was the result of negotiating with purveyors. Quality means freshness, and freshness means a fine-tuned, extensive, and trustworthy network of suppliers.

A meal in which the consumer knows all the ingredients and all but cooks the meal whose elements have been personally grown or gathered is a dream of absolute individualization. That the undertaking is utopian in no way diminishes the longing for autonomy. To control one's food is to control one's self. The complexity of the contemporary food world, characterized by the inescapable interdependence of its parts and immense inequality in agricultural resources, makes the very thought of autonomy illusory. The vision is all the more seductive.

The spirit of culinary individualism touches food contexts that have nothing to do with gastronomy. Take the allergies that, in the United States at least, threaten to become ubiquitous. Only a few decades ago, restaurateurs paid little attention to diners' individual allergies, dislikes, distastes, and dietary preferences. Today, the situation is nothing like. Peanuts alone have generated vast networks that dispense advice to the afflicted and directives to institutions on how to avoid crises. Individuals and institutions have brought allergy consciousness to an all-time high. This consciousness raising has also promoted a conviction that the individual has a right to protection from contamination.

I am not speaking of collective interdictions—most often religious in nature—in which the community sees to its own protection and the collectivity dictates culinary choice. Nor am I referring to government surveillance of the food industry for the public good. The claims that I am targeting originate in the belief that choice is absolute and the insistence that the right of the individual should prevail.

Vegetarian, vegan, gluten free, peanut free, dairy free, locally sourced, humanely raised—taste preferences readily become desires and eventually demands. Requests become requirements, increasingly acknowledged, accepted, and acted upon. Whereas chefs impose their preferences on consumers with tasting menus, consumers dictate their own culinary requirements over the will of the chef. Diners simply assume that the menu will be modified according to their requirements.

If it seems reasonable enough to take account of physiological imperatives such as allergies, it is less evident for many that similar attention should be accorded likes and dislikes grounded in individual resolve with no medical, religious, or cultural justification. The restaurant chef cannot make a specialized meal for every customer, though home cooks have been known to do so. A hostess may feel obliged to cater to the culinary requirements of every guest; twenty years ago, she would not have even thought about it. Translating to home dining the choice that defines restaurant dining is problematic at least. Singular demands fall on one cook, not a team.

Although few consumers think of individual taste preferences in such drastic terms, much of contemporary American society effectively treats food preferences as a right of every individual, not excluding children. The constraints of so many varied and potentially conflictual directives might well give the most intrepid hostess pause before embarking on a dinner party. The larger the party, the bigger the nightmare. The costs of personalization must worry the restaurant chef concerned with salvaging the bottom line.

Whatever the response and the particular food at issue, the priority accorded the individual diner and singular ingredients puts us squarely in the world of haute food. Unlike haute cuisine, haute food need not be defined by elaborate preparations or extravagant settings. The actual food consumed need not be sumptuously presented. Indeed, it is often emphatically *not* luxurious, *not* opulent, and *not* splendid.

The Tuesday Vegetarian

Vegetarianism, to give one example, often draws its power from a vision of a simple life—simpler, in any event, than what is found in the urbanized, industrialized, and globalized world where most of us live. From this perspective, whether the preparation is plain or fancy, meat is a luxury in the most elemental sense. Given that our physiological well-being does not require meat, when we do eat meat, we are choosing luxury.

Many people today pay attention to what they eat, ever vigilant to make the right connection between diet and self. The regime of culinary individualism construes diet as an expression of self, not, as it might be in other instances, as an element in a broader cultural system. Jews and Muslims following kosher and halal food directives, Christians adhering to the proscriptions of Lenten abstinence—all eliminate foods that the collectivity has defined as inedible. The difference lies in the cultural nature of the validation. Respecting these collective directives joins the individual to the community. Haute food, on the other hand, sets the individual apart.

Of all the practices informed by haute food, vegetarianism may well be the most surprising. The variations on the basic choice of vegetarianism demonstrate the degree to which food choices have become individualized in contemporary American society. This once-marginalized, at times oppositional culinary practice has engendered social recognition and support unimagined a mere decade ago. An extensive network of specialized markets, suppliers, eateries, and blogs has moved vegetarianism from the wacky food practice that it represented for most Americans not so long ago to an acknowledged if marginal consumption category. Although this regime will remain a minority practice, vegetarianism of one sort or another is becoming a familiar option.

Individuals construe vegetarianism very differently from one another. The reasons for this choice remain, for the most part, stubbornly individual. For many, the health benefits of a plant-based diet loom large. Others are concerned above all with the treatment of animals. The practice, too, varies. Some will not consume cheese made with rennet (an animal enzyme used to coagulate milk into curds), insisting on cheese made with bacterial rennet derived from vegetables or doing without. Vegetarianism may be a question of taste ("These vegetables taste better"), health ("Vegetables are better for us"), or ideology ("Eating vegetables is better for the environment"). Given the strongly articulated ideological investments that shape so many practices of vegetarianism, it is remarkable how little attention has been paid to the ways that individuals fashion their own vegetarianism based on personal, idiosyncratic circumstances. Food is perhaps the least significant element.

A paper written by one of my students brought home to me the great many ways of doing vegetarianism and the fact that it is not merely a question of the specific foods that one does and does not eat. It is how and why one eats that produces the many varieties of vegetarianism. The small sample of her classmates whom my student interviewed about their relationship(s) to vegetarianism showed how apposite the plural is. Perhaps I should not have been, but I was astounded at the range of unique reasons given by these students for their variable adherence to a vegetarian regime. Embedded in a powerfully delineated social context, individual practice varied strikingly as a function of that context, regardless of the overall ideological commitment.

One of the respondents I dubbed the Friday Carnivore. A faithful vegetarian six days out of seven, this young man made a point of eating meat once a week. Every Friday when he joined his brothers for dinner, he joined them as well in eating meat—the meat that he knew they loved. It was not enough to join the others at table. A "real" meal, for him, required sharing their choice of food. This young man's solidarity with the others at the meal determined this private ritual. Subordinating his preferences, his customary practice, and his principles to those of the group, the Friday Carnivore chose not to set himself apart. He gave the group precedence over self.

The Tuesday Vegetarian offered a still more complex illustration of the varieties of vegetarianism. This young man did not opt out of meat every Tuesday; he opted into vegetarianism. The decision was neither accidental nor fortuitous. His dietary regime was more original than most. Vegetarian practice was not the way of life for him that it is for so many. It was, instead, a means of creating a singular occasion. Consuming a vegetarian diet was his way of honoring his grandmother in India. He followed her diet in a ritual observance that he had defined for himself. It was of no matter if his grandmother knew of his dietary decision. The choice connected continents and families. The Tuesday Vegetarian's grandmother was a steadfast vegetarian and so too, every Tuesday, was her grandson.

As far as varieties of vegetarianism may seem from haute food (and further still from haute cuisine), from another perspective the constraints of cooking without the resources of flavor and texture supplied by meat can also spur creativity. Like Carême two centuries ago, who took the lean meals imposed by Lent as a challenge to work wonders with fish and to be especially lavish with truffles, today's top chefs routinely take culinary restrictions as a springboard to innovation. The attention that falls on the singular element—individual diner, exotic ingredient, eccentric chef, unconventional cook—puts us in the land of haute food. From the Tuesday Vegetarian, with his meal of remembrance, to the celebrity chef devising an uncommon tasting menu or promoting a new technique or unfamiliar ingredient, haute food plays up the exceptional and the extraordinary.

At Table

Every one of us negotiates these extremes of community and distinction at every meal. We must reconcile the individualism that gives us license to indulge our appetites along with the sense of solidarity that takes others into account. The patterns of behavior that we call table manners evolved to formalize—that is, give form to and direct—our ways of eating so as to integrate individual behavior with collective needs, the individual diner with the others at table. The balance that concerns every society is no less essential than it is contested wherever individualism dominates.

The gains of culinary individualism are all around us—exciting exploration of new culinary territories, gratifying recognition of invention and reward for innovation, empowerment of the individual consumer as well as of the chef. So many new places to dine, and new products, dishes, and tastes—all to the good, surely.

Perhaps not entirely. Private gains incur public costs. Like Simmel's modern man, overwhelmed by the sheer numbers in the metropolis and pushed into eccentricity to make his presence felt, the haute foodist is effectively coerced into being ever more innovative, ever more singular. In the kitchen and at table, haute food struggles with the culture that haute cuisine represented and fortified. From Carême in the early nineteenth century to the proponents of modernist cuisine today, culinary individualists center attention on the food, the farm, the kitchen, and the plate. These claims for the primacy of the food oppose the meal as a collective enterprise. The archetypal meal creates a community, connecting individuals in a whole that is greater than the sum of its parts.

The theoretician of the meal as communal enterprise is Brillat-Savarin. A sociologist before sociology, he always considers food as a social phenomenon intimately tied to a particular social setting. Not that Brillat ignores food, but his primary interest is pleasure at table, just as his real subject is the meal, of which, he tells us again and again, food is only a part—a vital part, but a part. Food alone cannot make a meal because a meal is a social relationship. It must be understood in a vast network of social relationships that brings together chef and consumer, producer and cook, critic and restaurateur, publishers and publicists, not omitting waiter and dishwasher.

Pleasure at table is social. The meal—a good meal—satisfies a need for society, delight in communication, and above all joy in conversation. Gratification of sensual appetite is only one function of the meal, which Brillat considered preliminary to the creation of community at table. The least ideologically passionate of men, Brillat comes down firmly in favor of the collective over the individual, the social over the singular, the meal over the mouthful. An ideal gathering brings together people of all sorts and turns them into collaborators in a common endeavor.

Like the food consumed, the community formed at table inevitably perishes. As Virginia Woolf shows with such sensitivity in *To the Lighthouse*, a meal worthy of the name merges disparate parts into an incomparably greater whole. In doing so, it creates an event. It produces an occasion to remember. In the best of all possible meals, a moment comes when, as Woolf points out, "everything seem[s] possible. Everything seem[s] right." Individuals connect. The gathered guests become a gathering: "Some change at once went through them all, . . . and they were all conscious of making a party together in a hollow, on an island; had their common cause against that fluidity out there." An incomparable hostess, Woolf's heroine, Mrs. Ramsay, is well aware that the wonderful French stew that has taken so long for the cook to prepare "will celebrate the occasion." She feels "a curious sense rising in her . . . of celebrating a festival." Meals, like festivals, are communal affairs, vehicles for a collectivity to affirm its identity.

No one conveys better than Woolf the creation and almost immediate obliteration of pleasure at table. For an instant, time stands still—almost: "For the moment she hung suspended." Then, like the food that disappears, the meal turns into something else. It recedes into history. The food eaten, the wine drunk, and the hostess absent, nothing remains to hold the group together. The meal has ended, and the diners have become individuals once again, no longer part of something beyond themselves: "And directly she went a sort of disintegration set in; they wavered about, went different ways."

Talking Toques

Gone, but, thanks to the novelist, definitely not forgotten. The end of the meal, the food consumed—this is where food talk comes in. It makes meals memorable by creating taste memories. The most consequential food talk comes at the end of the meal, when the food is no more, the wine bottle is empty, the table is cleared, conversation has ended, and the diners have dispersed. The talk continues with the waiter who notes customers' reactions to be transmitted to the chef; with the critic who writes a review; with the technologically savvy diner who rushes to send text messages to sundry friends; with the blogger who spreads the word. The writer and the artist take longer to give the meal a new life, but if we (and the author) are lucky, it will be a life as long as Mrs. Ramsay's dinner has been for generations of readers.

Without food talk, from recipes to criticism, and without food talkers, from cooks to consumers, the most glorious meal would be forgotten. Just as cookbooks bring cooking out of the kitchen, so food talk memorializes the meal. It translates the experience for those who were not there, who neither partook of the food nor participated in the festival of the meal. Although food talk fixes neither food nor the meal for eternity or for the whole world, it works for a good while and reaches out to all kinds of listeners. Woolf's readers, too, sit at Mrs. Ramsay's table.

Not all societies value knowledge about what people do with the food that they produce and consume. They construe food in largely instrumental, material terms. The perception of food as a social form, a symbol of identity, and a matter of intellectual interest and aesthetic value mark some cultures strongly and others little, though globalization undoubtedly attenuates such differences. In one of the most striking developments of the past half century, food talk has turned to promoting the connection between food and place, between cuisine and country. Cuisines once defined and perhaps dismissed as regional are promoted to national honor. As one country after another offers its cuisine as an authentic product of place, food talk flourishes.

That France dominated the food world in the West for so long has much to do with the food talk that spread the good news about its portability and adaptability. The French made, and continue to make, a point of talking about their cuisine—its virtues, advantages, and superiority. Articulating the principles of cuisine, showing the effects of culinary creativity, draws attention to food and what it can become. Food in France—French food and other foods as well—retains its importance in large measure because it is so insistently and repeatedly identified with country. French culture has long made talking about food something of a national pastime. The film *Haute Cuisine,* discussed in chapter 1, is only the latest in a long line of such promotion.

It may be that France has shaped our world of culinary delights most decisively with its food talkers—not the talking heads of the political arena but the talking toques, the chatty chefs of a food world where chef's hats, metaphorical as well as real, abound. The repertory of dishes, the techniques of preparation, the organization of the kitchen, the professionalization of cooking, and the premium placed on tradition and creativity—all of these were necessary to French culinary hegemony. Necessary is not sufficient. Neither separately nor in concert do these undeniable contributions produce, or explain, the hold of France and its cuisine over the food world in the West. With no talking heads or culinary pundits to disseminate the fundamental principles and distinctive practices, with no chattering classes to spread the culinary gospel, with no chefs or cooks to recount their culinary expertise and experiences, French cuisine would never have exercised the influence that it did, and in many ways, still does.

Today, when more than one commentator takes evident pleasure in pointing to the decline of French culinary importance, it is all too easy to overlook this crucial element of French culinary presence. With more than a bit of schadenfreude, critics smugly note the mounting competition faced by French chefs and French restaurants. Paris no longer beckons as the undisputed culinary or gastronomic capital that it once was. Culinary risk takers modify the standard French dishes; the more radical dispense with them altogether. From *sous-vide* cooking to liquid nitrogen, the latest technological inventions contest the monopoly of the fundamental techniques of French cuisine. Prototypes other than the hierarchical kitchen brigade come into play.

The decline of the French, the rise of the Spaniards and the Scandinavians, the vibrancy of New York and America (not to mention Japan), the takeover of molecular gastronomy or modernist cuisine . . . the tale is true enough—as far as it goes. It does not, because it cannot, say anything much about the pull that France and French cuisine continue to exercise on culinary imaginations around the world. Because the ideal of wonderful food that French food talk conveys, the French model remains iconic, an exemplar of culinary excellence, invention, and tradition. And this is why the French paradigm remains a reference point, the one to learn from, the one to beat.

Though they may be more skeptical about French achievements than when France held the aces in the culinary game, people still listen. And they listen because French food talk has given the food world more than a particular cuisine, as remarkable as that cuisine was and is. For this food talk builds a community around the principles of culinary excellence, the joys of culinary pleasure, and the appreciation of culinary creativity.

And So?

When we ask ourselves, as we are bound to do, where this food world is headed, we come up against the persistence of the fundamental oppositions explored in *Word of Mouth:* cooking versus chefing, formality versus informality, tradition versus invention, culinary individualism versus communal conversation, conspicuous consumption versus conspicuous production, haute cuisine versus haute food, gluttony versus gastronomy, and the most basic dichotomy of all, the virtual food of talk and image versus the material food in the oven or on the plate.

Sustained by the economics as well as the politics of globalization, and exacerbated by the accelerating pace of change in everyday life, these tensions are here to stay. The hyperconnectivity of food talk in the age of the Internet provokes instant replay of every controversy and intensifies the fascination with celebrity of every sort—people, places, and foods.

At the same time there will be, indeed there already are, moves to reconnect with tradition. The films that I have discussed—*Haute Cuisine* and *Le Grand Chef* in chapter 1, *Chocolat* in chapter 2, and *Big Night* in chapter 6—each in its own way makes the most of tradition. Celebrity chefs look to the past for dishes lost to the novelty-seeking culture of haute food. Nevertheless, these traditions in the making will be infused with the spirit of today. They will address new publics and produce new cuisines.

Most of all, these new publics and cuisines will generate new food talk to comment on, criticize, and make sense of our food world and its cultures. They will promote new food stories to stage our food world. *Ratatouille*, as we shall see, is one such new food story—a tale of and for, a new, contemporary food world. Such a story also has the virtue of pulling everything back together.

Epilogue

LAST WORDS: *RATATOUILLE*

I began *Word of Mouth* with a vintage pop song that shows what food stories can tell us. My story ends with a contemporary popular film that dramatizes responses to questions about the ways that food shapes the world we live in. *Ratatouille* (2007) is recognizably a Disney production—a fantasy, to be sure, yet with enough bite to make it a fable for our times. Just as the early Disney movies gave us animals like Mickey Mouse and Donald Duck, with human inclinations and problems, so *Ratatouille* tells of a rat who, against all probability, becomes a celebrity chef. In Paris! There is the expected glorious animation, bright colors, insistent music, special effects, fast-paced action, exotic setting, deeds of derring-do, and unlikely oddball hero (in this event, two heroes). The requisite happy ending ties up loose ends, distributes rewards equitably, and ratifies the victory of good over evil, or at least better over bad.

Ratatouille does all of this and more. It reveals a food world in all of its complexity. *Our* food world. For our edification as much as our entertainment, it uncovers the structure and tensions of that world, its values and norms, heroes and villains, conflicts and rewards, people and places, as well as the many markets that it serves. In the past quarter century, a number of films have focused on food, most often for comic effect. *Ratatouille* is different. Beyond talking about food, beyond the comedy, this food story reaches to the heart of what it means to cook and dine in today's unsettled and unsettling food world. The film is a compendium of the ways that food talk helps cook and consumer alike to negotiate the contradictions of individual desire and communal constraints.

Finally, and even though it takes place in France, the story that *Ratatouille* tells is an American tale of success. The film reenacts the primal encounter of the New World and the Old. The fairy-tale ending notwithstanding, it presents a model of culinary connection that is simultaneously a paradigm for cultural understanding.

Ratatouille recounts the saga of Remy, a rat with a fine-tuned sense of smell and an intense ambition to undertake a most unrodent-like enterprise: cooking. Like other chefs who find themselves at odds with their milieu, this would-be chef is distinctly different from his fellow rats, who scrounge for whatever edibles they can find. Remy wants passionately to explore new flavors. This unusual rat wants to cook because he wants to create. The television cooking shows and cookbooks that he comes across in surreptitious visits to a nearby home whet his appetite. Following a harrowing trip via the sewers, Remy arrives in the capital of the food world, Paris. Providentially, he finds himself in the famed restaurant of Auguste Gusteau, alas deceased, but whose ghost obligingly reappears to counsel Remy as he copes with the stressful conditions of the high-end restaurant.

Having lost two of its five stars, Gusteau's restaurant is in crisis. Resting on laurels will not do in the fast-paced, highly competitive world of Parisian restaurants, where savvy customers demand more than the old standbys. Skinner, the villainous new chef, worries mostly about making the most of the Gusteau name by marketing frozen dinners—Gusteau's microwave burritos, corn puppies, barbeque spareribs, haggis bites, and tooth-pickin' chicken. Haute cuisine meets fast food, and haute cuisine is the loser. These abominations traduce Gusteau's legacy—the foods themselves complain. Yet Skinner has a point: Things have to change. The restaurant needs a makeover. Enter Remy—the outsider incarnate and everyone's worst nightmare: a rat in the kitchen. He joins forces with another outsider, the hapless and culinarily ignorant garbage boy and dishwasher, Linguini.

When Linguini is unaccountably asked to make the soup, Remy cannot resist taking over. Not only is disaster averted but the soup is a sensation. Orders fly. An important critic likes it. Everyone wants it. But how can the supremely inept Linguini reproduce Remy's superlative soup? As his name suggests and his body movements make clear, he has the backbone of a noodle.

The larger issue concerns the nature of creativity itself. Rationalization—in this case, coming up with a formal recipe—necessarily destroys innovation by making it routine. What to do? The restaurant kitchen depends on routine. It *has* to be organized, and there can be no doubt about the chain of command. As the lone female cook, Colette, explains to Linguini, cooks follow directions, while the chef supplies the unexpected. In this case, Remy's official nonexistence in this kitchen and Linguini's inexpertise rule out routinization. The solution has Remy directing culinary maneuvers from under Linguini's tall chef's hat. In the classic division of labor, Linguini's hands execute Remy's cuisine.

The once-diffident public flocks to the restaurant. Eventually, so does the most powerful critic in Paris—the acerbic, disdainful, self-centered, and aptly named Anton Ego, acknowledged guardian of Great Food. Following Gusteau's admonition that a great chef must be fearless, Remy serves Ego ratatouille, a casserole of ordinary vegetables, which he reimagines in a complex, elegant plating. And voilà! Haute ratatouille. Remy raises comfort food to new heights, turns plain fare into fancy. He transforms everyday cooking into haute cuisine. The combination is dynamite. Like the madeleine that transported Proust's narrator to his childhood, one bite takes the critic back to the ratatouille served at the kitchen table that turned the downcast boy into a happy child comforted by his mother's love.

For Ego, as for Proust's narrator, taste triggers conversion. Through this latest nouvelle cuisine, the critic at long last understands Chef Gusteau's motto (and title of his best-selling book): "Anyone Can Cook." Ego has a slight emendation: although not just anyone can become a great artist, "a great artist can come from anywhere." This one certainly did. Ego's review, with its admirable, moving mea culpa, ensures Remy's success—not in Gusteau's fancy restaurant, but in his own bistro. High above the city, "La Ratatouille" packs them in, run by the latest version of the culinary couple, Remy's Escoffier to Linguini's César Ritz.

Ratatouille reconciles the irreconcilable, joins the everyday and the exceptional, and preaches the democracy of opportunity and the elitism of achievement. If anyone can cook, becoming a great chef requires dedication. It requires expertise, which Colette demonstrates with her awesome knife skills and her analysis of how to judge fresh bread by listening to its "symphony of crackles." A professional chef has to know the conventions, rules, and techniques on which the restaurant depends. Colette sets Linguini straight: "You cannot be Mommy!" Chefing is not home cooking.

Artists are driven creatures. A classic overachiever, Remy wants more out of life. He dreams of putting his exceptional sensory gift to a purpose higher than sniffing out poison to keep the rat colony safe. Remy bares his soul to his brother. He wants to *make* food, as humans do, not simply to *take* food, the way rats do. He possesses a generosity of spirit that every great chef must have. In dramatizing culinary mobility, *Ratatouille* speaks to anyone who dreams of creating another world and another self.

The miracle of the restaurant lies in its work of synthesis. From many ingredients come dishes that are more than the sum of their parts. The motley crew in the kitchen fuses into a team that produces the miracle that is a meal. The kitchen crew in *Ratatouille* is nothing if not multicultural: Mustafa, the Arab saucier; Horst, the German *sous-chef* with a menacing past shrouded in secrecy; the African Django; and the traditional French Colette, François, and Larousse, who bears the name of the most venerable French-language dictionary. Skinner is the proverbial skinflint, skinning Gusteau's restaurant alive. The names themselves could fit in an old-fashioned morality play where epithets tell us what we need to know about the characters. Differences notwithstanding, this varied crew pulls together under the sign of taste that Gusteau's embodies. Taste, the restaurant sign enjoins customers, and taste with gusto.

The ultimate synthesis—that is, the meal—is possible only because the restaurant is so tightly organized. For consumers, production is inconspicuous, the kitchen out of sight. The dining room is the stage where the meal is performed. Backstage, in the kitchen, the military model remains in force. Introducing him to the restaurant kitchen, Gusteau puts Remy through his paces, identifying all the members of the kitchen brigade: chef, *sous-chef*, *saucier*, *chef de parti*, *demi-chef*, *commis*. Each occupies a strictly defined place in the hierarchy. Each has a job to do. The miracle is that, despite their many differences, all of these cooks work together to produce the meal.

Still, for all the emphasis on the sensuality of the food and the attention to the dynamics of the restaurant kitchen, it is the final meal that centers the most important story that *Ratatouille* has to tell. The elaborate hierarchy in the kitchen contrasts with the equality of the dining room. The whole film, we realize only close to the end, is Remy's telling of his epic rise to celebrity chef. His story, and the film, ends when he is called to supervise the dinner service.

Consider the transformations that have taken place. The rats no longer scarf garbage. They gather to listen to after-dinner talks. A sign of what they have learned, they dine on proper food at tables. They have learned to taste. They have come to appreciate, if not fully understand, Remy's gift. They are regular people with regular names—Remy and his brother Emile have common French names and the "Dad" they call their father is as ordinary as could be. These people have become a different community, one created by commensality and by the food talk that makes eating together a truly social occasion. Sooner the lion lie down with the lamb, you may object, than rats dine with humans. But in true Disney fashion, the impossible happens, though the two species do not actually dine together. They remain separate communities, connected by the chef-artist.

Ratatouille takes its place in a long line of works that proclaim the civilizing effect of cooking. The case for the transformative power of food has never been more forcefully presented than in this work, which brings contraries together and resolves the clash of individual appetite against collective good. The vision is undeniably, inescapably, and wonderfully utopic. Rats dining; humans lining up for "La Ratatouille," where, as the sign tells passersby, the chef-rat stirs his stew high up over Paris (the Eiffel Tower looms on the skyline). A guy from the boonies, an underdog, comes to literally dominate the world of French cuisine from the heights of Montmartre, where the miniskirts and berets sported by the arty young crowd make a decided contrast to the more formal dress of the older regulars at Gusteau's.

Is it too much to see in Remy an American hero? The gifted young outsider who, against all odds, conquers the bastion of French cuisine? Both he and Linguini have familiar American accents. They are "regular" guys, meaning not obviously educated, while Skinner's generic uncultured foreign and Ego's vaguely British accents, along with their pronounced un-French names, establish them as the real outsiders. Remy's rise to fame and fortune does not portend the Americanization of French food that is so feared in some quarters. If anything, it "Frenchified" American food talk. *Ratatouille* translates French food practices and French culinary ideals into an American idiom. This unabashedly American story uses a French model to make claims about the very nature of creativity.

That Remy tells his own story reminds us of the importance of food talk in creating and shaping our food world as well as his. *Ratatouille* hits all the themes and conflicts of *Word of Mouth:* professional expertise versus innate gift, sensuality and pleasure versus food fears, creativity versus convention, cooking versus chefing, the meaning of the meal, the dynamics of a restaurant, the power of the critic, the tribulations of the chef, and the epiphanies of the consumer. In its assumption of interest on the part of a broad public, this film, by its mere existence, shows how far culinary America has come in knowledge and sophistication about food.

But the most important message of this film, its greatest story, is that learning to cook and to dine is learning to live. Good food and good meals, *Ratatouille* shows us, are essential ingredients of a good life. Together they join pleasure for the senses and sustenance for the soul.

ACKNOWLEDGMENTS

So many friends, colleagues, students, and even mere acquaintances have contributed to *Word of Mouth* that I feel rather like a chef in a kitchen full of cooks and critics pushing me to get the meal on the table.

For their part in culinary conversations over the years, I am especially grateful to Kyri Watson Claflin, who shared her research with me and cheerfully scrutinized parts of the manuscript with her historian's eye; Sharon Zukin, an interlocutor on things culinary of many years standing; Julia Abramson, whose insightful reading for the University of California Press pushed me to refine my presentation; and Bénédict Beaugé, Pierre-Michel Menger, and Denis Saillard, who brought very different expertise to the table that I was figuring out how to set.

Then there are those who have shared both food and food talk: longtime friends Barbara Mittman, Susan Welch, and Lois Widdemer responded to my queries and questions about their cooking careers with good grace and special insight; Carolyn Betensky, Susan Hiner, and Masha Belenky turn consumption into a ritual of friendship and conversation; Chris Curro at the Mohawk Harvest Coop has shown me how food and food talk create a community.

This book would not be what it is without the interest and enthusiasm of my students over the past several years. One of those students, Jonathan Mandell, came up with a title that crystallized the book's message for me and sent it forth to the world.

At the University of California Press, I have been the grateful beneficiary of Darra Goldstein's key support of the project and Kate Marshall's skillful shepherding of my work from manuscript to printed page.

Finally, as ever, thanks and love to Robert A. Ferguson, for being there, always willing to try out yet another culinary idea, on the table or in the text.

New York
December 2013

NOTES

PROLOGUE

Stories about Food

Marcel Mauss first identified "total social phenomena" in *The Gift* ([1925] 1990). Mauss analyzed the structure of gift exchange, but he might as well have been talking about food. He wrote: "In these 'total' social phenomena, as we propose calling them, all kinds of institutions are given expression at one and the same time—juridical, religious, and moral, which relate to both politics and the family; likewise economic ones, which suppose special forms of production and consumption, or rather, of performing total services and distribution. This is not to take into account the aesthetic phenomena to which these facts lead, and the contours of the phenomena that these institutions manifest" (3–4).

A live performance of "Bread and Butter" is available on YouTube at www.youtube.com/watch?v=LdXWojZKNGE. The Newbeats were Larry Henley (lead singer) and brothers Dean and Mark Mathis (backup singers), all Southerners. "Bread and Butter" was written by Larry Parks and Jay Turnbow.

I discovered the song and video together in 2010 as I was surfing the Internet in search of a song about mashed potatoes. Based on my admittedly idiosyncratic survey, "Bread and Butter" turns out to have had an extensive public. At last count, one of the several YouTube video sites devoted to this song had over

900,000 hits. Even discounting my own repeated views, that is not an insignificant audience. To judge by the comments posted in response to the video, many of the listeners had known only the melody and paid no attention to the lyrics, which told a tale of masculine woe. Until these listeners discovered the video years later, they had assigned the voice that they heard to a black woman. Many registered total surprise when they discovered that the lead singer was in fact a young white guy singing falsetto. None of these listeners seems to have had a clue about the intimate, essential role that food plays in the breakup, though one commenter did wonder (on an earlier version of the site, which has now been dropped because of copyright infringement) if the song was "really about food."

Sociological Understandings
Benjamin's *Arcades Project* (1999) comes close to realizing his dream of writing a book comprised entirely of quotations. He foraged in the Bibliothèque Nationale in Paris, picking up whatever he found. It was a thrill, when I was doing research for my book on Paris, to call up the books that I had first encountered in Benjamin.

Benjamin's words were: "To seize the essence of history, it suffices to compare Herodotus and the morning newspaper" (1999, 14). Probably basing his claim on a 1924 work by Rémy de Gourmont (see Benjamin 1999, Convolute S1a 2), Benjamin (mis)attributes the claim to Schopenhauer. Whatever the source (which remains unidentified), the idea is very much Benjamin's.

In fact, Herodotus is not as far from the morning paper as Benjamin (or the faux Schopenhauer) implies. A greater historian for his marked ethnographic bent, Herodotus was an attentive listener and a tireless teller of stories—some of which were every bit as lurid, violent, and improbable as anything the tabloid press could come up with. The sustained attention that Herodotus paid to the stories told in different societies that he visited or heard about makes him the first ethnographer.

With my emphasis on forms and types of behavior I part company with the perceptive analyses of Johnston and Baumann (2010), who see "foodies" as a social grouping and attribute the tensions in the contemporary food world to the greater access to culinary goods that implies democratization and the exclusivity entailed by the new distinctions created around food. This tack also sets my work apart from that of Michael Pollan (2009, 2013), who seeks to make connections to the natural, not the social, world.

Simmel's "The Metropolis and Mental Life" ([1903] 1950) speaks with especial directness to those students from small towns who find themselves living in New York City for the first time. It is especially illuminating read alongside Fyodor Dostoevsky's *Crime and Punishment*. Had he read the novel, Simmel would certainly have recognized the urban universe that Dostoevsky constructed.

No single individual or institution realizes completely any one of the three types of authority proposed by Weber (1978), but the interplay among traditional, rational-legal, and charismatic authority has proved a potent instrument for the analysis of political life and the forms and functions of leadership. Where would political campaigns be without a leader that we'd like to think of as charismatic, even though we know that no one person fills the bill?

Of course, the concern with forms, types, and structures marks sociology more generally. The roll call of "founding fathers" has to include Émile Durkheim. In what is perhaps a Simmelian reading, Durkheim, too, can be seen to analyze structures and types. Every sociologist learns the four types of suicide that frame Durkheim's statistical analyses in *Suicide* ([1897] 1951) and is well aware that Durkheim explicitly rejects any explanation that veers into the psychological. It is telling that Durkheim draws on literary works—that is, highly constructed representations in no way to be confused with actual cases—to illustrate the types of suicide. Moreover, the very title of his monumental work, *The Elementary Forms of Religious Life* ([1912] 1995), alerts the reader to Durkheim's subordination of doctrines, beliefs, and rituals to the forms of social interaction beyond the particulars.

Connecting to Simmel's formal analysis, Erving Goffman (1959) best conveys the strategy behind the ostensibly random promenade through the social world, asserting that "the illustrative materials used in this study are of mixed status: some are taken from respectable researches . . .; some are taken from informal memoirs . . .; many fall in between. . . . The justification for this approach (as I take to be the justification for Simmel's also) is that the illustrations together fit in a coherent framework that ties together bits of experience the reader has already had" (xi–xii).

CHAPTER ONE. THINKING ABOUT FOOD

Scholars of every stripe have weighed in on globalization—its contents, discontents, and malcontents. On McDonald's adaptations to the South Asian market, see the articles in Watson (1997), especially Ohnuki-Tierney (1997), and Watson's own update (2000). Issenberg (2008) vividly details the sushi takeover of the United States. Whereas consumption practices ally sushi with fast food, production, especially the requirement of personnel of great skill, connects it to highly professionalized cooking.

My discussion of Spam draws heavily on Ong (2010), specifically his personal experience, research, and interviews with Spam aficionados and practitioners, for which I am most grateful.

"Imagined communities" is the happy coinage of Benedict Anderson (1983), who argues with telling case studies that we cannot fully belong to a country unless we believe in some way in its difference from other countries or nations.

Culinary France

The assertions of superiority of French cuisine are in order from Massialot ([1691] 1698, ii) and Carême ([1828] 1986, i). The larger notion of cuisine as the "culinary conscience" of France derives from Norbert Elias's (1994) discussion of the concept of civilization as the self-consciousness of the West.

For the development of cookbooks, see Hyman and Hyman (1999). The dismissal of foreign sauces is found in Carême ([1828] 1986, 25–28).

The quotations from the introduction to *La vie et la passion de Dodin-Bouffant-Gourmet* may be found in Rouff ([1924] 1994).

Marthe Allard Daudet was the second wife of the writer and politician Léon Daudet, who was also director of the right-wing journal *L'Action française*. (The word *pampille* refers to ornamental fringe or decorations.) For a more extensive discussion of Pampille, see Ferguson (2008). King (2006) translates and adapts Pampille's recipes to American kitchens. For Proust's references, see Proust ([1913-1927] 1987-1989, 3:293 and 2:792). Proust also calls Daudet a "true poet" (3:546).

Trubek (2000) examines the changes in the profession and details the significance of cross-cultural connections and tensions during the mid to late nineteenth century, when considerable numbers of French chefs worked in England. For career details on Carême and Escoffier here and below, see Ferguson (2004); on Soyer, see Cowen (2006).

Capatti and Montanari (2003) make a case for the existence of a distinctive Italian cuisine as early as the Renaissance, though Diner (2001) claims that a truly national Italian cuisine emerged only in the immigrant communities in the United States.

Judt's assessment is in his memoir (2009): "Like most Englishmen of my generation I now think of takeout or delivered Indian food as a native dish imported centuries before. I am English enough to think of Indian food in particular as an aspect of England that I miss here in the US where Chinese is the ethnic dish of local preference."

On Indian philosophies concerning food, see Khare (1992); on Chinese cuisine, see Chang (1977) and Waley-Cohen (2007). Arjun Appadurai (1988) argues that the cuisine identified as Indian around the world owes much to a cadre of professional women whose English-language cookbooks in the 1960s and 1970s created a semifactitious Indian cuisine, most recognizable as such from abroad.

Albala (2002) traces the shift from a food system defined by the humors to a modern understanding of food relations.

Those inclined to see wine as a "natural" product would do well to consult Paul (1996) on the intersection of science, state authority, and the production of wine beginning in the early nineteenth century.

For the *appellations d'origine contrôlées*, see the official site of the Institut national de l'origine et de qualité, www.inao.gouv.fr.

On the chocolate battles, see "EU'S Chocolate Dispute," TED Case Studies, No. 521, www1.american.edu/TED/chocolat.htm. From a close analysis of applications by members of the European Economic Community for protected status for distinctive foods, DeSoucey (2010) gives top ranking to France, Italy, and Spain as the strongest advocates of their foods.

On the French campaign to have UNESCO list French gastronomy as part of the world cultural heritage, see Sciolino (2008) and the official UNESCO site for Intangible Cultural Heritage, www.unesco.org/culture/ich/index.php

COMPETITIVE COOKING
On the MOF, see Hohenadel (2010) and the official site, www.meilleursouvriersdefrance.info, as well as the recent documentary film *The Kings of Pastry*, by Chris Hegedus and D. A. Pennebaker. As the documentary makes clear, the world of competitive cooking is intensely masculine. Only one woman has ever won the Bocuse d'Or.

As the New York-based Ethiopian-Swedish chef Marcus Samuelsson recounts in his biography (2012), he learned to cook in Swedish kitchens dominated by classical French cuisine. The Swiss kitchens where he trained were equally French. Even so, and although he was already a chef in a highly regarded New York restaurant, Samuelsson felt that he needed to go to France to work, because "anyone who wanted to know greatness had to go to France" (153). Despite his reservations about the French cuisine as he knew it from his training, Samuelsson went to France on an (unpaid) internship at the three-star restaurant of Georges Blanc (chapter 16).

The Bocuse d'Or is not the only contest to take the Olympics as a model. The annual Internationale Kochkunst Ausstellung (IKA) International Culinary Exhibition is commonly known as the "culinary Olympics." Its U.S. sponsor is the American Culinary Federation.

For a breathless blow-by-blow account of the 2009 Bocuse d'Or competition from the American point of view, see Friedman (2009). Paul Bocuse made a notable investment in American participation in the Bocuse d'Or when he drafted celebrity chefs Daniel Boulud and Thomas Keller to spearhead the American effort. Their work did not go unnoticed. In a signal honor for a foreigner (Alice Waters and Julia Child are the only other Americans from the food community to be so recognized), in March 2011 Paul Bocuse bestowed the Legion of Honor on Chef Keller.

In the competition, which takes place over two days, twenty-five judges from around the world assess the taste, presentation, and representation of the identity of the country. The highest and lowest marks are eliminated. Of the forty-two medals awarded from 1987 to 2013, ten have been won by France, including seven gold, the most recent in 2013; eight by Norway, including four gold, the most recent in 1997; six by Belgium (no gold); five by Sweden, including one gold in 2009; and four by Denmark, including one gold in 2011; 2011 was notable for a straight sweep of the Scandinavians (Denmark, Sweden, and Norway in first, second, and third place, respectively).

The idea of French cuisine as following the rules of harmony (solfège) is taken from my September 1991 interview with André Jammet, then owner of the esteemed restaurant La Caravelle. La Caravelle closed in 2004 after forty-three years at the heart of elegant French dining in Manhattan.

I take the French terms from the well-worn edition of *The Joy of Cooking* (Rombauer 1943) that I inherited from my mother.

HAUTE CUISINE

Haute Cuisine (*Les saveurs du palais*) was released in September 2012 (September 2013 in the United States), a "free adaptation" (according to the final credits) of a memoir with recipes by Danièle Mazet-Delpeuch, who wrote of her two years (1988-1990) as the private chef to President François Mitterrand. The identification with Mitterrand is inescapable, especially given his well-known love of both great (French) food and great (French) literature. Some of the recipes in the film from Mazet-Delpeuch's book can be found on the Marmiton website at www.marmiton.org/magazine/dossiers-marmiton_les-saveurs-du-palais-les-recettes_1.aspx:

Chaudrée Charentaise [chowder from the Charentes region]
Chou farci au saumon braisé aux petits lardons [cabbage stuffed with salmon, cooked with fatty bacon]
Crème de Mémée [Granny's custard sauce]
Pommes de terre Julia [Julia's potatoes]
La tarte au chocolat Julia [Julia's chocolate tarte]

Mazet-Delpeuch would not divulge Mitterrand's tastes, beyond that he was "a gourmet, highly cultured and unfailingly polite" ("gastronome, lettré, et d'une politesse irreprochable"). See Pham (2012).

The film cuts back and forth between Hortense's time at the Élysée Palace and her later stint as cook at a French scientific base in Antarctica. The farewell dinner at the base that we see her preparing features many of the traditional dishes of French cuisine, including a St. Honoré cake—named in this case, as she clarifies, for the address of the Élysée Palace (55 Rue du Faubourg Saint-Honoré). The glories of French cuisine, the film tells us, are not just for the powerful ("Up yours" is my translation of the French "La DuBarry, elle vous emmerde!").

The director, Christian Vincent, insisted that the food in this film be good to look at and good to eat. See interview with Caroline Broué on the podcast *La Grande Table*, 19 September 2012, www.franceculture.fr/emission-la-grande-table-2eme-partie-entretien-avec-christian-vincent-realisateur-du-film-les-saveur. See also Luciani (2012).

On the continued significance of the meal in French culture, in addition to the recognition by UNESCO, see Adam Gopnik's love letter to French food, *The Table Comes First: Family, France, and the Meaning of Food* (2011). Amy Trubek's aptly named *Taste of Place: A Cultural Journey into Terroir* (2008) follows the extension of *terroir* from France to America.

See the epilogue of Ferguson (2004) for my analysis of *Babette's Feast*. Better than any cultural document that I know, certainly better than any other film, *Babette's Feast* conveys the alchemy by which food transforms itself and the world. The material is spiritual, aesthetic, and celestial, even as it remains insistently sensual. As the principal guest at this feast notes in a state of euphoria, "In this beautiful world of ours, all things are possible." Hortense is no Babette. Yet, like *Babette's Feast, Haute Cuisine* celebrates the possibilities of this world made more beautiful, and especially more pleasurable, by the cook.

The broad sense of *logos* emerges in the *Histories* of Herodotus (484–425 B.C.E.), the writer often called the Father of History, albeit with some misgiving. In his use of the stories that he picked up on his travels from those whom we would call native informants, Herodotus is certainly the direct ancestor of ethnography and sociology. His *logoi* (plural of *logos*) were the stories that he heard from the peoples he visited and retold in the larger historical or ethnographical narrative.

Sociology, baptized around 1830 by the French philosopher Auguste Comte, divides its etymological allegiance between Latin and Greek. This template holds for other disciplines as well (anthropology, biology, psychology). If I call myself a "cuisinologist" (again split between languages), it is because I work to tell food stories that are also interpretations.

Culinary America
I discuss reactions to the arrival of the Michelin Guide in New York in Ferguson (2008). I draw on Davis, McBride, et al. (2008), who report the results of a small survey of Americans at a food conference asked to define American cuisine.

The standard version of "America the Beautiful" memorized by generations of American schoolchildren was first published as music and lyrics in 1910. The first stanza and the refrain go as follows:

> O beautiful for spacious skies,
> For amber waves of grain,
> For purple mountain majesties
> Above the fruited plain!
>
> America! America!
> God shed His grace on thee,
> And crown thy good with brotherhood
> From sea to shining sea!

Though there had been a number of presidential proclamations of thanksgiving since 1777 and many states had decreed their own thanksgiving holidays over the years, not until 1863 did President Abraham Lincoln declare a national commemoration. In the middle of a devastating civil war, the president seized the opportunity to reiterate his faith in the union. He enjoined all Americans, at home and abroad, to gather together, honor their country, and give thanks for divine mercy. Lincoln acted at the fervent urging of prominent magazine editor Sarah Josepha Hale, who promoted a national thanksgiving in several editorials in *Godey's Ladies Book*. For the text of Lincoln's 1863 proclamation, see "Proclamation of Thanksgiving," Abraham Lincoln Online, http://showcase.netins.net /web/creative/lincoln/speeches/thanks.htm.

By contrast, Canada proclaimed Thanksgiving officially only in 1957, and even then the whole country does not observe the holiday (Prince Edward Island, Newfoundland, Labrador, and Nova Scotia opt out). There is no ritual meal and no historical occasion that is commemorated—only the time-honored tradition of offering thanks for a bountiful harvest. Smith and Boyd (2009) make extensive comparisons of the two holidays.

COMPETITIVE EATING

Competitive eating got a big push in 1997 with the founding of the International Federation of Competitive Eaters (IFOCE), the governing body of Major League Eating (MLE), based in New York City. MLE currently backs over eighty events a year, calling on competitors to consume almost any imaginable food, from mayonnaise to pretzels.

Prizes intensify the competition—Nathan's Super Bowl gives $10,000 to the winners (along with the Mustard Belt for the men's champion and the Pink Belt for the women's), $5,000 to the runner-up, and $2,500 to third place. According to the IFOCE, an estimated 40,000 people watch the contest on site and 1.7 million watch it on ESPN, the sports channel (and on YouTube). The current record, set in 2013 by Joey "The Jaws" Chestnut, is sixty-nine hotdogs.

Fans of the Food Channel in the United States will object that there is, in fact, a great deal of competitive cooking in America. They are right, but as with *Iron Chef,* the Japanese import that started the vogue, in 1993 (in Japan) and 1999 (in the United States), the emphasis falls squarely on spectacle.

POW! quotations are, in order, from the following pages of Yan (2012): 280, 288, 291, 287.

Culinary Nationalism
Matsuhisa is quoted by White (2009). On culinary culture in Japan, see also Surak (2012) on the tea ceremony.

LE GRAND CHEF
Around the time that *Le Grand Chef* was made, South Korea embarked on a campaign to make Korean cuisine better known abroad and better practiced at home. A campaign by the Ministry of Food, Agriculture, Forestry and Fisheries spent ten million dollars in 2009, including on grants and scholarships for South Koreans to travel and attend cooking school. See Moskin (2009b).

The unequal relationship between myths and calories was noted by Alain Senderens (1993), at the time a three-star Michelin chef and president of the Conseil National des Arts Culinaires.

CHAPTER TWO. THE PERILS AND PLEASURES
OF CONSUMPTION
Here and below, the discussion works off the identification by Paul Rozin (1997) of the "omnivore's paradox." That is, humans, as omnivores, need to consume a broad range of nutrients. That need for variety increases the potential for ingesting noxious food. Unlike most animals (rats being the big exception), humans must be exceptionally vigilant about the foods that they consume. Humans oscillate between neophilia—the adventurous spirit—and neophobia—the fear of trying new things that marks us all. Michael Pollan (2006) translates the omnivore's paradox into the dilemmas faced by every culinary consumer.

Ferrières ([2002] 2006) examines exemplary food fears from the Middle Ages to the twentieth century. As she notes, drawing on the observations of historian Lucien Febvre, such fears are a function of the way we manage risk in everyday life. There is by now a vast bibliography of works that deal with one or another aspect of contemporary food safety, from food-industry exposés (Nestle 2002) to the best-selling works of Michael Pollan (2001, 2006, 2009), which show an

increasing concern for the effects of food beyond the individual and for engagement with issues of sustainability as well as safety.

Food Fears
Fans of detective novels will know the arsenic exception. One can mithridatize—
that is, inoculate—oneself by repeatedly consuming small quantities of certain
poisons. Talk about premeditation! Dorothy Sayers's *Strong Poison* (1930) is an
archetypal narrative of mithridatization.

"Weapons of the weak" is the felicitous concept of James C. Scott (1985).

On President Obama's trip to Paris in 2009, a taster was reported in attendance
in one restaurant, though it was never clear what, exactly, the taster was supposed to taste *for*.

The saga of the pea eater (summer 2010) made the media rounds in the United
States and the United Kingdom. See Paddock (2010).

Three of the medical mysteries unraveled by Edlow (2009) concern food. What is
striking is the great array of individual experts and governmental institutions at
every level that is required to determine the origin of food-borne illness. Even
then, questions abound, and answers remain speculative.

CHOCOLAT AND CHOCOLATE
Chocolat (2000), directed by Lasse Hällestrom, starring Juliette Binoche, Judi
Dench, and Johnny Depp, is based on the book of the same name (1999) by the
British-French writer Joanne Harris.

Pleasure Talk
Routinely attributed to the writer Dorothy Parker, and not only by my mother-
in-law, the ham quote has yet to find an unimpeachable attribution. The quip
certainly sounds like Dorothy Parker. One source pointed to Irma Rombauer's *Joy
of Cooking*, though I can find no reference in the editions of 1931, 1943, or 1964.

For a list of American food holidays and details about the mechanisms of nam-
ing, see "American Food Holidays," *The Nibble*, www.thenibble.com/fun/more

/facts/food-holidays.asp. Note that individual states also have their own rosters of symbols, and these often include foods. New York State, I found, designated an official muffin (apple-cinnamon) in 1987. See "State Symbols USA," www.statesymbolsusa.org/New_York/muffin_apple.html.

Weil (2010) kicked off National Ice Cream Month with a report on ice cream experiments apparently designed to stave off culinary boredom. Johnny Iuzzini, executive pastry chef at the Jean-Georges restaurant in Manhattan until 2012, felt almost trapped by the restaurant's signature chocolate cake. Every order of (the admittedly luscious) confection missed the excitement of his high-tech desserts and the possibility of a new taste sensation (see the interview in Powell 2010).

THE HAPPY GLUTTON

See A. A. Milne, *Winnie-the-Pooh* ([1926] 1992). Many of the "decorations" by Ernest H. Shepard for the first edition feature honey, and Pooh's lack of and search for honey are central to the Disney film (2011).

The comic strip *Blondie* began in 1930 with Dagwood as the playboy son of a billionaire railroad tycoon and Blondie as a frivolous flapper—not at all the Dagwood and Blondie whose ventures we follow today. See the discussion of *Blondie*'s origins on the King Features website: http://kingfeatures.com/comics/comics-a-z/?id=Blondie. As the son of the original cartoonist explains it, the Great Depression promoted a change in perspective. Dagwood was disinherited for marrying beneath his social class to that "gold-digger blond." The penurious newlyweds entered the ordinary life of Middle America, where they have been concerned these eighty years with the elemental tasks of working, raising a family, eating, and sleeping. To a certain extent, Dagwood's insatiable hunger can be seen as a response to food scarcity in the Depression, though in later times of relative prosperity, food fixation is simply his defining character trait. Blondie and Dagwood's marriage took place only after an almost monthlong hunger strike, which, for Dagwood, was nothing short of heroic.

It is noteworthy that for all that seems indelibly American about *Blondie*, the strip has a sizeable readership worldwide. Syndicated in over 2,300 newspapers, the comic strip is translated into 35 different languages in 55 countries and read by an estimated 280 million people every day.

CHAPTER THREE. TEXTS TAKE OVER

From Talk to Text
This dictum was articulated by the philosopher Ludwig Feuerbach (1804-1872), who wrote, "Der Mensch ist, was er isst." My thanks to Julia Abramson for this reference. For the history of the later phrase in English, see "You Are What You Eat," *The Phrase Finder*, www.phrases.org.uk/meanings/you%20are%20 what%20you%20eat.html.

Anthropologist Jack Goody (1975) argues forcefully that by allowing comparisons, written texts make critical thought possible.

THE ENTHUSIAST: ATHENAEUS'S CULINARY TOURISM

A modern translator and editor goes so far as to claim that "in some respects it [*The Deipnosophists*] is the most important work of later antiquity" (Athenaeus 1969, 1: xv). Especially when one considers that the text we have today is incomplete—of the fifteen books, only summaries exist for books one, two, and parts of three, eleven, and fifteen (Athenaeus 1969, 1:vii-xxi)—*The Deipnosophists* is staggering on every count. See Braund and Wilkins (2001) and Wilkins, Harvey, and Dobson (1995). Jeanneret ([1987] 1991) places Athenaeus within the tradition of the philosophical drinking party known as the symposium (see, especially, 67-70, 160-171).

Athenaeus came to general attention with translations of his work into Latin, in 1556 by Noël le Comte, and in 1612 by Jacques d'Alechamp and Isaac Causaubon. Michel de Marolles undertook the first translation into a modern language, with *Les quinze livres d'Athénée,* published in 1680. Although there was another full French translation in 1789-1791, and selections in 1828, *The Deipnosophists* did not appear in English until 1854. My thanks to David Konstan, who first suggested that a nonclassicist interested in food ought to explore Athenaeus.

The Loeb Classical Library (Harvard University Press) published a new translation by S. Douglas Olson in seven volumes under the title *The Learned Banqueters* (2007-2011).

All quotations in this section come from Charles Gulick's seven-volume edition of Athenaeus (1969) for the Loeb Classical Library (1929-1941) and are cited in the text by volume and page. The citations sometime cover up to four pages because they skip the facing original Greek text.

An oft-cited, more recent claim of the decisive effect of cooking on civilization turns up in James Boswell's definition of man as "a Cooking Animal" (1786): "The beasts have memory, judgment, and all the faculties and passions of our mind, in a certain degree; but no beast is a cook" (Sunday, the 15th of August). Pollan (2013) makes the case that we would all be better off, and healthier, if we cooked.

Dreams of abundance are a staple of every society subjected to episodic food scarcity. Another celebrated example, predating Athenaeus by several centuries, is found in book seven of *The Odyssey*. Odysseus is welcomed in the utopian society of Phaecia, where "luxuriant trees are always in their prime. . . . The yield of all these trees will never flag or die, neither in winter nor in summer, a harvest all year round." Such were the "glories showered down by the gods" on this realm (Homer 1996, 7:183).

THE VISIONARY: FOURIER'S GASTROSOPHY
All quotations in this section are from Fourier's complete works (1966–1968).

Although Fourier's first work, *Théorie des quatre mouvements et des destinées generals* (Theory of four movements and general destinies), appeared in 1808, his last, *Le nouveau monde amoureux* (The new world of love), remained in manuscript until 1967. Fourier's ideas circulated widely well before his disciples brought out an incomplete edition in the mid-1840s.

The gastronomic critic Charles Monselet (1859, 165) attributes Fourier's phalanstery as a "gastronomic throne surrounded by culinary institutions" to Eugène Woestyn's "Physiologie du dîneur" (1854).

THE PRACTITIONER: CARÊME'S TREATISE
Citations from Carême are from the following works: "man born to wealth . . . mediocrity": Carême (1833, 2:vi-vii); "modern cuisine will owe to me . . . ": Carême (1833, 2:13); "Nineteenth-century French cuisine . . . centuries to come": Carême ([1815a] 1841, dedication); "The analytical spirit of the 19th century":

Carême (1833, 1:lxvi); "every citizen . . . delicious food": Carême (1833, 1:lviii–lvix).

On the notable increase in the number of cookbooks published in France from in 1811 (when the *Bibliographie de la France* was first published) to 1898, see Ferguson (2004, 205–208).

Gigante's anthology of writings on food (2005), or in my terms, food talk, is a useful reminder that food inspired writers outside as well as inside France.

THE CRITIC: GRIMOD DE LA REYNIÈRE'S GASTRONOMIC CRITICISM

Quotes are from the title page and preface of *Manuel des Amphitryons* in Grimod de La Reynière (1977). On French gastronomic discourse generally, see Ory (1998).

The term *gastronomie* was resurrected from a sixteenth-century translation of *The Deipnosophists*, in which Athenaeus refers to a lost culinary treatise of Archestratus. The immediate source was a quite dreadful poem by Joseph Berchoux, "La gastronomie, ou l'homme de champs à table," published in 1801.

Grimod de La Reynière was the son of a wealthy aristocrat. (The home that his father built in Paris on the Champs-Élysées currently houses the U.S. Embassy.) Forced by the Revolution to find new sources of support, he launched his gastronomic career in 1803. That career ended in 1812. Though he lived for another quarter century, Grimod wrote nothing more. His food career spanned Napoleon's Empire (1804–1814).

THE ANALYST: BRILLAT-SAVARIN'S SOCIAL ANALYSIS

All citations in this section are from Brillat-Savarin, *Physiologie du goût* ([1826] 1839). The aphorisms are listed at the beginning of the work.

Brillat-Savarin had a much broader experience than Grimod de La Reynière. After having emigrated from his native province to the United States to escape revolutionary retributions, as he recounts in the *Physiology*, he was a magistrate in Paris for most of his adult life. Brillat was no revolutionary (he died within a month of the publication of the *Physiology*, having caught cold at a memorial mass for the martyred Louis XVI). Yet his vision of what he called "social gourmandise" was unmistakably modern. Not for nothing did the title page proclaim the *Physiology* "Meditations on transcendent gastronomy, a theoretical and historical work on the order of the day.""

The gastronomic critic Charles Monselet sets the parameters for the standoff between "grimodiens" and "brillatistes": "There has been a lot of talk recently of Brillat-Savarin, who, another Amerigo Vespucci, has inherited all the glory that belongs to Grimod de La Reynière. The clever author of the *Physiology of Taste*, with his assurances, his sophistication, his charm, opens the modern succession of genial temperaments, whereas the author of the *Almanach des Gourmands*, to the contrary, closes that of vigorous natures" (Monselet 1859, 103).

The rue Brillat-Savarin, located in the thirteenth arrondissement close to the southern edge of Paris, was dedicated in 1894. The rue Carême, near Les Halles, was unfortunately demolished in various urban renewal projects, though a tiny Passage Antoine Carême can be found today (with difficulty) in the first arrondissement near Les Halles, close to where the rue St. Honoré runs into the rue des Halles. The "Brillat-Savarin" cake, now known as a "Savarin," was created in 1845; Brillat-Savarin cheese is a triple-cream Brie first made in the 1930s by celebrated cheese maker Henri Androuët. Paris has no street for Grimod de la Reynière, his works are not readily available, and there is no English translation of his work (though one of the *Manuel* is under way, thanks to the historian Jennifer Davis).

THE ARTISTS: PROUST'S AND WOOLF'S CULINARY WORLDS
Quotations (in my translation) are from Proust ([1913–1927] 1987–1989, 1:437 and 4:612). In 1909, after a meal that must have provided the basis for the comparison in the novel, Proust wrote to his hostess that "I should like to succeed as well as you what I am going to do this evening, may my style be as brilliant, as clear, as solid as your aspic, my ideas as savory as your carrots and as nourishing and fresh as your meat" (4:1311).

Carême's architectural ambitions prompted him to self-publish a set of drawings for monuments, *Projets d'architecture dédiés à Alexandre Ier* (1821).

The Woolf quotes are from chapters 17 and 18 in the first section ("The Window") of *To the Lighthouse* ([1927] 1989, 125–168).

For the Brillat-Savarin quotes in this section, see "Portrait d'une jolie gourmande" (Brillat-Savarin [1826] 1839, 168) and "Du plaisir de la table" (197). Brillat refers to a *convive*—that is, someone with whom one lives for the time of a repast. The English word *companion* retains something of the food connection, meaning literally someone with whom one shares bread. On the duties of the host, see Brillat's Aphorism XVIII: "He who receives his friends and gives no personal care to the meal is not worthy of having friends." Mrs. Ramsay does her duty. Whether or not Woolf knew Brillat-Savarin, she was well aware of the stakes in dining: "A good dinner is of great importance to good talk. One cannot think well, love well, sleep well, if one has not dined well" (Woolf [1927] 1989, chapter 1).

The Food World as a Cultural Field
See Ferguson (1998) for an analysis of gastronomy in France as a cultural field in the making. Elaborated in its specifically sociological usage by Pierre Bourdieu, "field" designates the state of a cultural enterprise when the relevant productive and consumption practices achieve a degree of independence from direct external constraints (i.e., those of state and church for the arts in premodern Europe). As a "particular social universe endowed with particular institutions and obeying specific laws," a field translates external economic or political phenomena into its own terms (Bourdieu 1993, 162–163).

ADVENTURES IN CHOCOLATE
Quotations in this section come from publicity by chocolate purveyors at the Paris and New York Chocolate Shows in 2007. Besides outrage at the performances of Karen Finley slathered in chocolate and nothing else, Catholics protested at the Holy Week 2007 exhibition in a Manhattan gallery of a life-sized chocolate sculpture of a naked Jesus. The sculpture, *My Sweet Lord* by food artist Cosimo Cavallaro, was not displayed.

For examples of overt, even suggestive appeals to sensuality and sexuality, one need only turn on the television and succumb to advertisement after advertisement that show, usually in close-up, a beautiful woman biting into a piece of dark chocolate with a creamy filling, her eyes closing in evident ecstasy. Dove is notably adept at representing orgasmic chocolate experiences. For one among many clips available on YouTube, see www.youtube.com/

watch?v=VbgM1ulaBVc&NR=1. Chocolate World Expo, held at the Meadowlands Stadium in New Jersey, brings together seventy-plus vendors, from artisans to farmers. For a video celebrating all the chocolate shows (Paris, Bordeaux, Cannes, Lille, Lyon, Nantes, Marseilles, New York, Bahia, Bologna, Cairo, Seoul, Shanghai, Tokyo, Zurich), see the Salon du Chocolate website, www.salonduchocolat.fr/accueil.aspx.

CHAPTER FOUR. ICONIC COOKS

Women's Work and Women's Words
As many studies have demonstrated, and as everyday observation will verify, the feminization of a profession leads to its decline in attractiveness (often tied to a decline in remuneration). One need only think of nursing, teaching, and secretarial work. Despite increasing numbers of women working as chefs in higher-end restaurants, the world of the professional chef remains overwhelmingly male.

Chefing is the term that I use to translate the oppositions that set the male *cuisinier* against (and usually superior to) the female *cuisinière*. The verb avoids the essentialist associations of status by focusing on the roles involved. See Ferguson (2004, 131–147).

Subsequent cookbooks strengthen the sense of connection that Massialot claims between *la grande cuisine* and *cuisine bourgeoise*. Menon wrote *La cuisinière bourgeoise* (1746), a best seller for over a century, and a few years later *Le manuel des officiers de bouche* (1759). Although the title of the last cookbook specifically addresses the professional chef—the officers in charge of provisions—the lengthy subtitle reaches much further: *Ou le précis de tous les apprêts que l'on peut faire des alimens pour servir toutes les tables, depuis celles des grands seigneurs jusqu'à celles des bourgeois* (Or, a summary of all the dishes that can be made of foods to serve all tables from those of the great lords to those of the bourgeois). The third subtitle looks back to the great and their chefs: *Ouvrage très-utile aux maîtres pour ordonner des repas & aux artistes pour les exécuter* (Very useful work for masters ordering meals and for artists to execute them).

Sarah Josepha Hale (1788–1879) is better known as the longtime editor of the magazine *Godey's Ladies Book*. It was from this position of considerable influence that she relentlessly lobbied President Abraham Lincoln to declare a national holiday for Thanksgiving.

Donna Gabaccia (1998) examines the impact of immigrant cuisines in the United States. See, in particular, her chapter 5, "Food Fights and American Values." Hasia Diner (2001) tells the story of unequal culinary assimilation from the immigrants' perspective.

NEW CULINARY CONNECTIONS

Given the importance of household management, cookbooks were invariably more than just collections of recipes. For a sense of these works, there is no better place to begin than the Historic American Cookbook Project, an incomparable resource at Michigan State University for the study of American cookbooks from the nineteenth century. See "Feeding America: The Historic American Cookbook Project," MSU Libraries, http://digital.lib.msu.edu/projects/cookbooks/. On the women whose cookbooks did so much to shape American cookery, see the introduction by culinary historian Jan Longone, http://digital.lib.msu.edu/projects/cookbooks/html/intro_essay.html.

Culinary Translations

FANNIE FARMER

Working from cookbooks, magazine columns, and articles, as well as voluminous correspondence, Laura Shapiro (2008) examines women's cooking, and the relationship between women and cooking, from the late nineteenth through the early twentieth century, following Fannie Farmer's career and assessing her influence. See especially her chapter 5, "The Mother of Level Measurements" (100–119).

The full text of the original 1896 edition of *The Boston Cooking-School Cook Book* has been digitized by the Michigan State University Libraries and is available at http://digital.lib.msu.edu/projects/cookbooks/html/books/book_48.cfm. The full text of the 1918 edition, the last completely authored by Farmer, is available on Bartleby.com at www.bartleby.com/87/. *The Boston Cooking-School Cook Book* has been published in thirteen editions: 1896, 1906, 1918, 1923, 1930, 1936, 1941, 1946, 1951. 1959, 1965, 1979, 1990, with a reissue in 1996 to celebrate the hundredth anniversary of publication. Since 1959, Fannie Farmer has been elevated to the title.

Farmer's epigraph is taken from Ruskin's *Ethics of the Dust: Ten Lectures to Little Housewives; On the Elements of Crystallization* (1865). The work is presented as a series of conversations with girls at a school. The discussion of cooking comes in the seventh lecture, on "Home Virtues." One does wonder at Ruskin proposing these four women for his supposed public of young girls. All bona fide enchantresses, none was associated with cooking. Medea was credited with poisons; Helen charmed with her beauty and also (in book 2 of the *Odyssey*) with opiates; and Circe's food turned Odysseus's men into pigs (in book 10). Though she had no connection to cooking, at least the Queen of Sheba did not wreak havoc. According to Laura Shapiro (personal conversation), the passage circulated widely at this time, particularly among advocates of scientific cookery.

My thanks to Iberechi Ihezie for his suggestion that the Ruskin quote implies a narrative of ultimate culinary empowerment.

A Modern Culinary Education
David Strauss (2011, chapter 3) reconstructs the male-dominated world of fine dining that prevailed when Rombauer and Fisher started writing. This was the food world of men's clubs and wine societies, catered by professional—and often French—chefs, which did not admit women. The Wine and Food Society, the Amis d'Escoffier, and the Confrerie du Tastevin were founded or set up American branches in the 1930s. Their French inflection further separated professional chefs' organizations from domestic cooking.

Sidonie Naulin's analysis (2012) of blogs and restaurant reviews in France over the past decade shows this bifurcated universe in a different time and place. The blogs, with their commentary and recipes, are overwhelmingly written by women; the restaurant reviews are penned by professionals, which means men.

Quotations from M. F. K. Fisher ([1954] 1976) in this section are as follows: "taste-blind": 59; "missionary . . . not too despicable": 59.

IRMA ROMBAUER

Anne Mendelson (2003) does an amazing job of sorting out Rombauer's complicated, confused, and contentious relations with her publisher, Bobbs-Merrill. More generally, Mendelson's masterful examination puts Rombauer and her daughter and eventual coauthor, Marion Rombauer Becker, in the broader social context. She connects the laconic presentation of nineteenth-century cookbooks, with their lack of detail, to the extended family often working together in the kitchen, many of whom would know how to use summary directions and therefore would not need the specifications that came later. As cookbook after cookbook stressed, twentieth-century cookbooks addressed an audience of individual women working alone at home.

Edgar R. Rombauer Jr. gives this sales figure in footnote 4 in his foreword to the facsimile edition (1998). The seventy-fifth anniversary edition, published in 2006, continues to sell briskly. The second edition, first revision, appeared in 1936; the third was published in 1943. That this devoted reader and lover of cookery is a carefully crafted persona becomes clear when we realize that before *Joy*, Rombauer had a reputation as a hostess, not as a cook.

Child (1975) called Rombauer *Mrs. Joy* in her October column in *McCall's*, in which she reviewed the latest edition of *The Joy of Cooking*. My thanks to Amy Trubek for sending me a copy of this column. Child notes, as many have before and since, that the later editions written with her daughter, Marion Rombauer Becker, mute when they do not altogether eliminate the personal voice that made the early editions (through 1951) so engaging.

For Franklin's account of his childhood dinner table, see Franklin (1961, 24). Subsequent to this first part of the *Autobiography*, which dates from 1771, Benjamin Franklin spent considerable time in France, where he was lionized as an American *philosophe* and was reluctant to leave. For his disobliging reflections on American foodways, see Cooper ([1938] 1956, 162–163).

M. F. K. FISHER

Quotations from M. F. K. Fisher ([1954] 1976) in this section are as follows: "so ungastronomic a nation": 320; "We and almost all American Anglo-Saxon children . . . ": 320; "drown the devil": 321; "birds in a tree," 6; "taste-blind" and "innumerable tin cans": 59; "balanced meals": 189–91; "my own exhilarated senses and my pleased mind": 179; "about eating and about what to eat": 6.

On fine dining in the United States, see the analysis of New York restaurant menus over the nineteenth century by Freedman and Warlick (2011) and more generally on dining in New York by Grimes (2009).

Fisher's success at getting Americans to join her can be seen in the regular publication and especially republication of her work. The aptly named *Art of Eating*, containing five of her best-known works, came out in an omnibus edition in 1954, with an introduction by writer-critic Clifton Fadiman and an appreciation by James Beard. Reissued two decades later, in 1976, *The Art of Eating* subsequently celebrated its half century with another edition in 2004.

Culinary historian Joan Reardon (1994) explores the connections between M. F. K. Fisher and Julia Child (along with Alice Waters), although she focuses more on the culinary and personal relationships that bound them, especially Fisher and Child, who were of the same generation. See Gabaccia (1998) on the often bumpy path of the Americanization of foreign cuisines.

Laura Shapiro (2004a) speaks of a "genuine cult" around Fisher and her works beginning in the 1980s.

Fisher's translation of *The Physiology of Taste*, first published in 1949, has been reissued regularly, most recently in 2011, with a foreword by Bill Buford. Fisher herself recounts the prejudice against women as picky or unenthusiastic eaters. See "César," *Serve It Forth* (Fisher [1954] 1976, 116–120).

For James Beard's "Appreciation" of M.F.K. Fisher, see Fisher ([1954] 1976, xvii-xviii).

David Bouley paid tribute to Fisher in an author interview conducted at Bouley Restaurant, 31 May 1991.

Quotations, unless otherwise indicated, are from the foreword to *Mastering the Art of French Cooking*.

Shapiro (2008) has the best introduction to Child's work and impact. See also Fitch (1999) and Spitz (2012). Dana Polan (2011) analyzes her television career in detail and depth.

In England the cookbooks of Elizabeth David, like *Mastering* in the United States, turned French ways of doing food to English culinary account. The British had the advantage of being close to the Continent, where they could go see—and eat—for themselves. Americans, at a greater distance, needed more explanation, more hand-holding, more step-by-step instruction, more explanations of what were, to most American cooks, exotic ingredients.

It is useful to compare the commitment to explanation in various cookbooks. Take the recipe for béarnaise sauce: *Mastering the Art of French Cooking* requires four-and-a-half big pages, large format and large type, set up with ingredients on the left in bold and instructions on the right. The first three-and-a-half pages deal with hollandaise (sixty-one lines plus nineteen on the version made in the blender), which supplies the principle for béarnaise (and an additional nineteen lines on what to do when you mess up); then almost an entire page (thirteen lines) focus on the specifics of béarnaise. By contrast, Escoffier's *Guide to Modern Cookery* (1903, 1909, translation) takes care of béarnaise in sixteen lines over two narrative paragraphs. Prosper Montagné's *Larousse gastronomique* ([1939] 1961) dispatches it in seventeen lines of one of two columns on the page, in very small type. Cookbooks aimed at the domestic market, American as well as French, also assumed experience in the kitchen: Fannie Farmer (1930) devotes seven lines to béarnaise in one recipe, eleven lines for hollandaise sauce plus one line to turn hollandaise into béarnaise; and Irma Rombauer (1931) has only nine lines for hollandaise plus one extra for béarnaise.

Cookbooks aimed at the French domestic market also assumed culinary knowledge and know-how. A good example is Émile Dumont's extraordinarily perennially popular *La bonne cuisine française: Tout ce qui a rapport à la table; Manuel-guide pour la ville et la campagne*. Although Dumont died in 1887, the book lived on. The twenty-sixth edition—the one that I have at hand, probably from the 1920s—expedites sauce béarnaise in a single paragraph of six lines, only hinting at difficulty in a second paragraph that notes that the sauce "should be made with great care"; Pampille ([1913] 2008) devotes a half page, seventeen lines in good size type; Ginette Mathiot, whose *Je sais cuisiner* (I know how to cook) first appeared in 1932 and has remained a staple of the French housewife ever since, requires a mere eight lines of actual instruction in addition to ingredients and times (4th ed., 1984).

Elizabeth David's recipes, like most others, are summary next to those of *Mastering the Art of French Cooking*. Not surprisingly, David's *Italian Food*, published in 1958, did not sell well in the United States. Its focus on high-end Italian cooking did not resonate in an America that, at the time, did not see anything Italian much beyond spaghetti (Shapiro 2011). The film *Big Night* (1996) dramatizes the difficulty of getting Americans to eat anything authentically Italian in the 1950s.

Child's insistence on detail and extensive preparation takes her close to traditional bistro or restaurant cuisine. The dishes are French staples, to be sure, but they push everyday life up a notch or two. See the discussion of Julia's boeuf bourguignon in contrast with a recipe from a well-known and much-used French cookbook in Moskin (2009a).

See Child's memoir with Alex Prudhomme (2006) for her introduction to French cuisine and French foodways and the transformations they brought to her life. Not for nothing does Laura Shapiro (2004b) put Julia Child and Betty Friedan in the same chapter. However unlikely the connection, Child and Friedan both liberated American women by giving them a different perspective on their lives as women, wives, and homemakers.

My connections with Julia Child were limited but, like those of everyone else who came in contact with her, memorable. When I sent her a copy of an article on French cuisine that I had written, she wrote back—a real letter, before the days of email—saying if I was ever in Cambridge, let her know. I was and I did, and she invited me to dinner. The experience was repeated in France a couple of years later.

Vexed question: how much of *Mastering* is Julia's, as the American public assumed? Louisette Bertholle withdrew to a less active contribution (with 18 percent of the royalties), which left Simone Beck and Julia. Wherever the recipes came from (all thoroughly tested), the writing that shaped the book was Child's. Child's promotional personality soon turned her from an author into a cultural phenomenon. See Polan (2011).

Cooks Watching Cooks Cooking
Arthur Frommer's *Europe on 5 Dollars a Day* in 1957 was a landmark publication to be found in virtually every traveling American's pocket or backpack.

My thanks to Barbara Mittman, Susan Welch, and Lois Widdemer, superlative cooks and hostesses all, for sharing their cooking journeys with me, not to mention culinary conversations and glorious meals over many years.

Readers were quick to understand what this approach to cooking could do for them. My friend Barbara thought that she was a pretty good cook pre-Julia, but Julia made the difference, because she showed exactly "how to do the good 'ole boeuf bourguignon, . . . how to wow your friends with oeuf en gelée, etc."

For Julia Child's turn on the David Letterman Show in 1987, see www.youtube.com/watch?v=SHXopv8_JOE.

In his extensive discussion of the early history of culinary TV, Dana Polan (2011) makes clear both how new the medium was and how different Julia Child was in her understanding of it. Jeanne Schinto (2011) considers the early fame and subsequent decline of Dione Lucas as a culinary figure. Lucas was authoritative, close to authoritarian, and a perfectionist who did not fail to express her displeasure.

The overwrought title and subtitle of David Kamp's *The United States of Arugula: The Sun Dried, Cold Pressed, Dark Roasted, Extra Virgin Story of the American Food Revolution* (2007) sum it all up. Kamp tracks in great detail the foods and individuals who were the prime movers in this revolution.

CHAPTER FIVE. CHEFS AND CHEFING

On the conditions and consequences of professionalization, three sources prove especially illuminating. The uncertainty that Pierre-Michel Menger (2014) sees as the structuring condition of the career of the artist can be usefully applied to the world of restaurant chefing, despite the differences in the market structures of each. Andrew Abbott's now-standard study (1988) adopts a comparative perspective to examine the conditions of professionalization and the status of the profession. Gil Eyal's recent critique (2013) proposes the analytical superiority of "expertise"—conceived as a broad, heterogeneous, and shifting network of agents, concepts, knowledge, and institutions—over the more usual focus on attributes of a profession (codes of ethics, monopoly of knowledge, specific sites of training, recruitment, and accreditation). Experts need not be professionals.

The Dramas of Chefing

Robert Altman's film *Gosford Park* (2001) and the British television series *Upstairs, Downstairs* (1971-1975; reprise 2011) and *Downton Abbey* (2009-2013) are only the most recent illustrations of the divorce of production from consumption. Twenty-first-century viewers, of course, get to partake of both, but it is crucial that production and consumption take place in separate worlds, for this separation legitimates consumption as "pure" pleasure.

Martin Scorsese's 1993 film adaptation of Edith Wharton's 1921 novel, *The Age of Innocence*, gives an idea of just how lavish these intimate dinners could be. The kitchen scenes that figure prominently in the movie are nowhere to be found in the novel, which remains firmly focused on life "upstairs."

MAKING MEALS MATTER

No consideration of dining can overlook Georg Simmel's idiosyncratic piece on the "Sociology of the Meal" ([1910] 1997). Thorstein Veblen's *Theory of the Leisure Class* ([1899] 1979) makes an argument specific to the elites of the late nineteenth century, who sought to signal their distinction from others and their separation from productive work. Conspicuous consumption has come to have a much broader application. As the discussion here illustrates, the concept considers dining as power politics.

Chandra Mukerji (1997) argues that the elaborate formal gardens at Versailles, as well as their technological infrastructure, produced the very power relations that they expressed.

In seventeenth- and eighteenth-century France, the centerpieces were called *parterres* (flower beds) or *dormants* (sleepers) and were made of *pastillage* (mostly flour and sugar). Edible in theory, the culinary constructions that the nineteenth century called *pièces montées* were not meant to be consumed, though Carême notes that he made it a point to make edible pastry "from time to time." Edible constructions are, as Carême makes sure to mention, much more difficult to produce (Carême [1815a] 1841, xxiv).

Modern Chefing
Quotations are from Carême (1833, 2:xvii).

A strict hierarchy determined status in great households. Cooks were separate from the other servants. Series 1 of the BBC historical melodrama *Downton Abbey*, set between 1912 and 1914, produces a skirmish of sorts when a new cook takes over the kitchen. Accustomed to a small kitchen and no staff, Mrs. Bird dines with the valet. In the grander household, as is pointed out to her with considerable asperity, the kitchen staff dines apart from the servants, quite as Carême had required.

Rambourg (2010) contends that, at least since the seventeenth century, French cuisine has been driven by a heightened sense of self-worth on the part of its practitioners.

COMPETITIVE DINING
The classic locus for the division between production and consumption remains George Orwell's *Down and Out in Paris and London* (1933). It is no wonder that the great sociologist Erving Goffman, in his own classic work, *The Presentation of Self in Everyday Life* (1959), uses Orwell's description of a waiter entering the dining room to illustrate the division between backstage (the kitchen) and front stage (the public dining). Orwell (who had worked in Parisian restaurant kitchens) stressed the instant transformation in passing from one to the other.

Bénédict Beaugé (2013, part II) considers at length the Guide Michelin and cookbook production as vehicles of the democratization of French cuisine.

Media manipulation is also a matter of economic survival. The more haute the cuisine, the more expensive it is to run the restaurant. Supplemental income must come from outside sources—consulting, sales of cookbooks, appearances on the lecture circuit, and contracts with the food industry.

Although much has changed on the Manhattan restaurant scene since then, not least through the work of these chefs, the articulation of models of what a restaurant should do and be makes the interviews as illuminating now as two decades ago.

Consulting for airlines catering to the luxury market of business and first-class passengers is increasing. Foreign airlines have taken to recruiting top chefs—Joël Robuchon and other top French chefs for Air France; Gordon Ramsay, among others, for Singapore Airlines—and American airlines are following suit. See Mouawad (2012).

Chef Thomas Keller elaborates this ethic of the pursuit of unattainable perfection in an interview on the DVD of *Ratatouille*. Joël Robuchon claims happiness as the chef's goal ("on devient marchand de bonheur") in Robuchon and de Meureville (1995, 33).

FROM CULINARY CONNECTION TO SOCIAL TIE
Quotations in this section come from the following interviews with chefs:

Interview, Jean-Georges Vongerichten, chef-restaurateur, New York City, 29 August 1991, at his restaurant JoJo. As of January 2013, Vongerichten runs eight restaurants in New York City, one in Chicago, two each in the Bahamas, Las Vegas, Shanghai, and French West Indies, and one in Paris, plus sixteen others in collaboration with Culinary Concepts Hospitality Group.

Interview, Jean-Michel Bergougnoux, executive chef, Le Cygne, New York City, 24 July 1991. Three stars from the *New York Times* and twenty years in business did not keep Le Cygne from closing only a couple of weeks after our discussion, in early August 1991. Today Bergougnoux owns and runs L'Absinthe, a brasserie-restaurant on the Upper East Side of Manhattan.

Interview, Daniel Boulud, 21 October 1991, at Le Cirque, where he was then executive chef. As of January 2014, Boulud runs eight restaurants in New York, and one each in Miami, Palm Beach, Beijing, Singapore, London, Montreal, and Toronto.

Interview, Gilbert LeCoze, June 7, 1991, at his Manhattan restaurant Le Bernardin. LeCoze died of a heart attack only a few years later, at the age of forty-eight. Under LeCoze's successor, Chef Eric Ripert, Le Bernardin remains one of the top restaurants in New York City, with three Michelin stars and four from the *New York Times*. It is regularly ranked in the top ten best restaurants by Zagat's.

For Danny Meyer's comments on food trends, see the interview with Deborah Solomon (2006). Meyer began his restaurant empire with the 1985 opening of Union Square Café, which regularly figures among Zagat's favorite restaurants in Manhattan. As of 2012, Meyer's hospitality group has ten restaurants in New York, and his burger-milkshake Shake Shack has, at this writing, seven locations in New York, two in Washington, DC, and one each in Miami, Westport, CT, the racetrack at Saratoga, Kuwait, and Dubai.

Fisher makes her commentary in "The Perfect Dinner" ([1954] 1976, 736–744).

Culinary mavens will object to lumping into a single category culinary tendencies that are quite different, and while it is true that modernist cuisine (Myhrvold 2012), molecular gastronomy, and constructivist cuisine (This 2005, 2009) pursue different culinary ends, they share a determined, relentless focus on the culinary as opposed to the convivial and the social.

Keller's comments are from his interview with Shelasky (2011).

EXPLORATION AND EXPERIMENTATION
Ferran Adrià is not the only representative of this hypercreative cuisine, but he is the most visible and the most outspoken, and his kitchen has trained numerous

chefs who are now spread about the world. My discussion draws on M. Pilar Opazo's extensive research (2014) on elBulli restaurant and its transition to elBulli Foundation. All quotations in this section are from Opazo's wonderfully evocative interviews with Ferran Adrià and members of his team at elBulli and from Adrià's comments at a "Times Talk" on 1 October 2011 at the Food and Wine Festival in New York City (Opazo 2014).

Ferran Adrià offered his course at the Harvard School of Science and Engineering. See "Science and Cooking 2013 Lecture Series" course description and syllabus at www.seas.harvard.edu/cooking. Other chefs who participated include David Chang, Wylie Dufresne, Heston Blumenthal, and Nathan Myhrvold.

The kitchens of elBulli have been a training ground as important as Escoffier's in London at the end of the nineteenth century. Said David Chang: "More people have gone through Ferran's kitchen than any other kitchen. No question. . . . At the very minimum, you can say that Ferran opened the door for chefs in ways that the French chefs never did before" (Chang et al. 2012, 9–10).

The "young chef," Daniel Patterson of Coi in San Francisco, talked about Adrià's impact on how people think about cooking in a freewheeling conversation with four peers. (Chang et al. 2012, 9).

In 2013, Albert Adrià, Ferran's brother and erstwhile partner, opened a restaurant featuring Japanese-Peruvian cuisine (the cuisine that evolved from Japanese emigrants to Peru a century ago) in Barcelona. It emerged in the wake of elBulli and is distinct from it, especially in the modesty of the two tasting menus, the price, and its location in an unchic area of a major city. See Sexton (2013).

Extreme Cuisines
The parallels between cuisine and fashion that Bénédict Beaugé (2013) elaborates at length underscore the extreme volatility of both cultural phenomena.

The quote from the anonymous, "grateful" chef in New York City is taken from Opazo (2014).

Like many celebrity cookbooks aimed at the domestic market, Jean-Georges Vongerichten's recent entry (2011) into the cookbook market emphasizes family gatherings. His children and wife contribute recipes, and the photographs highlight the conviviality no less than the food.

One may wonder how much these cookbooks are actually used for cooking. The Vongerichten book, for instance, lists quantities in such fine, elegant, and light type as to be unreadable in the flurry of preparation. I ended up penning the ingredient measurements in bold ink and readable size, spoiling the presentation to make the cookbook usable. Every ambitious chef has to balance the working document against the coffee-table trophy. Even Ferran Adrià (2011) has produced a cookbook for home use.

HOW FAR IS TOO FAR?

Given the strong presence of tradition in French cuisine, it is understandable that extreme cuisine does not have a strong French inflection and that its most celebrated practitioners (Ferran Adrià; René Redzepi, of Noma in Copenhagen; Wylie Dufresne, of WD-50 in Manhattan; Nathan Myhrvold, head author of *Modernist Cuisine at Home* [2012]) are not French. However, French chemist (not chef) Hervé This (2005, 2009) first came up with the term *molecular gastronomy*.

CHAPTER SIX. DINING ON THE EDGE

For an extensive discussion of the implications of democratization of the food world and the inevitable conflict with the equally powerful urge for distinction, see Johnston and Baumann (2010). Pearlman (2013) explores in great detail the downscaling, or "casualization," of dining, which I call "informalization," from changes in restaurant design (open kitchens; sleek, ostentatiously modern décor), dress (the tie is now an endangered species), and behavior across the United States. The contrast with the often elaborate and invariably expensive food is all the more striking. Informalization may seem to be the road to democratization, but in fact it redefines the distinctions of elite dining. Pearlman is especially concerned with the contradictions of the "foodie" subculture in the United States.

Robert Altman's film *Gosford Park* (2004) is exemplary for its presentation of a succession of meals at a country estate in England in the late 1920s, including a picnic with staff in attendance and most of the appurtenances of formal dining (silver and glassware, floral centerpieces, butler and servers). The clueless American guest receives his comeuppance when he orders breakfast from the butler. "No Englishman," he is told sharply, "is ever served at breakfast." Other depictions of formal dining at home include Martin Scorsese's *The Age of Innocence* (1993), adapted from Edith Wharton's novel set in late nineteenth-century New York, and the 2010-2012 BBC costume drama series *Downton Abbey*, set in England before and after the Great War.

These imaginative reconstructions have a solid historical basis. Anyone wishing to compare to the "real thing" would do well to visit the Musée Nissim de Camondo, in Paris, where "below stairs" of a turn-of-the-century mansion has been completely restored to its modernized state circa 1910, from kitchen to service pantry and staff dining room, including a telephone for the chef to communicate with the butler "above stairs."

Thiébaut (1994) documents the ever-more-elaborate cutlery and dinnerware that came into fashion over the nineteenth into the twentieth century. See also Girveau (2001). For an example of a middle-class dowry (marriage in 1906), I put forward my grandmother's silverware with its thirty-six "nutpicks" [sic] and hand-embroidered (by her) heavy linen tablecloth and napkins.

Going "Out," Staying "In"

One indicator after another points to the increasing incidence of eating outside the home in contemporary postindustrial societies. A 2002 survey by the U.S. Department of Agriculture shows that eating out has steadily increased since 1972 and now accounts for fully half of all food expenditures in the United States. Some three-quarters of Americans eat out at least once a week. Nor are Americans alone in their fondness for consuming food in public places, lagging as they do behind the Japanese, who head the list.

See Stewart, Blisard, and Jolliffe (2006) on changing American culinary habits. With 196 meals out every year, the Japanese head the list, followed by Americans at 119; the Germans, British, Italians, and French clock in between 80 and 85; and the Dutch and the Belgians come in last with between 66 and 75 meals eaten out per year (Millstone and Lang 2008, 92-93). Figures are for 2005. In the Netherlands alone, from 1951 to 1981 the number of restaurants increased over 150 percent, that of café-restaurants more than doubled, and small food outlets increased almost twenty-fold (Albert de la Bruhèze and Otterloo 2003, 320).

Many of these establishments were classified according to the kinds of drinking they provided as well as their food: *guinguettes* were popular cabarets in the outskirts of Paris, where people ate and often danced as well; *auberges* were inns; *estaminets* were lower-class cafés in Northern France and Belgium focusing on beer and tobacco; *gargotes* were greasy spoons serving bad food; *bouchons* were small restaurants characteristic of Lyon; and *bouillons* were big restaurants serving traditional dishes such as *bouillon* (broth).

Jean-Paul Aron (1975) proposed the restaurant as a safety valve for an increasingly compartmentalized and gender-segregated bourgeois society. The club in England, arguably, served the same purpose. Both ratified the increasingly strict separation of the private sphere, to which women were relegated, and the public sphere, dominated by men, in which political, professional, and commercial life took place.

The traditional food culture in Norway only very recently adopted the practice of eating out based on (post)modern models that favor professionalized food preparation and make claims to gastronomic excellence. The results have been nothing short of spectacular (Amilien 2003). Surely this intense interest in food played a role in Norway's stellar performances at the recent cooking competitions of the Bocuse d'Or. Norway may have lagged behind other European countries in its culinary sophistication on some measures, but it certainly caught up fast: the Norwegian entrant has now won the gold medal at the Bocuse d'Or four times, most recently in 2009. Norway captured eight out of forty-two medals awarded from 1987 to 2013, second only to the ten total medals of the French.

Moveable Feasts
See Spang (2000) on the development of the restaurant in Paris and Grimes (2009) on restaurants in nineteenth-century New York.

READING MEALS
Pierre Bourdieu ([1979] 1984) applies the dichotomy between luxury and necessity specifically to matters of taste, identifying tastes of liberty or luxury *(goûts de luxe / liberté)* in contrast to tastes of necessity *(goûts de nécessité)*. For an exploration and critique of this division, see the articles in Ferguson and Régnier (2014).

Culinary Individualism

Flandrin (2007) tracks the times of meals in France from the Middle Ages through the nineteenth century, with a few cross-European comparisons.

The Paris restaurant Le Taillevent featured scrambled eggs (*oeufs brouillés*) on the menu as of December 2010.

INFORMALIZATION

See Garofalo (2011). Restaurant Daniel will not change its everyday dress code (jackets for dinner). That the dress code remains a bone of contention in the restaurant world is brought vividly to mind in *A Table in Heaven*, a documentary film about Sirio Maccioni's fabled restaurant Le Cirque and the decision to open a new Le Cirque in 2006. Maccioni stood firm for formality (jackets required), while his sons pushed for informality, arguing that it would bring in a younger crowd. Maccioni won the argument despite the list of the flexible dress codes at competitors' restaurants. Other restaurants compromise. Asked what he would do if a customer in a T-shirt refused to wear the jacket that that restaurant provided, a head waiter at Le Bernardin said that he'd put the jacket on the back of the chair.

NEW MENUS, NEW MEALS

For Le Bernardin's menus, see its website, at le-bernardin.com. As at all top-flight restaurants, the menu changes with the season. For a discussion of the makeover of Le Bernardin in 2011, comparing old and new décor, see Fabricant (2011).

For a revelatory introduction to *sole meunière*, see Child (2006) and the film version of the encounter in *Julie and Julia* (2009), in which the butter all but drips off the screen. For the repertory of French cuisine, see Montagné ([1939] 1961, but any edition will do). Counting is complicated because not all preparations have labels and there are repeats. Still, the point holds.

Georges Briguet, the French-Swiss owner of the restaurant Le Périgord in New York (author interview, 22 July 1991) further commented on the increasing importance of eye appeal: "A lot of restaurants are only interested in making the dish look like a Picasso painting. You look at the painting, but you eat your dinner. It makes no difference how beautiful a steak with cucumbers looks!" Briguet's respect for culinary tradition led him to a certain skepticism about the vogue for experimentation: "The chefs get carried away," not at the great restaurants, "but a lot of others don't pay attention."

Increasingly vivid photographs in magazines such as *Gastronomica* and *Saveur*, both aimed at the general foodphilic public, seek to convey distinctive textures with close-ups. Today's conception of presentation reaches beyond pastry to every dish.

André Jammet, the owner of the New York restaurant La Caravelle, gave the American preoccupation with new things as a reason for redecorating the restaurant (author interview, 16 September 1991). In 2004, La Caravelle closed, after forty-four years as what the media generally referred to as a "temple" of distinctive French haute cuisine.

Between Charisma and Routine
On the chef as brand, see Carter (2012).

BEYOND THE KITCHEN
In my interviews, chefs and restaurateurs alike invoked the importance of regular diners. In New York, where so many eat out virtually every night, treating regulars well is crucial to keep them returning. That this special treatment goes against the grain for many Americans is made clear in the controversy surrounding the 2013 review of Daniel by the *New York Times* restaurant critic Pete Wells (2013). In the assessment demoting the restaurant to three stars (from the four that it had held for over a decade), Wells noted the different treatment that he received as a critic from that of a friend, unknown to the restaurant, dining at the same time at another table. The friend did not complain about not receiving some of the over-the-top gestures that Wells got (a finger bowl, for one), but many of the comments on the review did complain. As any restaurateur will tell you, regulars are absolutely essential to the survival of any restaurant, low-end or high. The meal is part of a social context. Frank Bruni (2013), the former *New York Times* restaurant critic, identifies the pleasures of familiarity and of being known when dining out.

The terms from a range of restaurants underscore the importance of designating important customers. See Schott (2012).

The special language applies also to the dishes, and, as a trip to any diner will confirm, is not confined to upscale establishments. My favorite is from the Viand diners in Manhattan: "whiskey down" is rye toast ("whiskey" is rye bread). For a list of flavorful diner lingo, see "Diner Lingo," *The Free Dictionary*, http://encyclopedia.thefreedictionary.com/diner+lingo.

Although culinary memoirs date back at least to Carême, they have by and large focused on the professional development of the chef. Escoffier's *Souvenirs inédits* (1985) are a good example. The very definition of culinary relevance changed with Anthony Bourdain's vivid and salacious (lots of drugs and sex) "tell-all" memoir, *Kitchen Confidential* (2000). So unusual was Bourdain that one commentator (Fine 2008, xi) divides culinary history in the United States, into eras before and after *Kitchen Confidential*. Notable memoirs on the American culinary scene include those by Jacques Pépin (2003), Bill Buford (2006), Gabriella Hamilton (2011), Adam Gopnik (2011), and Marcus Samuelsson (2012). There will assuredly be more.

Daniel Humm is quoted by McBride (2012): "Humm is changing his game plan yet again, turning the meal at Eleven Madison into "an extravagant, participatory, close-to-four-hour ode to the romance and history of New York." See Gordinier (2012).

CHAPTER SEVEN. HAUTE FOOD
The characterization of "endless reinvention" is from Eleven Madison chef Daniel Humm riffing off Miles Davis's model for jazz. See Wells (2013).

New Food in New Places
The menu from Restaurant Jean-Georges is taken from the restaurant's listing on *New York Magazine*'s website, http://nymag.com/listings/restaurant/jean-georges/menus/main.html Spring 2012.

Vongerichten reordered menus beginning with his time at the Lafayette Hotel, where he set up the menu in four blocks—vinaigrettes, infused oils, bouillons, and vegetable reductions—to guide diners and to keep them from doubling up on any one ingredient (say, ordering a vinaigrette in a salad and a fish cooked with the same vinaigrette). "The menu let people make their own choice," he said. "And it worked" (author interview, Jean-Georges Vongerichten, 29 August 1991).

The emphasis on generosity came out in my interviews with chefs. Sharon Zukin and I shared cappuccinos with David Bouley (interview, 31 May 1991); Sharon had a dinner at Le Cirque after her interview with restaurateur Sirio Maccioni; and I had lunch in a private dining room at Le Bernardin during my interview with Gilbert LeCoze (7 June 1991).

Consideration of interconnected reciprocal obligations attendant upon the giving and receiving of gifts starts with Marcel Mauss's extraordinary essay *The Gift* ([1925] 1990).

Haute Food and Everyday Life

General references to "haute" tend to be more casual than analytical (a blog with food paintings or photographs of food or cartoons such as the one that opens this section). I use the term "haute food" to refer to the abstraction of the individual dish from a traditional or conventional culinary context. There are, of course, other models of meals. Spanish tapas and Chinese dim sum exemplify meals that do not follow the order that dominates in Western cuisines.

Samuelsson (2012) makes a point about the care taken to calibrate an innovative menu. However, the frame—the menu—needs to be within the "comfort zone" of the diner. So, for a 1990s restaurant public, salmon brushed in miso, wrapped in Thai basil, served with fennel and a broth of kaffir lime leaves, lemongrass, galangal, and yuzu would turn up on the menu as crispy salmon with orange broth and grilled fennel. Wasabi went public as horseradish. Samuelsson explained: "The key was presenting these things in accessible, understandable terms, which kept customers in their comfort zone." The young chef (he was only twenty-four when he took over as executive chef at Aquavit in Manhattan) was acutely aware of the need to balance his responsibility to the customer with the (greater) responsibility to upgrade the food, and aware too of the difficulty of achieving that balance (Samuelsson 2012, 188).

Samuelsson worked long and hard to come up with the signature dish that every ambitious chef needs to make his mark in the world, to set himself against the competition and anchor his reputation. It is not easy, and Samuelsson makes a point of noting just how unusual it is to come up with something that does more than simply "tweak" well-known dishes.

Traditional cuisine is both opportunity and constraint (Michael Romano, interview, 30 May 1991). In a younger generation, chef Marcus Samuelsson (2012), born and raised abroad, explicitly addresses the constraints of French cuisine. He grew up with Swedish home cooking, learned French techniques and dishes in professional kitchens in Sweden and in Europe, and cooked French cuisine everywhere but sought out local ingredients. However, he did not actually work in a top French kitchen until he was in New York. Much later still he discovered his native Ethiopia and its cuisine.

My interview with Jean-Georges Vongerichten took place on 29 August 1991 at his restaurant JoJo. Vongerichten spent two years in Bangkok, one in Singapore, and another in Hong Kong.

ORDINARY LUXURY
See Murphy (2012) for Wendy's Surf & Turf Burger. Wendy's manager discussed the transformation from mass-market business to gourmet market, intended to meet Japanese expectations of quality and variety. The proven business model of fast food marketing had to be adapted to Japanese tastes. The lobster and caviar burger was a LTO (limited-time offer).

Boulud's upscale burger is found at db Bistro Moderne and at his Miami and Singapore restaurants. See his website, www.danielnyc.com, for details about Daniel Boulud's ever-expanding culinary empire, in the United States and abroad, which included as of 2012, eight restaurants in New York City, two in Florida, and five abroad.

Chicago mayor Richard Daley declared the foie gras ban "silly," and it was repealed in 2008.

In July 2012, a foie gras ban, voted in 2004, went into effect in California.

Culinary Individualism
Amy Trubek (2008) explores the assimilation of the French concept of *terroir* (more usually associated with wine) into an American lexicon.

On Paul Bocuse's career and influence, see Mognard (2012).

René Redzepi of Noma explains his philosophy and practice in the film *Three Stars* (2010), where he is shown foraging in what seem to be the suburbs around Copenhagen. The restaurant's website (http://noma.dk/) clarifies his perspective: "In an effort to shape our way of cooking, we look to our landscape and delve into our ingredients and culture, hoping to rediscover our history and shape our future." Noma currently occupies the top position on the San Pellegrino list of fifty best restaurants in the world. It attained first place in 2010, when it took over from elBulli, which had occupied the top spot five times between the 2002, the award's first year, and 2010, the year that Ferran Adrià closed his restaurant. See "The Worlds Fifty Best Restaurants," www.theworlds50best.com/awards/1-50-winners/.

Michelin three-star French chef Alain Passard (author interview, 13 March 2001) talked about the need for identifying the "passport" of the foods that he served so that he would know how to treat them. It was vital for him to have been on the fishing boat and to have seen the exact spot off the Ile d'Yeu on the Atlantic coast where his fish had been caught. The quotation from Charlie Trotter comes from the author interview, 9 November 1991 at his restaurant in Chicago.

The interview with Gilbert LeCoze took place on 7 June 1991, at Le Bernardin, New York City.

The Fulton Fish Market where LeCoze sourced his fish was established in 1822 in Lower Manhattan. In 2005 all operations were moved to the Hunts Point Food Distribution Center in the Bronx, where the fish market shares space with markets for produce and meat. The newly expanded Fulton Fish Market Cooperative is the largest wholesale fish market in the United States and second in size world-wide only to Tokyo's Tsukiji wholesale seafood market. My thanks for insight into the wholesale food market as an organization to Daniel Leong (2010).

The success of Michael Pollan's works (2006, 2013) testifies to the hold of the utopian vision of self-sustainability. It is symptomatic that the meals whose loving preparation takes up both books are largely a one-man enterprise.

The increasing incidence of allergies has occasioned a great deal of controversy. I am interested in the ways in which the consciousness of what might be called allergy rights has affected culinary practice. Allergy sensitivity, individually and collectively, varies greatly both across and within cultures.

While the religious directives are well-established and reinforced by rituals and by organization of the food system, in certain milieus vegetarianism has elaborated both rituals and social organization sufficiently robust to support a collective definition. See Abramson (2012).

THE TUESDAY VEGETARIAN
On these varieties of vegetarianism see Ricker (2010). *The Vegetarian Times* reported a 2008 study showing that 3.2 percent of American adults (7.3 million) follow a "vegetarian-based diet" (of whom 1 million, or 0.5 percent of American adults, are vegan), while another 10 percent (22.8 million) follow a "vegetarian-inclined" diet. See "Vegetarianism in America," *Vegetarian Times,* www .vegetariantimes.com/article/vegetarianism-in-america/. Government-mandated practices such as food labeling facilitate this (and other) diet individualization.

AT TABLE
In one of the clearest presentations of the tension between solidarity and individualism, Simmel ([1904] 1957) characterizes fashion as a product of this dynamic between the inclination to participation in a collective enterprise and the will to sever one's self from that collectivity. The model analysis of the meal is Simmel ([1910] 1997).

The quotes in this section from *To The Lighthouse* are from chapters 17 and 18 of Woolf ([1927] 1989, 99–102, 104–107, 111, 112).

TALKING TOQUES

For other organizational models of the professional kitchen, I think of the only three-star restaurant featured in the documentary film *Three Stars* (2010) in which the chef-restaurateur is a woman. Chef Luisa Valazza's mode of operation in her Piedmontese restaurant, Al Sorriso, downplays hierarchy and an elaborate division of labor (her mother works in the kitchen, as does her son; her husband is the manager). This internationally recognized chef runs her restaurant almost like a family.

Even though Anne-Sophie Pic's kitchen is rigorously organized on the traditional brigade system, the only woman in France to have received three Michelin stars (of a total of twenty-five in France) deviates from what she considers a masculine model. Pic explains that her conception of cuisine is feminine, by which she means privileging emotion over technique. See Becky Anderson (2012). In an interview soon after her restaurant received the coveted third star (in 2007), Pic argued that women feel no need for the yelling and posturing that marks the (male) professional kitchen. See Euan Ferguson (2007). This article also covers Michelin three-star women chefs in Europe, including Luisa Valazza.

AND SO?

On the revival of tradition among contemporary chefs, see Buford (2013), who recounts Daniel Boulud's search for three classic recipes of French cuisine that have fallen out of favor: *chartreuse*, a game-bird confection inside a vegetable mold; *coulibiac*, salmon in pastry; and *canard à la presse*, a roast duck whose juices are extracted by a very special duck press. For each of these dishes, considerable historical research informed the work in the kitchen.

EPILOGUE. LAST WORDS: *RATATOUILLE*

Ratatouille, directed by Brad Bird and Jan Pinkava (also screenwriter and writer, respectively), won the Oscar for Best Animated Film. Readers should consult the DVD of the film, which features extensive interconnected interviews between Bird and the film's culinary consultant, chef Thomas Keller, whose two restaurants (the French Laundry, in Napa, California, and Per Se, in New York City) have both received three Michelin stars. Preparation involved sending key staff animators to observe chef Keller at the French Laundry to observe how food looks as it is cooked. An obligatory trip to Paris gave the animators a sense of place and of the cuisine that they would be working to convey.

There is a significant body of literature on "food films." For a start, see the articles in Bower (2004) and my discussion of "Babette's Feast" (Ferguson 2004) and "Eat Drink Man Woman" (Ferguson 2011).

The comic associations of food that dominate discussion and representation reach far into the past. The eight hundred or so works that Athenaeus refers to in *The Deipnosphists* (see chapter 3) are mostly comic, and *Ratatouille* works off and with those associations. Cartoons have their requirements, after all. But the analysis of creativity—what it is, where it comes from, how it is nurtured—and the dynamics of cooking and dining take the film far beyond facile body associations. No wonder A. O. Scott (2007) called *Ratatouille* "one of the most persuasive portraits of an artist ever committed to film."

The discussion of the characters' names draws on my article with Gary Alan Fine, "Sociology at the Stove" (Ferguson and Fine 2008). However important the association in the film, there is no connection between rats and ratatouille, a vegetable stew of tomatoes, onions, eggplant, and zucchini. The word *ratatouille* entered French in the late eighteenth century as a variant of the verb *touiller* or *ratouiller*, meaning "to stir."

A. O. Scott (2007) called *Ratatouille*'s sensibility "both exuberantly democratic and unabashedly elitist, defending good taste and aesthetic accomplishment not as snobbish entitlements but as universal ideals."

Abbott, Andrew. 1988. *The System of Professions: An Essay on the Division of Expert Labor*. Chicago: University of Chicago Press.

Abramson, Julia. 2012. "Food and Ethics." In *Routledge International Handbook of Food Studies*, edited by K. Albala, 371–378. London: Routledge.

Albala, Ken. 2002. *Eating Right in the Renaissance*. Berkeley: University of California Press.

Albert de la Bruhèze, Adri, and Anneke H. van Otterloo. 2003. "Snacks and Snack Culture and the Rise of Eating Out in the Netherlands in the Twentieth Century." In *Eating Out in Europe: Picnics, Gourmet Dining and Snacks since the Late Eighteenth Century*, edited by Marc Jacobs and Peter Scholliers, 317–334. Oxford: Berg.

Amilien, Virginie. 2003. "The Rise of Restaurants in Norway in the Twentieth Century." In *Eating Out in Europe: Picnics, Gourmet Dining and Snacks since the Late Eighteenth Century*, edited by Marc Jacobs and Peter Scholliers, 179–193. Oxford: Berg.

Amilien, Virginie, Silje Skuland, and Sigurd Bergflødt, eds. 2012. "Nordic Food Cultures." *Anthropology of Food* S7. http://aof.revues.org/6950.

Anderson, Becky. 2012. " 'World's Best Female Chef' Shares Recipe for Success." CNN, April 10. www.cnn.com/2012/04/10/world/europe/anne-sophie-pic /index.html.

Anderson, Benedict. 1983. *Imagined Communities: Reflections on the Origin and Spread of Nationalism*. London: Verso.

Appadurai, Arjun. 1988. "How to Make a National Cuisine: Cookbooks in Contemporary India." *Comparative Studies in Society and History* 30 (3): 3–24.

Aron, Jean-Paul. 1975. *The Art of Eating in France: Manners and Menus in the Nineteenth Century*. Translated by Nina Rootes. London: Owen.

Athenaeus of Naucratis. 1969. *The Deipnosophists of Athenaeus of Naucratis*. Translated and introduced by C. B. Gulick. 7 vols. Cambridge, MA: Harvard University Press.

Beaugé, Bénédict. 2013. *Plats du jour: Sur l'idée de nouveauté en cuisine*. Paris: Métaillié.

Beaugé, Bénédict, and Sébastien Demorand. 2009. *Les cuisines de la critique gastronomique*. Paris: Presses de Sciences Po.

Benjamin, Walter. 1999. *The Arcades Project*. Cambridge, MA: Harvard University Press.

Bestor, Theodore C. 2000. "How Sushi Went Global." *Foreign Policy* 121 (Nov.-Dec.): 54–63.

Bidgood, Jess. 2012. "Oxen's Fate Is Embattled as the Abattoir Awaits." *New York Times*, 28 October. www.nytimes.com/2012/10/29/us/oxens-possible-slaughter-prompts-fight-in-vermont.html.

Boulud, Daniel. 2003. *Letters to a Young Chef*. New York: Basic Books.

Bourdain, Anthony. 2000. *Kitchen Confidential: Adventures in the Culinary Underbelly*. New York: Bloomsbury.

———. 2010. *Medium Raw: A Bloody Valentine to the World of Food and the People Who Cook*. New York: Harper Collins.

Bourdieu, Pierre. (1979) 1984. *Distinction: A Social Critique of the Judgement of Taste*. Cambridge, MA: Harvard University Press.

———. 1993. *The Field of Cultural Production*. New York: Columbia University Press.

Bower, Anne L. 2004. *Reel Food: Essays on Food and Film*. New York Routledge.

Braund, David, and John Wilkins, eds. 2001. *Athenaeus and His World: Reading Greek Culture in the Roman Empire*. Exeter: University of Exeter Press.

Briffault, Eugène. 1846. *Paris à table*. Illustrated by Bertall. Paris: Hetzel.

Brillat-Savarin, J. A. (1826) 1839. *Physiologie du goût ou, Mèditations de gastronomie transcendante; ouvrage théorique, historique et à l'ordre du jour, dédié aux gastronomes parisiens, par un professeur.* Paris: Hetzel.

———. (1949) 2009. *The Physiology of Taste: Or, Meditations on Transcendental Gastronomy.* Translated and edited by M. F. K. Fisher and introduced by Bill Buford. New York: Knopf.

Bruni, Frank. 2013. "Familiarity Breeds Content: Frank Bruni, Former Restaurant Critic, on the Joys of Repeat Visits." *New York Times,* 17 September. www.nytimes.com/2013/09/18/dining/frank-bruni-former-restaurant-critic-on-the-joys-of-repeat-visits.html.

Buford, Bill. 2006. *Heat.* New York: Knopf.

———. 2013. "Cooking with Daniel." *New Yorker,* 29 July, 46–55.

Capatti, Alberto, and Massimo Montanari. 2003. *Italian Cuisine: A Cultural History.* Translated by Aine O'Healy. New York: Columbia University Press.

Carême, M. A. (1815a) 1841. *Le pâtissier royal parisien, ou Traité élémentaire et pratique de la pâtisserie ancienne et moderne, de l'entremets de sucre, des entrées froides et des socles suivi d'observations utiles aux progrès de cet art, d'une série de plus de soixante menus, et d'une revue critique des grands bals de 1810 et 1811.* 2 vols. Paris: No publisher given.

———. (1815b) 1842. *Le pâtissier pittoresque.* Paris: Chez l'Éditeur, rue Thérèse, n. 11.

———. (1822) 1842. *Le maître d'hôtel français Traité des menus.* 2 vols. Paris: J. Renouard et Cie.

———. (1828) 1986. *Le cuisinier parisien, ou l'art de la cuisine française au dix-neuvième siècle.* Lyon: Éditions Dioscor.

———. 1833. *L'art de la cuisine française au dix-neuvième siècle: Traité élémentaire et pratique suivi de dissertations culinaires et gastronomiques utiles aux progrès de cet art.* 2 vols. Paris: Chez l'auteur.

Carter, Adrienne. 2012. "Marcus Samuelsson, a Chef, a Brand and Then Some." *New York Times,* 5 August. www.nytimes.com/2012/08/05/business/marcus-samuelsson-both-a-chef-and-a-brand.html.

Chang, David, Sat Bains, Claude Bosi, and Daniel Patterson. 2012. "Chef Rant." *Lucky Peach* 3 (Spring): 4–13.

Chang, K. C., ed. 1977. *Food in Chinese Culture: Anthropological and Historical Perspectives.* New Haven: Yale University Press.

Child, Julia. 1975. "How Good is the New *Joy of Cooking?*" *McCall's*, October, 63–68.

———. 2006. *My Life in France*. With Alex Prudhomme. New York: Knopf.

Clark, Priscilla P. 1987. *Literary France: The Making of a Culture*. Berkeley: University of California Press.

Colapinto, John. 2012. "Check, Please." *New Yorker*, 10 September, 58–65.

Cooper, James Fenimore. (1838) 1956. *The American Democrat: Or, Hints on the Social and Civic Relations of the United States of America*. New York: Vintage.

Cowen, Ruth. 2006. *Relish: The Extraordinary Life of Alexis Soyer, Victorian Celebrity Chef*. London: Weidenfeld and Nicolson.

Davis, Jennifer J. 2013. *Defining Culinary Authority: The Transformation of French Cooking*. Baton Rouge: Louisiana State University Press.

Davis, Mitchell, Anne McBride, et al. 2008. "The State of American Cuisine." White paper, James Beard Foundation. http://homestaging.iceculinary.com/news/articles/article_53.shtml.

———. 2009. "Eating Out, Eating American: New York Restaurant Dining and Identity." In *Gastropolis: Food and New York City*, edited by Annie Hauck-Lawson and Jonathan Deutsch, 293–307. New York: Columbia University Press.

DeSoucey, Michaela. 2010. "Gastronationalism: Food Traditions and Authenticity Politics in the European Union." *American Sociological Review* 75 (June): 432–456.

Diner, Hasia R. 2001. *Hungering for America: Italian, Irish, and Jewish Foodways in the Age of Migration*. Cambridge, MA: Harvard University Press.

Dumas, Alexandre. (1873) 2000. *Grand dictionnaire de cuisine*. Paris: Phébus.

Durkheim, Emile. (1897) 1951. *Suicide: A Study in Sociology*. Translated by John A. Spaulding and George Simpson. Glencoe, IL: Free Press.

———. (1912) 1995. *The Elementary Forms of Religious Life*. Translated by K. Fields. New York: Free Press.

Edlow, Jonathan. 2009. *The Deadly Dinner Party: And Other Medical Detective Stories*. New Haven: Yale University Press.

Elias, Norbert. 1994. *The History of Manners*. In *The Civilizing Process* (1939), translated by E. Jephcott, 1–256. Oxford: Blackwell.

Escoffier, Auguste. 1985. *Souvenirs inédits: 75 ans au service de l'art culinaire*. Marseille: Éditions Jeanne Laffitte.

Eyal, Gil. 2013. "For a Sociology of Expertise: The Social Origins of the Autism Epidemic." *American Journal of Sociology* 118 (4): 863–907.

Fabricant, Florence. 2011. "A Transformed Bernardin Is Set to Reopen." *New York Times*, 6 September. www.nytimes.com/2011/09/07/dining/le-bernardin-reopens-after-makeover.html.

Ferguson, Euan. 2007. "Michelin Women." *The Observer*, 24 March. www .theguardian.com/lifeandstyle/2007/mar/25/foodanddrink.features11.

Ferguson, Priscilla Parkhurst. 1998. "A Cultural Field in the Making: Gastronomy in 19th-century France." *American Journal of Sociology* 104 (3): 597–641.

———. 2004. *Accounting for Taste: The Triumph of French Cuisine*. Chicago: University of Chicago Press.

———. 2008. Introduction to *Les Bons Plats de France* (1913), by Pampille, 5–14. Paris: CNRS Éditions.

———. 2011. "The Senses of Taste." *American Historical Review* 119 (April): 371–384.

———. 2012. "La Gastronomie." In *Dictionnaire des cultures et des modèles alimentaires*, edited by J. P. Poulain, 616–622. Paris: Presses Universitaires de France.

Ferguson, Priscilla Parkhurst, and Gary Fine. 2008. "Sociology at the Stove." *Contexts* 7 (1): 59–61.

Ferguson, Priscilla Parkhurst, and Faustine Régnier, eds. 2014. "Manger entre plaisirs et nécessités." *Sociologie et sociétés* 47 (September).

Ferrières, Madeleine. (2002) 2006. *Mad Cow, Sacred Cow: A History of Food Fears*. Translated by Jody Gladding. New York: Columbia University Press.

Fine, Gary Alan. 2008. *Kitchen: The Culture of Restaurant Work*. 2nd edition. Berkeley: University of California Press.

Fischler, Claude. 1990. *L'Homnivore*. Paris: Odile Jacob.

Fischler, Claude, and Estelle Masson, eds. 2007. *Manger: Français, Européens et Américains face à l'alimentation*. Paris: Odile Jacob.

Fisher, M. F. K. (1954) 1976. *The Art of Eating*. New York: Random House.

Fitch, Noel Riley. 1999. *Appetite for Life: The Biography of Julia Child*. New York: Doubleday.

Flandrin, Jean-Louis. 2007. *Arranging the Meal: A History of Table Service in France*. Translated by Julie E. Johnson. Berkeley: University of California Press.

Flandrin, Jean-Louis, and Massimo Montanari, eds. (1996) 1999. *Food: A Culinary History*. New York: Columbia University Press.

Fourier, Charles. 1966–1968. *Oeuvres completes.* 12 vols. Paris: Anthropos.

Franklin, Benjamin. 1961. *The Autobiography and Other Writings.* New York: Signet.

Freedman, Paul, ed. 2007. *Food: The History of Taste.* Berkeley: University of California Press.

Freedman, Paul, and James Warlick. 2011. "High-End Dining in the Nineteenth-Century United States." *Gastronomica* 11 (1): 44–52.

Friedman, Andrew. 2009. *Knives at Dawn: America's Quest for Culinary Glory at the Legendary Bocuse d'Or Competition.* New York: Free Press.

Gabaccia, Donna R. 1998. *We Are What We Eat: Ethnic Food and the Making of Americans.* Cambridge, MA: Harvard University Press.

Garofalo, Christina. 2011. "Dine in Blue Jeans with Daniel Boulud." *Robb Report*, 15 February.2011.http://robbreport.com/Fine-Dining/Dine-in-Blue-Jeans-with-Daniel-Boulud.

Gigante, Denise. 2005. *Gusto: Essential Writings in Nineteenth-Century Gastronomy.* New York: Routledge.

Girveau, Bruno, ed. 2001. *A table au XIXe siècle.* Paris: Flammarion.

Goffman, Erving. 1959. *The Presentation of Self in Everyday Life.* New York: Doubleday-Anchor.

Goody, Jack, ed. 1975. *Literacy in Traditional Societies.* Cambridge: Cambridge University Press.

Gopnik, Adam. 2011. *The Table Comes First: Family, France, and the Meaning of Food.* New York: Knopf.

Gordinier, Jeff. 2012. "A Restaurant of Many Stars Raises the Ante." *New York Times,* 27 July. www.nytimes.com/2012/07/28/dining/eleven-madison-park-is-changing-things-up.html.

Grimes, William. 2009. *Appetite City: A Culinary History of New York.* New York: North Point Press.

Grimod de La Reynière, Alexandre Balthazar Laurent. 1997. *Écrits gastronomiques.* Edited by Jean-Claude Bonnet. Paris: UGE-10/18.

Hamilton, Gabrielle. 2011. *Blood, Bones, and Butter: The Inadvertent Education of a Restaurant Chef.* New York: Random House.

Han, Katherine. 2008. "*Sik Gaek:* Family, Legacy, and Identity in a Korean TV Series." Paper, Sociology 2230, Columbia University, Fall.

Hohenadel, Kristin. 2010. "Rigor Required, Cream Puffs Need Not Apply." *New York Times*, 1 September. www.nytimes.com/2010/09/05/movies/05pastry.html.

Homer. 1996. *The Odyssey*. Translated by R. Fagles. New York: Penguin.

Hyman, Mary, and Philip Hyman. 1999. "Printing the Kitchen: French Cookbooks, 1480–1800." In *Food: A Culinary History*, edited by J. Flandrin and M. Montanari, 394–402. New York: Columbia University Press.

Issenberg, Sasha. 2008. *The Sushi Economy: Globalization and the Making of a Modern Delicacy*. New York: Penguin.

Jacobs, Marc, and Peter Scholliers. 2003. "*Vaut ou ne vaut pas le détour:* Conviviality, Custom(er)s and Public Places of New Taste since the Late Eighteenth Century." In *Eating Out in Europe: Picnics, Gourmet Dining and Snacks since the Late Eighteenth Century*, edited by Marc Jacobs and Peter Scholliers, 1–15. Oxford: Berg.

Jeanneret, Michel. (1987) 1991. *A Feast of Words: Banquets and Table Talk in the Renaissance*. Translated by J. Whiteley and E. Hughes. Cambridge: Polity Press–University of Chicago Press.

Johnston, Josée, and Shyon Baumann. 2010. *Foodies: Democracy and Distinction in the Gourmet Foodscape*. New York: Routledge.

Judt, Tony. 2009. "Food." *New York Review of Books* blog. www.nybooks.com/blogs/nyrblog/2009/nov/25/food.

Kamp, David. 2007. *The United States of Arugula: The Sun Dried, Cold Pressed, Dark Roasted, Extra Virgin Story of the American Food Revolution*. New York: Broadway Books.

Khare, R. S. 1992. *The Eternal Food: Gastronomic Ideas and Experiences of Hindus and Buddhists*. SUNY Series in Hindu Studies. Albany: State University of New York Press.

King, Shirley, ed. and trans. 2006. *Pampille's Table: Recipes and Writings from the French Countryside from Marthe Daudet's* Les Bons Plats de France. Lincoln: University of Nebraska Press.

Leong, Daniel. 2010. "With: Mechanisms of Inclusion and Community at the New Fulton Fish Market." Paper, Sociology 2230, Columbia University, Spring.

Luciani, Noémie. 2012. "'Les Saveurs du palais': La cuisinière du président d'un autre temps." *Le Monde*, 18 September. www.lemonde.fr/culture/article

/2012/09/18/les-saveurs-du-palais-la-cuisiniere-du-president-d-un-au-
tre-temps_1761523_3246.html.

Massialot, François. (1691) 1698. *Le Cuisinier roïal et bourgeois*. 3rd. ed. Paris:
Charles de Sercy.

Mauss, Marcel. (1925) 1990. *The Gift: The Form and Reason for Exchange in Archaic
Societies*. Translated by W. D. Halls. New York: W. W. Norton.

McBride, Anne. 2012. "An Interview with Daniel Humm." *Gastronomica* 12 (2):
96–99.

Mendelson, Anne. 2003. *Stand Facing the Stove: The Story of the Women Who Gave
America* The Joy of Cooking. New York: Scribner.

Menger, Pierre-Michel. 2002. *Portrait de l'artiste en travailleur: Métamorphoses du
capitalisme*. Paris: Le Seuil.

———. (2009) 2014. *The Economics of Creativity: Art and Achievement under Uncertainty*. Cambridge, MA: Harvard University Press.

———. 2013. "The Power of Imagination and the Economy of Desire: Durkheim
and Art." In "*Durkheimian Studies/Études Durkheimiennes* 19 (Winter):
77–94.

Mennell, Stephen. 1985. *All Manners of Food: Eating and Taste in England and France
from the Middle Ages to the Present*. Oxford: Basil Blackwell.

Miller, William Ian. 1997. *The Anatomy of Disgust*. Cambridge, MA: Harvard University Press.

Millstone, Erik, and Tim Lang. 2008. *The Atlas of Food: Who Eats What, Where, and
Why*. Berkeley: University of California Press.

Milne, A. A. (1926) 1992. *Winnie-the-Pooh*. New York: Penguin-Puffin.

Mintz, Sidney W. 1996. *Tasting Food, Tasting Freedom: Excursions into Eating, Culture, and the Past*. Boston: Beacon.

Mognard, Élise. 2012. "Paul Bocuse." In *Dictionnaire des cultures alimentaires*,
edited by J. P. Poulain, 188–192. Paris: PUF.

Monselet, Charles. 1859. *La cuisinière poétique*. Paris: Michel Lévy Frères.

Montagné, Prosper. (1939) 1961. *Larousse gastronomique*. Edited by C. Turgeon and
N. Freund. New York: Crown Publishers.

Montanari, Massimo. 2010. *L'identitá italina in cucina*. Rome: Laterza.

Moskin, Julia. 2009a. "A Boeuf Bourguignon In (Gasp!) Five Steps." *New York
Times*, 26 August. www.nytimes.com/2009/08/26/dining/26fren.html.

———. 2009b. "Culinary Diplomacy With a Side of Kimchi." *New York Times*, 22 September. www.nytimes.com/2009/09/23/dining/23kore.html.

Mouawad, Jad. 2012. "Beyond Mile-High Grub: Can Airline Food Be Tasty?" *New York Times*, 11 March. www.nytimes.com/2012/03/11/business/airlines-studying-the-science-of-better-in-flight-meals.html.

Mukerji, Chandra. 1997. *Territorial Ambitions and the Gardens at Versailles.* Cambridge: Cambridge University Press.

Murphy, Eamon. 2012. "Lobster and Caviar Burgers? Wendy's Menu Goes Upscale in Japan." *DailyFinance*, 8 August. www.dailyfinance.com/2012/08/08/wendys-lobster-caviar-burgers-japan.

Myhrvold, Nathan. 2012. *Modernist Cuisine at Home.* With Maxime Bilet. Bellevue, WA: The Cooking Lab.

Naulin, Sidonie. 2012. "Le journalisme gastronomique: Sociologie d'un dispositif de médiation marchande." Thesis, Docteur de l'Université, Université Paris-Sorbonne.

Nestle, Marion. 2002. *Food Politics: How the Food Industry Influences Nutrition and Health.* Berkeley: University of California Press.

Ohnuki-Tierney, Emiko. 1997. "McDonald's in Japan: Changing Manners and Etiquette." In *Golden Arches East: McDonald's in East Asia*, edited by James L. Watson, 61–82. Stanford, CA: Stanford University Press.

Ong, Bao. 2010. "SPAM: Asia and America in a Can." MA essay, School of Journalism, Columbia University.

Opazo, M. Pilar. 2012. "Discourse as Driver of Innovation in Contemporary Haute Cuisine: The Case of elBulli Restaurant. *International Journal of Gastronomy and Food Science* 1 (2): 82–89. http://dx.doi.org/10.1016/j.ijgfs.2013.06.001.

———. 2014. "Appetite for Innovation." PhD dissertation, Columbia University, Department of Sociology.

Ory, Pascal. 1998. *Le Discours gastronomique français des origines à nos jours.* Paris: Gallimard-Archives.

Paddock, Catharine. 2010. "US Man Discovers He Has Pea Plant Growing in His Lung." *Medical News Today*, 12 August. www.medicalnewstoday.com/articles/197623.php.

Pampille [Marthe Allard Daudet]. (1913) 2008. *Les bons plats de France: Cuisine régionale.* Paris: CNRS Éditions.

Parasecoli, Fabio. 2009. "The Chefs, the Entrepreneurs, and Their Patrons: The Avant-Garde Food Scene in New York City." In *Gastropolis: Food and New York City*, edited by Annie Hauck-Lawson and Jonathan Deutsch, 116–131. New York: Columbia University Press.

Paul, Harry W. 1996. *Science, Vine, and Wine in Modern France*. Cambridge: Cambridge University Press.

Pearlman, Alison. 2013. *Smart Casual: The Transformation of Gourmet Restaurant Style in America*. Chicago: University of Chicago Press.

Pépin, Jacques. 2003. *The Apprentice: My Life in the Kitchen*. New York: Houghton-Mifflin.

Pham, Anne-Laure. 2012. "Danièle Mazet-Delpeuch: 'Je n'ai touché à une casserole qu'à 19 ans.'" Interview, *L'Express*, 19 September. www.lexpress.fr/styles/saveurs/daniele-mazet-delpeuch-je-n-ai-touche-a-une-casserole-qu-a-19-ans_1163241.html.

Polan, Dana. 2011. *Julia Child's* The French Chef. Durham: Duke University Press.

Pollan, Michael. 2001. *The Botany of Desire: A Plant's-Eye View of the World*. New York: Random House.

———. 2006. *The Omnivore's Dilemma: A Natural History of Four Meals*. New York: Penguin.

———. 2009. *Food Rules: An Eater's Manual*. New York: Penguin.

———. 2013. *Cooked: A Natural History of Transformation*. New York: Penguin.

Poulain, Jean-Pierre. 2012. "La gastronominalisation des cuisines de terroir." In *Dictionnaire des cultures alimentaires*, edited by Jean-Pierre Poulain, 622–628. Paris: PUF.

Powell, Robert M. 2010. "What Makes a Dessert? A Study of Five of New York City's Top Pastry Chefs." Paper, Sociology 2230, Columbia University, Spring.

Proust, Marcel. (1913–1927) 1987–1989. *A la recherche du temps perdu*. 4 vols. Paris: Gallimard-Pléiade.

Quellier, Florent. 2010. *Gourmandise: Histoire d'un péché capital*. Paris: Armand Colin.

Rambourg, Patrick. 2010. *Histoire de la cuisine et de la gastronomie françaises*. Paris: Éditions Perrin.

Rao, Hayagreeva, Philippe Monin, and Rodolphe Durand. 2003. "Institutional Change in Toqueville: Nouvelle Cuisine as an Identity Movement in French Gastronomy." *American Journal of Sociology* 108 (4): 795–843.

Ray, Krishnendu, and Tulasi Svrinivas, eds. 2012. *Curried Cultures: Globalization, Food, and South Asia*. Berkeley: University of California Press.

Reardon, Joan. 1994. *M. F. K. Fisher, Julia Child, and Alice Waters: Celebrating the Pleasures of the Table*. New York: Harmony Books.

Redfield, James. 1985. "Herodotus the Tourist." *Classical Philology* 80 (2): 97–118.

Ricker, Isabel. 2010. "The Part-time Vegetarian." Paper, Sociology 2230 Columbia University, Spring.

Robuchon, Joël, and Elisabeth de Meureville. 1995. *Le carnet de route d'un compagnon cuisinier*. Paris: Payot.

Rombauer, Edgar. 1998. Foreword to the facsimile edition of *The Joy of Cooking* (1931), by Irma Rombauer. New York: Scribner.

Rombauer, Irma. 1931. *The Joy of Cooking: A Compilation of Reliable Recipes, with a Casual Culinary Chat*. St Louis: A. C. Clayton.

———. 1943. *The Joy of Cooking*. Indianapolis: Bobbs-Merrill.

Rouff, Marcel. (1924). 1994. *La vie et la passion de Dodin-Bouffant-Gourmet*. Paris: Le Serpent à Plumes.

Rowley, Anthony. 1994. *À table! La fête gastronomique*. Paris: Gallimard.

Rozin, Paul. 1997. "Why We Eat What We Eat, and Why We Worry about It." *Bulletin of the American Academy of Arts and Sciences* 50 (5): 26–48. www.jstor.org/stable/3824612.

Ruskin, John (1865) *The Ethics of the Dust: Ten Lectures to Little Housewives*. Project Gutenberg. www.gutenberg.org/cache/epub/4701/pg4701.html.

Samuelsson, Marcus. 2012. *Yes, Chef! A Memoir*. New York: Random House.

Schott, Ben. 2012. "Terms of Service." *New York Times*, 6 August. www.nytimes.com/interactive/2012/08/06/opinion/06schott-terms-of-service-restaurants.html.

Sciolino, Elaine. 2012. "Culinary Battles of Mitterrand's Chef Go From Kitchen to Screen." *New York Times*, 27 October. www.nytimes.com/2012/10/27/world/europe/culinary-battles-of-mitterrands-chef-go-from-kitchen-to-screen.html

Scott, A. O. 2007. " 'Ratatouille': A Portrait of an Artist as a Culinary Rat." *New York Times*, 29 June. www.nytimes.com/2007/06/29/arts/29iht-flik30.1.6405896.html.

Scott, James C. 1985. *Weapons of the Weak: Everyday Forms of Peasant Resistance.* New Haven: Yale University Press.

Senderens, Alain. 1993. "Nous consommons plus de mythes que de calories." *L'Expansion*, 13 July. www.lexpansion.com/economie/nous-consommons-plus-de-mythes-que-de-calories_1263.html.

Sexton, Josie. 2013. "After the Foam and Fame, a New Direction." *New York Times*, 16 April. www.nytimes.com/2013/04/17/dining/after-el-bulli-its-peruvian-cuisine-with-a-japanese-twist-at-pakta.html.

Shapiro, Laura. 2004a. "'Poet of the Appetites': The Art of the Meal." *New York Times Book Review*, 12 December. www.nytimes.com/2004/12/12/books/review/12SHAPIRO.html.

———. 2004b. *Something from the Oven: Reinventing Dinner in 1950s America.* New York: Viking.

———. 2008. *Perfection Salad: Women and Cooking at the Turn of the Century.* 2nd ed. Berkeley: University of California Press.

———. 2009. *Julia Child: A Life.* New York: Penguin.

———. 2011. "Importing Italian Cuisine." *New York Times Book Review*, 20 November. www.nytimes.com/2011/11/20/books/review/culinary-alliance.html.

———. 2012. "The Pillsbury Bake-Off." Oxford Symposium on Food and Cookery, 7 July. http://vimeo.com/55665342.

Schinto, Jeanne. 2011. "Remembering Dione Lucas." *Gastronomica* 11 (4): 34–45.

Shelasky, Alyssa. 2011. "Thomas Keller Will Feed You Burnt Steak, a Bowl of Wheaties, or Gluten-Free Whatever." *Grub Street*, 1 November. www.grubstreet.com/2011/11/thomas_keller_will_feed_you_a.html.

Simmel, Georg. (1903) 1950. "The Metropolis and Mental Life." In *The Sociology of Georg Simmel*, edited and translated by Kurt H. Wolff, 409–424. New York: Free Press.

———. (1904) 1957. "On Fashion." *American Journal of Sociology* 62 (6): 541–558.

———. (1907) 1997. "Sociology of the Senses." Translated by M. Ritter and D. Frisby. In *Simmel on Culture*, edited by David Frisby and Mike Featherstone, 109–120. London: Sage.

———. (1908) 1950. "The Stranger." In *The Sociology of Georg Simmel*, edited and translated by Kurt H. Wolff, 402–408. New York: Free Press.

——. (1910) 1997. "The Sociology of the Meal." Translated by M. Ritter and D. Frisby. In *Simmel on Culture*, edited by David Frisby and Mike Featherstone, 130–135. London: Sage.

Smith, Andrew, and Shelley Boyd. 2009. "Talking Turkey: Thanksgiving in Canada and the United States." In *What's to Eat? Entrées in Canadian Food History*, edited by Nathalie Cooke, 116–144. Montreal: McGill-Queen's University Press.

Solomon, Deborah. 2006. "Eat, Drink, Manhattan: Questions for Danny Meyer." Interview, *New York Times*, 10 September. www.nytimes.com/2006/09/10/magazine/10wwln_q4.html.

Spang, Rebecca. 2000. *The Invention of the Restaurant: Paris and Modern Gastronomic Culture*. Cambridge, MA: Harvard University Press.

Spitz, Bob. 2012. *Dearie: The Remarkable Life of Julia Child*. New York: Random House.

Stewart, Hayden, Noel Blisard, and Dean Jolliffe. 2006. *Let's Eat Out: Americans Weigh Taste, Convenience, and Nutrition*. United States Department of Agriculture Economic Research Service *Economic Information Bulletin*, no. 19 (October). www.ers.usda.gov/Publications/EIB19.

Strauss, David. 2011. *Setting the Table for Julia Child: Gourmet Dining in America, 1934–1961*. Baltimore, MD: Johns Hopkins University Press.

Surak, Kristin. 2012. *Making Tea, Making Japan: Cultural Nationalism in Practice*. Stanford, CA: Stanford University Press.

Takats, Sean, 2011. *The Expert Cook in Enlightenment France*. Baltimore, MD: Johns Hopkins University Press.

Thiébaut, Philippe. 1994. "De 1920 à 1990: A la recherche d'un style de vie contemporain." In *Histoire de la table: Les arts de la table des origines à nos jours*, edited by Pierre Ennis, Gérard Mabille, and Philippe Thiébaut, 317–355. Paris: Flammarion.

This, Hervé. 2005. *Molecular Gastronomy: Exploring the Science of Flavor*. Translated by Malcolm DeBevoise. New York: Columbia University Press.

——. 2009. *Building a Meal: From Molecular Gastronomy to Culinary Constructivism*. Translated by Malcolm DeBevoise. New York: Columbia University Press.

Trubek, Amy B. 2000. *Haute Cuisine: How the French Invented the Culinary Profession*. Philadelphia: University of Pennsylvania Press.

———. 2008. *The Taste of Place: A Cultural Journey into Terroir*. Berkeley: University of California Press.

Veblen, Thorstein. (1899) 1979. *The Theory of the Leisure Class*. New York: Penguin.

Vongerichten, Jean-Georges. 2011. *Home Cooking with Jean-Georges: My Favorite Simple Recipes*. New York: Clarkson-Potter.

Watson, James L. 2000. "China's Big Mac Attack." *Foreign Affairs* 79 (3): 120–134.

Watson, James L., ed. 1997. *Golden Arches East: McDonald's in East Asia*. Stanford, CA: Stanford University Press.

Waley-Cohen, Joanna. 2007. "The Quest for Perfect Balance." In *Food: The History of Taste*, edited by Paul Freedman, 99–133. Berkeley: University of California Press.

Weber, Max. 1978. *Economy and Society*, vol 1. Edited by Guenther Roth and Claus Wittich. Berkeley: University of California Press.

Weil, Elizabeth. 2010. "I'll Take a Scoop of Prosciutto, Please." *New York Times Magazine*, 4 July. www.nytimes.com/2010/07/04/magazine/04icecream-t .html.

Wells, Pete. 2012. "Talking All Around the Food." *New York Times*, 17 September. www.nytimes.com/2012/09/19/dining/at-the-reinvented-eleven-madison-park-the-words-fail-the-dishes.html.

———. 2013. "Serving the Stuff of Privilege: Restaurant Review; Daniel on the Upper East Side." *New York Times*, July 23. www.nytimes.com/2013/07/24 /dining/reviews/restaurant-review-daniel-on-the-upper-east-side.html.

White, Merry. 2009. "Writing Food as History in Japan." Paper delivered at the annual meeting of the American Historical Association, New York, 3 January.

Wilkins, John, David Harvey, and Mike Dobson, eds. 1995. *Food in Antiquity*. Exeter: University of Exeter Press.

Woolf, Virginia. (1927) 1989. *To the Lighthouse*. New York: Harcourt Brace.

———. 1929. Chapter One. *A Room of One's Own*. eBooks@Adelaide. http://ebooks .adelaide.edu.au/w/woolf/virginia/w91r/chapter1.html.

Yan, Mo. 2012. *POW!* Translated by Howard Goldblatt. New York: Seagull.

"You'll never pea-lieve it!" 2010. *New York Post*, 11 August, 3. http://nypost .com/2010/08/11/youll-never-pea-lieve-it/

FILMS

1993. *The Age of Innocence*, dir. Martin Scorcese

1996. *Big Night*, dir. Campbell Scott and Stanley Tucci

2000. *Chocolat*, dir. Lasse Hallström

2001. *Gosford Park*, dir. Robert Altman

2007. *Le Grand Chef*, dir. Yun-su Chong

——. *Ratatouille*, Disney-Pixar

2010. *Three Stars (Drei sterne-die köche und die sterne)*, dir. Lutz Hochmeister

——. *El Bulli: Cooking in Progress*, dir. Gereon Wetzel

——. *The Kings of Pastry*, dir. Chris Hegedus and D. A. Pennebaker

2012. *Haute Cuisine (Les saveurs du palais)*, dir. Christian Vincent

Franklin, Benjamin: on proper meal, 99–100
French gastronomic meal, 5, 38

gastronomic field, 73
gastronomy, as male preserve, 227
generosity, 31; of host, 174–75; necessity for chef, 126, 173; Remy (*Ratatouille*) and, 200, 244
glutton: happy, 45–49
Grimod de la Reynière, A.B.L., 58; career, 222; criticism of, 62–64, 122–23; gastronomy as social practice for, 65, 73; lack of reputation, 66
Guérard, Michel, 160
guest: at Athenaeus banquet, 54; duties of, 62; Mrs. Ramsey and, 69–70; participation of in meal, 52; president as special, 22; transformation of, 70

Hale, Sarah Josepha: cookbook of, 83, 216; as lobbyist for Thanksgiving holiday, 276
haut chocolat, 75
Haute cuisine, 17–23, 74, 148, 194, 213–14
haute cuisine: absence of women in, 124; compared to cuisine bourgeoise, 21–22, 177; compete with haute food, culinary ideal, 176; definition of, xxiv; ethos of, 182–87; from haute cuisine to haute food, 170–96; ratatouille as, 160
haute food, 13, 243–44; definition of, xxiv, 170–96; compete with haute cuisine, 170, 176, 182–83, 17, 190–91; and everyday life, 176–82, 184; and tradition, 177–78
haute ratatouille, 199
Herodotus, xix, 208

host: chef as, 165, 170, 173–74; decisions of, 187; duties of, 62–63; Mrs. Ramsay as, 68, 80, 192; restaurants as liberation from tyranny of, 145; table show off, 114, 117–18, 121, 125, 143
Humm, Daniel, 167

informalization, 141, 151, 238; effects on dining, 153–55, 176; limit to, 181
innovation, 4; commercial, 57; in Fannie Farmer, 88–89; pressure for, 165–66, 170, 177, 183, 190; restaurant as, 133–36, 152, 174; routinization destroy, 199

Jean Georges: menus, 127, 171–72, 176. *See also* Vongerichten, Jean-Georges
Judt, Tony: on curry as English cuisine, 12, 211

Keller, Thomas, 130, 213, 235–36

Le Bernardin, 127, 155–59, 161, 171, 185, 236; menu of, 156–59. *See also* LeCoze, Gilbert
Le Coze, Gilbert, 113, 127–28, 185, 236
Le Grand Chef, 29–31, 74, 196, 217
Letterman, David, 110–11
Locusta, 35–36

Massialot, François, 82
Matsuhisa, Nobu, 29
Mauss, Marcel, xv
McDonald's, xxii, 3–4, 23, 84, 210
meal: Brillat-Savarin as theoretician of, 191; create community, 65, 128–29; in *Ratatouille*, 202; sequence in, 146; Simmel on, 115–16; Virginia Woolf on, 191–92

menu: elBulli, 133; at Eleven Madison Park, 168; as food talk, 148; functions of, 34, 39-40; Grimod de la Reynière on, 63; at House of Representatives, 19; as instrumental text, 146-49, 153; at Jean Georges, 171-72, 176; at Le Bernardin, 155-61; in restaurant, 123; in Rombauer, 31

menu French, 148-49, 156, 159-60

Meyer, Danny: on hospitality, 127, 236

MOF [Meilleur Ouvrier de France], 14-16, 27, 183, 212

Nathan's Hot Dog contest, 25, 216

Pampille [Marthe Allard Daudet], 8-9, 210-11; Proust praise of, 8, 211

Parker, Dorothy: on ham as eternity, 43, 218

Passard, Alain, 246, 262

Pasteur, Louis, 13

pleasure talk, 42-44, 74-76, 218-19,

poison, fears of, xxii, 35-36, 40, 89, 200, 218

production: conspicuous,114, 118, 121; inconspicuous, 164, 195

Proust, Marcel: and Carême, 66-70; madeleine tasting, 136, 199; on Pampille, 8, 211

Ratatouille, xxiv, 197-203

Redzepi, René, 185, 246

restaurant: choice as central to, 24; conspicuous production in, 114-15, 118; Daniel Boulud on, 127; elBulli, 131-34; Gilbert LeCoze on, 113; Grimod de la Reynière on, 64; jargon at, 164-65; Jean-Georges Vongerichten on, 126-27; male domain, 80, 98, 102; Michelin stars and, 15, 131, 135;

nineteenth-century innovation, 143-46, 49-53; redefine consumption, 121-23; reshaped by food talk, 144; as sector gastronomic field, 73; spectacle of, 114

Restaurant Guy Savoy, 175

Ritz, César: partnership with Escoffier, 123

Robuchon, Joël, 22; chefs as sellers of happiness, 125

Rombauer, Irma, 17, 91-98, 230 personal relation to reader, as Mrs. Joy, 228

Rouff, Marcel, 8

Ruskin, John, 88-90, 227

Samuelsson, Marcus, 178-79, 212, 243-5

Saveurs du palais (Les). See *Haute cuisine*

Scott, Walter: cited by M.F.K. Fisher, 100

service: à la française, 61, 117; à la russe, 121; costs of, 187; personalization of in restaurants, 165-66

Simmel, Georg, xx, 113, 191, 209-10, 247; *Sociology of the meal*, 233

sociability: as goal of meal, 126

Soyer, Alexis (chef), at Reform Club, 9

SPAM, 5

sushi, 3-5, 111, 182, 21

tasting menu: elBulli,133, 167; Eleven Madison Park, 168; Jean Georges, 171-72, 176; as negation of consumer choice, 174, 186

total social phenomenon, xv, 207

Trotter, Charlie, 185

UNESCO, 5, 138, 212

Veblen, Thorstein, 149, 233

vegetarian diet, 3, 186-90, 247